AUSTRALIA'S **50** INFLUENTIAL WOMEN ENTREPRENEURS

{ Inspiring women entrepreneurs }

Rare Birds - Australia's 50 Influential Women Entrepreneurs
First Publication 2015

Inspiring Rare Birds Pty Ltd
Level 2, 131 York Street Sydney NSW 2000, Australia

Publisher: Jo-Ellen Burston
Managing Editor: Brittany Lee Waller
Assistant Editor: Louise Taffa
Copy Editor: Alice Fraser
Content Advisor: Dr. Richard Seymour
Editorial Assistant: Merissa Johnston
Creative Director: Toby Hook
Designer: Danielle Hurps
Photographer: Rebekah Schott
Contributors: Emily Ralph, Donna Lu, Jessie Attwood

Printed in Hong Kong

ISBN 978-0-646-93306-1

For every 100 books sold, Rare Birds will donate a book to an Australian public education institution.

FOUNDER'S LETTER

—

Elizabeth, Love your work! Love Jo ox #rfshecanican

I am a very proud Australian and global citizen.
I have no sense of entitlement, I am privileged.
I am an entrepreneur. I am a woman.

I have what one of my inspirations, David Hieatt, calls "cold passion". He says I am a purpose-driven entrepreneur, and that my head and heart are working together. He believes when our purposes are clear the rest will be great, not easy.

This book is for hearts and heads. It's a call to action, a call for celebration. It's a call for us each to ensure that every woman is given the opportunity to be an entrepreneur by choice. It won't be easy, but it will be great.

It's aimed at every school in Australia, every library, every corporate book shelf, every woman. It's aimed at the little boys and little girls who are the future of this magnificent planet. So that one day, when they start to think about their journey in life, they understand and truly believe that "If she can, I can". It's so that, even while still at school, they practice how to Ask - Try - Do; the simple learning cycle of the entrepreneur.

It's aimed at future changemakers and entrepreneurs to give them the inspiration, skills and resources to create a job, rather than get a job. It's aimed at those who know, or want to know, where they are most alive: That place between love, action and the zeitgeist.

I welcome you to 'Rare Birds - Australia's 50 Influential Women Entrepreneurs'. I believe this is the first piece of written narrative celebrating the women entrepreneurs of our 'clever' country.

The 50 women you will meet and get to know - they are truly inspiring. They shape vision into reality. They influence their industries and their communities. They have economic and social impact way beyond their footprints.

Throughout the interviews and conversations collected to write this book, I have laughed my sides off, cried, reflected endlessly with empathy and affinity. I am enormously honoured and humbled that these women have trusted me to tell their stories. Here we see their steely strengths, vulnerable weaknesses, and their powerful lessons from success as well as failure. But mostly we see their diehard belief in who they are and what they do. Never once do they apologise for being different, or for doing things differently.

Traversing the globe to capture these stories, what became very apparent, very early on were three things. Firstly, women entrepreneurs want to celebrate and support other women. Secondly, the time is right for this book. And thirdly, these women are passionate about ensuring Australia fosters the next generation of emerging women entrepreneurs.

These women are special. They should be our role models: cherished and celebrated. They are my friends, they are my tribe, they are Rare Birds.

——

Fly high and fly fast,
Jo Burston

CONTENTS

—

ACKNOWLEDGEMENTS

—

Andrea Culligan for creating a killer brand that will stand the test of time.

Andy Lark for being there, always, offering insight and thought leadership.

James Aldridge, Benjamin Chong, James Cooper, Eris Hess, Craig Rochat, Andrew Styliano, Brian Super for encouragement, respect and sharing lessons of life and business.

Brittany Lee Waller for being the words bird. For believing, doing, being utterly brilliant and being the best comrade an entrepreneur can fly with.

Carden Calder for being at the very first step of my journey of purpose and backing my spirit.

Carol Schwartz for having my back gently.

Dr Richard Seymour for giving us some feet to go with our wings.

Jamie Yoo and **Louise Taffa** for working with an entrepreneur, growing with me and growing within you.

Joanna Moore for being as steady as they come.

Lauren Fried for all things pure and Hemingway.

Lawrence Wolf for taking a chance and giving some film work to the project.

Lynn Kraus for taking the journey with us.

Rare Birds interns who gave their time and we gave our opportunity of experience to grow with Rare Birds.

Rebekah Schott for her stunning photography and making our women see themselves a little differently.

Sally-Ann Williams for reminding me of the value of the collective global community, its influence and why women nerds are cool.

Sir Richard Branson for my time on Necker Island and the opportunities and doors it has opened globally.

Tim Oxford for filming.

Toby Hook for his creative genius and leading our design team.

Topaz Conway for believing in my vision and sharing it abundantly.

Ursula Hogben for her legal legwork and guiding us through risk and reward.

DEDICATIONS

—

This book is dedicated to all influential entrepreneurs globally. To my tribe of women entrepreneurs, past, present and aspiring. To those that are purpose-driven, the ones that totally fall in love with what they set out to change. The ones that persevere, that never quit, that go over, under, around or smash right through all barriers they come up against. The ones that can build profitable businesses with a smart heart. The ones that have so much love for what they are doing that their purpose fuels endless, obsessive passion and abundance in the world in which they operate. The ones with an augmented sense of reality. The ones that see the zeitgeist.

To my mum and (my late) dad, who gave me the opportunity to know real love. Their pride fuels my courage.

Finally, to my mentor, whom never stops believing in me, whom fuels my relentlessness to be the top of all things worthwhile. He taught me to fight like Ali, care unconditionally and understand how to play my own game and make my own rules. Not only in business, but in life.

———

Jo

SUPPORTERS

—

The myth of the entrepreneur is that they are predominantly young males. That couldn't be further from reality. The majority are females. But what we need is a movement that helps those women understand that they are entrepreneurs building businesses that can scale - creating opportunity for themselves and their communities. The impact of these sustainable and scaled businesses can be transformative.

Entrepreneurs need an understanding of financial basics and funding models. Simple things like how to invoice and when; what to watch for contractually; the value of equity; and marketing basics. They need to be able to cut through what the media presents - which are often false positives - and get to the heart of qualifying ideas and managing within constraints. These are a few of what needs to be taught. Mostly they are going to need to know how to nurture patience and perseverance in the face of constant adversity.

Australia's size means it's large enough to support great entrepreneurs, but small enough that you can spot them. Its economic footprint mean there is plenty of available market against which to launch and scale ideas. And capital, while difficult to access, is here and available. What's missing is the right context for an entrepreneur to fail. Most fail but remain hidden. Other markets wear failure with pride. Here it is still viewed with shame. As a result few come back for a second try. We need to foster an environment where women entrepreneurs are supported not just once, but many times.

—

Andrew Lark
CMO XERO

———

This is not about gender equality or levelling any playing fields. This is tapping into new insights, new ways of thinking, new ways of managing and leading, and new ways of engaging with customers and society. This diversity creates value differently, and it shares it more broadly and collaboratively.

We need more women to grasp opportunity and lead their own futures through their own passions and foresights. It can be a tough journey, and even tougher if it is done alone. Rare Bird's mission plays a key role in building the required entrepreneurial communities of practice, care and interest. Community is the key feature of the ecosystem.

As an educator, we know from our teaching and research that successful entrepreneurs master a multitude of 'learning by doing'. They develop their functional skills such as marketing, strategy and finance. They polish their social skills including negotiation, team building and leadership. And, they mature their curiosity, passion and wisdom. This learning cannot be done alone; it cannot be done solely in a classroom, or from just copying others, it is done together. Women entrepreneurs can change the rules of the game by being more aware, more collaborative, more inclusive, and I think more creative. Seeing these attributes being applied would give me more confidence in the future success of Australian businesses here, and globally.

———

Dr. Richard Seymour
Senior Lecturer and Program Director of Entrepreneurship & Innovation at The University of Sydney Business School, Australia.

I believe that having more female entrepreneurs embracing risk and succeeding will open minds, add to the diversity of thought, challenge tired assumptions and lead us to better practices in Australia both economically and as a society.

The greatest potential for positive impact lies beyond individual women mustering courage.

It lies in their ability to maintain and share it through collaborating with communities and organisations. I believe that the structure, understanding, encouragement and combined wisdom offered by Rare Birds will benefit the members most and have the greatest social and economic impact over the longer term.

—

Matt Jackson
Founder of Affectors

I'm inspired to be part of the Rare Birds movement because of the passion and belief of its founder, Jo Burston. The vision to give women the opportunity to become an entrepreneur by choice is a magnificent one. I see Rare Birds as a vehicle to encourage, identify and help grow entrepreneurs in the early stages of their journey. I believe its greatest strength will lie in harnessing the collective passion and talent of its luminaries and creating many generations of entrepreneurs who will help inspire and grow others. I would hope the early Rare Birds of today will be the luminaries of tomorrow.

Creating an environment where people are open to the idea that entrepreneurialism is a possible path is one of the biggest changes we can make. If we can help young people see that becoming an entrepreneur is a valid option, then we've probably removed one of the biggest challenges.

Joey Moore
Founder of Moore Thoughts

FOREWORD

—

I wish "Rare Birds" came along two decades ago! I love how it truly inspires women entrepreneurs, I love the fact that Jo Burston is making this into a movement. I love the ripple effect that the stories of successful Australian women entrepreneurs will do not only for the nation of Australia, but for entrepreneurs of all ages around the world.

As Jo has alluded to in her book "Rare Birds", we came to know each other through the Entrepreneurs Organization (EO), a global organization where peers engage one another to learn and grow together. What binds us together beyond our boundaries is the experiences of owning and running our own endeavors....our companies, which sometimes we call our babies. It feels lonely on this entrepreneurial journey, and when we find peers that understand us, it empowers us. Imagine the power of the collective experience when shared, and how exponentially it helps each other learn and grow and be the most influential community of entrepreneurs. It's so empowering and life changing to a point where we can say nothing is impossible for us!

Jo is an inspiring example of that empowerment, this book is the catalyst to start the movement that will build a community for women to choose entrepreneurship for their life journey. The 50 stories found in this book will excite you, inspire you, as they're written in a beautifully authentic tone. I saw myself in the stories, I was edified, and it fed the passion in me.

I had the privilege of leading this amazing Entrepreneurs Organization as the Global Chairperson in 2013-14, the first Asian woman to do so. The opportunity to lead EO as the chairperson came as a surprise and I took it on with the grace of God, to fill a need and help EO embrace globalization. I was elated when Jo expressed how I have inspired her, in truth all I shared was my journey and my story. And here, she is sharing her own story and many stories like ours. Admirably, this book will truly engage women entrepreneurs around the world to boldly nurture the ecology of entrepreneurs. Through the power of stories, we hope they will plant a thought and encourage you to embrace entrepreneurship and move you to greater dreams.

Rosemary Tan
Global President 2013-2014
Entrepreneurs Organisation

INTRODUCTION

—

It has been difficult to ascertain the true definition of an entrepreneur. While the Merriam-Webster Dictionary may define them as "one who organises, manages and assumes the risks of a business or enterprise," this book demonstrates they are much more than this. To understand the entrepreneurs in this book, Merriam-Webster might need to consider rewriting their Dictionary.

This book tells the stories of 50 Rare Birds, each with a uniqueness of colour and song. These Rare Birds are not just sharing their entrepreneurial stories with you, they are humbly and joyfully unveiling their dreams, achievements, vulnerabilities and mistakes. Throughout their journeys you will find the highs and lows, the heartache and the joy, the hard work and the lessons that have built 50 remarkable women. They are a taste of the future, one that depicts the potential of a strong and diverse entrepreneurial landscape.

From the very beginning we always had you in mind; you that sort inspiration, information and connectedness. Something you were searching for, but was hard to find elsewhere. We want to bring you into the hearts and minds of these magnificent women as we expose their subject matter expertise, what makes them influential and unwind the threads of their 'secret sauce'.

We chose to use the word 'influential' because these women are indeed people of influence. There is no hierarchy, we do not 'rate' or prioritise according to their successes, each Rare Bird holds the capacity to affect someone differently. They are memorable, they add and convey value, they are market leaders and compassionate humans that never give up. Not only are they inspirational, but they have seismic influence. These women affect the communities in which they revolve in. They contribute to positive social and economic change, increased employment, amended government policies and initiatives, innovation, technology and an overall sense of prosperity, both locally and globally. For this reason they are Australia's 50 influential women entrepreneurs.

Their entrepreneurial journeys, insights and experiences are yours to explore. We trust you will see some of what it is to be an entrepreneur. Understand their strength, recognise their spirit, learn from their wisdom, be inspired by their tenacity. But above all, see how these women are motivating and supporting the next generation of entrepreneurial leaders.

Beyond these 50 women lie many more just like them. A tribe growing at a phenomenal rate. Rest assured, we will be here and ready to tell their stories, and we hope that one day that will be yours too.

—

Brittany Lee Waller
Managing Editor

THE 50

FLAVIA ABBATE

Founder of City Clinic and BodyBolster

Flavia Abbate is known for her considerate and tender temperament amongst friends, someone that will always go out of her way for others. An identical twin, she's always focused on those around her, and thrives on a collaborative approach.

Though soft hearted in day to day life, in business, she is something quite else, energetic, persistent and never takes no for an answer. Always willing to take risks, Flavia set out on her entrepreneurial journey in 1998, founding City Clinic, an Australian first in its patient-centric, multi-disciplinary approach to integrated injury management. Flavia launched Bolster Trading Pty Ltd, born from a notion to empower people by providing self-help tools and resources in order to recover and rehabilitate from health issues. This added a product range to the staple health services, complementing the original client-centric philosophy to meet the client where they are.

CITY CLINIC AND BODYBOLSTER

Founded
1998 AND 2003

Awards
MANY INCLUDING 2011 WINNER OF THE MICROSOFT IT INNOVATION AWARD

Inspiration
A DESIRE TO MAKE A DIFFERENCE TO PEOPLE ON A PERSONAL LEVEL

In the genes

Flavia's entrepreneurial acumen was seeded from a young age in the home.

"I caught the entrepreneur gene because I was born in Italy and my dad had a very large family of eight brothers and one sister. He was a twin himself and you can imagine in a family like that, that it was very competitive and yet very structured and disciplined as well. My grandmother used to tell stories about them growing up: There would be two of them sweeping, two of them organising dishes and two of them going to get the shopping. That whole idea of contributing to something that isn't just for yourself really came through my father. When we were little, all he might be doing was drilling a hole in the wall, but he had to have everyone there participating in it, "is this straight?" he would ask, then point to me and say, "you hold that there", so there was this whole thing of collaborating and doing things together."

Flavia promotes the importance of growing up in an open learning environment. "We thought we were hanging out and goofing around but there it was, we would talk about anything and everything. To us, anything was possible. Dad had made the trip out to Australia and not known anyone. There weren't these constraints. The safety net was having a family to go back to, we could really do anything we wanted."

As with most startups, City Clinic was born from a casual conversation based on a personal experience noting a lack of an integrated approach to injury management/ rehabilitation. The Sydney-based City Clinic Centre was the first of its kind in Australia to offer a patient-centric model, offering a multidisciplinary approach to injury management-all under one roof.

An opportunity to acquire a business which had been supplying City Clinic, presented itself in 2001 and with this acquisition Bolster Trading Pty Ltd was established. The flag-ship product is the BodyBolster, which was originally created by a team of physiotherapists to promote movement and support the back 'actively.'

CityClinic practitioners were already using and recommending it to patients prior to the acquisition, so in the tradition of the 'Gillette story' she says "we loved it so much we bought the company."

Prior to starting City Clinic with her sister, Flavia had had a successful career in media and management consulting, in communications, spending a great deal of time in magazine advertising. As a result, when she stepped off the career track, she felt well equipped to lead City Clinic. In 2001, Flavia acquired a major supplier, expanding the business and adding the title of CEO of Bolster Trading Pty. Ltd. to her belt.

Flavia firmly believes that everything we do in life prepares us for where we are now - so while media introduced her to consumer mindsets and psychographics, management consulting exposed her to business, strategy and critical thinking, all of which would form the framework and reference points for setting up future businesses. With the

PEOPLE WITH A POSITIVE MINDSET GIVE YOU ENERGY, IDEAS AND ENCOURAGEMENT

two businesses now operating successfully, Flavia has realised her life ambition; to make people's lives better, and healthier.

"This exposed us to a whole new world and soon after, we identified an opportunity to further our interest in the rehabilitation/wellbeing sector. Our flagship product, the BodyBolster is advanced 'active' technology in back pain management, recommended by OHS consultants and physiotherapists all around the world." Bolster Trading Pty Ltd. are manufacturers and distributors of a range of exercise tools and educational resources for allied health professionals and end users. Bolster's products are designed to specifically improve posture and physical function and are developed with the end-user in mind, to educate, offer comfort and optimise therapeutic

results. Bolster Trading is committed to reducing 'new age' musculoskeletal disorders born from today's sedentary lifestyle.

Having her twin sister Elizabeth by her side has helped her tremendously on her own journey. "It's very rare in life you move from one thing to another and have all your past shape you and have someone to bear witness to that. We still do and check in with one another and we could always bounce ideas off each other," says Flavia.

Ups and downs

Of course, the early stages of her journey as an entrepreneur were filled with the typical ups and downs characterised by a business that is growing organically, which Flavia

knows "will test your stamina, motives and the relationship with your bank manager." But, like most entrepreneurs, obstacles did not squash Flavia's desire to innovate.

"I'm fueled by ideas and that's where it stems from: having family discussions all through my childhood and even still now, sometimes they could be about nothing, but then a lot of times it could get quite weighty. We used to talk about corruption or the political situation in Italy. So our childhood was very happy, family orientated and dad opened up several businesses. Obviously, that's where I get it from."

On a personal level, the most rewarding thing for Flavia is the knowledge that what she sells has such a positive impact, and that, "it isn't just another 'widget'," she says.

{ We are Inspiring Rare Birds }

She had no idea that the first 18 months would be spent dealing with manufactures, patent attorneys and medical device legislators. Life had not prepared her for this, but she ground her teeth through it all recognising the necessary challenges that comes with the territory.

Above all, Flavia says it's important to surround yourself with positive people. "People with a positive mindset give you energy, ideas and encouragement. It is also important to be with like-minded people so investing in a business coach or a mentor is a great way to learn from other people's experience. Most importantly, you must understand that success does not happen without hard work,

challenging times that will have you in a fetal position under the desk, and also complete commitment. Having your own business means that work becomes a great part of your life there is no distinction between weekends and weekdays. If you are prepared for all this, then you are bound for success. In short, being an entrepreneur is not for everyone."`

Lessons from Flavia:
- Surround yourself with positive people.
- Understand that success does not happen without hard work.
- Take risks, and don't be afraid to try something completely new.

The BodyBolster is now sold in 13 countries and the business is steadily growing. The main distribution channel has been through allied health practitioners, who act as the pseudo sales force and educators. More recently, with the advent of social media and YouTube, the company is leveraging new mediums to educate and sell online.

NATALIE ARCHER

Founder of Bendelta

Funny, smart, beautiful, humble, these are all words you could use to describe Natalie Archer the co-founder of Bendelta, but perhaps the most pertinent word is 'extraordinary'.

Natalie, or Nat, is a New Zealander by birth. She has the wild ability to welcome you with her warmth while regaling you with stories and anecdotes which will leave you in a fit of laughter in minutes. Nat began Bendelta 11 years ago with her business partner Anthony Mitchell. The consulting company the two had worked for had exited the Australian market, which left a niche open for a firm with a focus on tailor-made strategic advice. The company specialises in helping organisations in the public and private sectors build capability and adjust quickly when change is called for. Bendelta has been awarded one of Anthill's 100 coolest companies.

BENDELTA

Founded
2003

Inspiration
A DESIRE TO COMBINE SUCCESS AND SIGNIFICANCE BY CREATING A MANAGEMENT CONSULTANCY THAT WOULD BE BOTH A COMMERCIAL SUCCESS AND MAKE THE WORLD A BETTER PLACE

Nat grew up in a family where 'business talk' was part of every day life, and the idea of forging a new path or a new business was warmly accepted. She remembers, "My father was a managing director and in his early thirties he went out on his own and set up as a business. I grew up talking business; I was always fascinated with it, and he was a guy who worked hard and did well and also had freedom, flexibility and spent time with us as a family."

Nat feels the entrepreneurial spirit is about spotting an opportunity where you are willing to put yourself on the line. Soon after moving to Australia, Natalie was asked by a New Zealand consulting firm to start up their Australian branch. She leaped at it. "I love consulting. Consulting is about going into people's businesses and looking around,

seeing what's happening, what's good, what works and being able to partner with those organisations. So, for me it's really stimulating."

Nat was thrown into the deep end of business development, responsible for everything from setting up premises to meeting with lawyers, accountants, business developers. "I had no idea what I was doing. I was 21 at the time and absolutely loved it, worked until 2 am in the morning, I did that for two and a half years and then [despite continued business growth] New Zealand wanted to pull out because it was a higher risk so that created another decision point and I was like okay, that's fine, what a great opportunity to give it a go."

After her dry run with the NZ firm's Australian startup, Nat had all the tools to set up her own consulting business with Anthony. They started

out with a tiny office and two laptops and took it from there. "We had a lot of contacts which was helpful. We called it Bendelta, so it's a mix and match of Latin and Greek, 'bene' meaning positive or well and 'delta' meaning change, so positive change."

Womanhood and the entrepreneurial challenges

Nat relates that there can be times in your life that are better for starting businesses, particularly for women. "Those early years in start-up can be brutal. Timing is so important. For me the perfect timing to do those years was in my 20s because it was full on. If you didn't invest to that extent fully and pulled back early it would be quite fragile and if you push through that you get to a different stage of stability with the business and then you can

HIGH ACHIEVEMENT, A PLAYERS AND VALUES DRIVEN AROUND MAKING AN IMPACT IS WHAT I TAKE, THEN I DELVE DEEP AND TAKE LOTS AND LOTS OF EXAMPLES ON HOW THAT'S PLAYED OUT IN PEOPLE'S LIVES

be more deliberate around how you design it, having other resources involved, stepping back a little bit, you have more choices."

On the disparity between male and female entrepreneurs in the Australian landscape, Nat doesn't see a huge difference but indicates that women are slightly more relational - a powerful parallel noted amongst many women entrepreneurs. "What you do find is that the more females you are associating with in a similar line of work or entrepreneurship, the more connected you become. Men tend to be more task orientated and women tend to be more relation oriented. Women entrepreneurs tend to talk about the whole picture rather

than just the business, how is being an entrepreneur serving your whole life? - that's a very female oriented conversation. "

"For me I think a lot of women do it for those same reasons, where it's not just about a successful business idea it's about wanting to have a really successful life and to do that as well as manage other priorities - family, wellbeing - it's quite a good path to choose - I think. Even though you'll work harder and longer hours than you ever will working for someone else if you work for yourself."

"If you're doing it because you think it's going to be an easy run then you are going to find it interesting.

There's a psychological freedom - that's a different type of freedom. You'll work like a demon running across town and be working like a mad-woman. The psychological freedom matters more to me than freedom because you're making choices as to how you want to design your day and do things differently. That's why a lot of women get into it, that's why entrepreneurship serves a lot of women well because they manage their businesses and lives holistically. It's a wonderful life if you can get it right for yourself."

Failure and learning

Nat has come across her fair share of obstacles, but mentions that often an overlooked hurdle is managing growth.

Growth can be a bottleneck, Nat says, "...in the sense of structures which won't allow other people to thrive and grow within a business. There was a period of time where my business partner and I held onto how we were running the business, which was having direct control and just getting to a point where the rubber band stretches and you say, I can either keep running a small business or if I want to get to the next stage then it's really about designing it to be a bigger business. We set the goal back then to be a ten million dollar business and invest in the infrastructure, the people, system, processers and new roles to take the pressure off and be able to grow."

For her personally, Nat's next step is around advancing herself in terms of leadership, which, she says, is always changing and evolving.

Inspiration and lessons

Nat has a passion for creating a positive work environment, something Bendelta has allowed her to do; she believes the sustainability of the enterprise is highly linked to this. Bendelta is built off a strong core of like-minded people.

Lessons from Natalie:
- Spot an opportunity where you are willing to put yourself on the line.
- Business is an amazing opportunity to be able to craft a life for yourself with interesting work, growing and evolving.

Nat understood that if you hire people that are very contribution and achievement-driven, you don't need to do anything other than support them. Encouraging excellence in their staff is also an attribute to Bendelta's success. Consistently measuring and revisiting what works and what doesn't in staff hiring and treatment has been key to Bendelta recruitment. "The work is fun and attracts people who are interested in the intersection between strategy and people. It's all about how do you grow, develop and align people in that organisation" says Nat.

NARELLE ANDERSON

Founder of Envirobank

ENVIROBANK

Founded

2008

Awards

RUNNER UP 2011 FOR
INNOVATION WORLD
ENVIRONMENT DAY AWARD.
WINNER OF WORLD
ENVIRONMENT DAY AWARD 2012

Inspiration

TO DO WHAT OTHERS SAY
CAN'T BE DONE

Narelle Anderson started early in life with the determination to accomplish what other people said couldn't be done.

Since leaving home as a teenager, Narelle has gone onto own and manage her own promotions company before she was 20, buying and expanding CBDEnviro to more than six times its previous size and creating an innovative recycling solution to easily repair Australia's severe littering problem. In 2007, Narelle sold CBDEnviro to a public company, not yet finished and seeing there was more to be done in the recycling space she then began work on Envirobank: a provider of systems and technology to help improve the efficiency of recycling depots and minimise cost for brands . Envirobank offers public place recycling solutions to retail outlets, universities and councils, combined with a customer acquisition program for brands and stores.

An independent spirit

Before entering the waste management industry, Narelle was working full-time as a teenager and relished her newfound independence of managing her own income. She moved out and left school at 16, preferring to make her own way in the world.

"When you go out on your own, you have to learn to look after yourself, be independent and provide for yourself. That's what I did."

By the time she was 19, Narelle had started her own promotions company, which provided support to teams at events such as car shows and fashion parades. While her first business was initially successful, a critical injury from a horse riding accident forced her to close.

Down but not out, Narelle continued to follow her passion for sales and business management by going back to school to complete an MBA and was hired to run CBDEnviro. After two years of paying off the company's proprietor, Narelle became the official owner and implemented a new system that was fundamental in the company's survival.

"That business was taking a waste management company that had two trucks and I grew it to a business with 14 trucks. I had it for seven years and I sold it to a recovery facility."

Womanhood, Challenges and Motivation

Narelle reveals the obstacles and prejudices she has had to overcome throughout her career, her journey behind developing and implementing the advantageous Envirobank and the rewards of contributing to her community.

Despite being the cause of renewed productivity within CBDEnviro, Narelle still had to overcome a very common problem as a businesswoman. She describes the waste management industry as "very male dominated" and constantly had to demonstrate her role in securing her company's success to be taken seriously.

"When I first started, I was known as the secretary that bought the boss' business. I was never the secretary and he was never my boss… but that's about an industry trying to put everyone in a box."

While Narelle claims she doesn't "buy into the glass ceiling" she acknowledges that sexism within the workplace is one of the many instances of being dealt "a good hand and a crappy hand". Narelle claims to be no victim, however, and combats negativity with a strong entrepreneurial spirit to accept circumstances as they are and keep moving forward.

Her career so far has definitely progressed in an upward direction when Narelle decided to keep the distribution rights to CBDEnviro's reverse vending machines which would later become known as Envirobanks.

In what started as an effort to impact public place recycling became a popular quid pro quo system for communities to deposit garbage for small change across Australia.

Starting in the Northern Territory and progressing to multiple 7/11 outlets in NSW, Victoria and Queensland, Narelle decided to take her initial idea to the development stage after witnessing the difference in waste management between NT and the other Australian states.

"In the Northern Territory [they have a ten cent bounty on the container], you see very little litter on the ground. In other states, where they don't have a container deposit, all you see on the grounds is beverage container litter."

In the absence of container deposit legislation, Narelle began testing in Northern Territory with one of the machines, which offered a manual and labour intensive process for consumers to be served quickly and provide beverage companies a detailed report of what's being returned.

While Envirobanks have not yet reached Western Australia, Narelle is confident

Envirobank Recycling will become a national staple once the Australian government realises the Council's current system is not substantively effective.

"We have bins out at the moment but it doesn't work, so putting another 166,000 bins out won't work either. To change people's behaviours, you either need to reward them or fine them."

Rewarding consumers, Narelle strongly believes, will make a major difference in the country's littering problem.

"The ten cent bounty works because cash is king. Those that don't care will leave garbage behind but others will pick it up. You break that behaviour down to how kids do jobs around the house when you give them pocket money."

In terms of awareness, Narelle is adamant that communities within NT are realising what an effective recycling system could and should look like as Envirobank Recycling has automated the depot, an adjustment which will largely benefit younger generations. This is clear in the organisation's mission statement and Narelle's vision for the future.

"Envirobank is going to change the way we recycle in Australia through rewards and incentives for consumers and automating depots... In doing that, there are a number of charities and communities that can self-fund."

Social good, mentorship and economic change

While Envirobank Recycling may pave the way for self-funding, the company also contributes to Barnardos Australia; a not-for-profit child protection charity which seeks to prevent abuse in foster care. Narelle's personal focus on providing opportunities for disadvantaged children dates back to her own experiences of prejudice as a student.

"Having been a child being told you can't do this and you won't be able to do that is being pigeonholed into a class set. With my Indigenous background, I feel passionately about having positive conversations with young people."

When asked about her own mentorship experience, Narelle attributes the growing success and national impact of Envirobank Recycling to one-on-one guidance and a strong network of support. Her first mentor, Lyn Scott [owner of Creative by Design], provided Narelle

with the right tools to start her own business and the "discipline" she needed. Eventually, Narelle joined the Entrepreneurs Organisation [EO]; a global business network of 10,000 plus entrepreneurs which enables business owners to learn by sharing experiences and strategies. Through the connections she made at EO, Narelle found new ways to raise productivity in customer service, accounts and other fields of her business.

"Having mentorship is absolutely critical when you start out on your own; nobody in my family had owned or operated a business so I couldn't seek out advice there. It can be very rewarding and very tough."

On the road to building Envirobank Recycling, Narelle believes that the foundation of a strong support network is emphasising her philosophy behind business and forming solid relationships with her clients. Her advice for emerging entrepreneurs is to be "motivated by things others say cannot be done" and not to focus solely on the financial rewards.

"When owning a business, you don't need to be an entrepreneur, but there comes a level of responsibility to make a contribution to your team and community."

Lessons from Narelle:
- When you fall down, get back up.
- Good mentorship is essential.
- Don't buy into the story, write your own.
- Be motivated by things others say cannot be done, makes you want to work incredibly hard.

Almost as importantly, Narelle reinforces that no success has been achieved without "a lot of heartache and soul-searching" as an entrepreneur her own journey is an incredible example of how one can find their place in business without compromising their priority to help their environment. Her last piece of advice to those struggling against conforming to the expectations of others is:

"Don't buy into the story, write your own."

JACQUELINE ARIAS

Founder of República Coffee

Astonishing value comes from the country of Colombia. Home to an array of unspoiled coastlines, the magnificent Amazon jungle provides 20 percent of the world's oxygen, and is the second biggest coffee bean market in the world.

It's also where a conscientious, deeply passionate and forward-thinking woman was born. Jacqueline Arias knows that coffee is the most heavily traded food commodity in the world, grown in some of the poorest regions and extremely volatile in price. With this knowledge and a heart for social justice, Jacqueline founded República Coffee and is now making drastic changes to the coffee industry.

REPÚBLICA COFFEE

Founded
2007

Awards
OVER 15 INCLUDING
WINNER UNITED NATIONS
BUSINESS AWARD,
EXCELLENCE IN OVERALL
ENVIRONMENTAL MANAGEMENT

Inspiration
TO PROVIDE ETHICS
WITH IMPACT

Social justice beginnings

Former ABC journalist turned entrepreneur, Jacqueline has been motivated towards peace and prosperity within her home country since she was a young girl.

"The class system is very much a class system [there]. You have the very wealthy and the very poor people and my father divorced himself from that and moved us to Chile to where it was the only country that had a social scale at the time. As a young child, I remember going on marches in the street holding up banners, chanting for the rights for the poor, chanting for the rights for the workers, I remember my mother signing petitions for women's rights. I think that all built the character of the person I am today. That's what my parents taught me. There wasn't a light bulb moment where I thought I'm just going to do this. The moment isn't now or wasn't five years ago, it happened when I was a child," Jacqueline retells.

While her curiosity blossomed into a career as one of Australia's leading journalists, after eight years Jacqueline sought a more direct route to the justice she craved. "Journalism for me, it's still a great passion of mine: Once a journalist, always a journalist. But I think above being a journalist, what I am connected to is justice. Journalism was perfect for that transition I made to a business woman. I was doing stories about social justice when I was a journalist, now I have a business that brings about social justice".

Profit for purpose catalyst

Jacqueline is opportunistic and focused on strong execution. She starts with a clear goal. After traveling back to Colombia with her family, the expectation of tasting the rich quality of the Colombian coffee bean was soon darkened by the reality of farming and production conditions for the workers. Jacqueline was faced with poor farmers who were clearly not receiving adequate reward for their work, drinking poor tasting instant coffee, burdened by serious social problems.

"That just didn't make sense to me, that coffee is grown and harvested in Colombia, but the instant coffee, it's really bad instant. At best, most of it goes outside to first world countries and supposedly the good instant is made overseas from Columbian product and is then shipped back to Colombia and sold to the locals at inflated prices."

That was the trigger and catalyst for Jacqueline. "I thought, that doesn't quite make sense. It's unjust that the people that grow most of the products that we consume and, come from these third world countries, don't get paid anything. Coming back to Australia from that trip I resigned from my previous career at the ABC and started searching for what I was going to do that was different," Jacqueline recounts.

República's journey; making Australian history

Driven by determination and distinguished by ethics, República Coffee was established in 2007. It's important to understand that Jacqueline not only launched a brand, but was the driver of impact within the coffee industry in Australia, something that will leave a strong legacy for the future. "All of our products at República are 100 percent organic, 100 percent carbon neutral, certified by the Australian Government, fair trade and 100 percent Australian owned." República leads the market in environmental outcomes, becoming the first certified carbon neutral business in Australia.

"We are very committed to being carbon neutral. It's something I am extremely proud of and it's something I did during a time when the Australian climate was politically anti-carbon anything. I know what's going on with climate change."

In a relatively mature Australian coffee market, Jacqueline knew the business she was to build needed an edge and a point of difference. With her dual passion for sustainability and helping those without a voice, fair trade delivered that point of difference.

THE MORE YOU TALK TO PEOPLE AND ALLOW THEM TO GUIDE YOU, THE MORE CONFIDENCE YOU WILL HAVE IN YOURSELF

"We are talking 2005 and 2006, [fair trade] just didn't exist in Australia and I had never heard of fair trade. Fair trade is all about ensuring that farmers in third world countries are paid a fair price for their produce. That made perfect sense to me because I could go into business but I didn't have to compromise my ethics and they are paramount to me."

It became Jacqueline's mission for herself and her business to make "fair trade accessible to local Australians in their supermarket and that's been my driving motto ever since."

For Jacqueline, the fact that her business is financially successful is a bonus. The fact that it is ethical is paramount. "For me the idea was very different and it was about fair trade, organics, carbon neutral, recycling...it was all about ethics. Money is not my driver, so that was really interesting learning for me that I operate differently to my fellow entrepreneurs. Would I start another business? Online seems to be a very attractive space to be in but at the end of the day for me to keep the momentum, the passion, for me to wake up in the morning with any sort of interest I need to be motivated by a bigger purpose than making money."

A larger vision for ethical outcomes has lead to Jacqueline focusing on the social justice outcomes of her fair trade business transactions, including giving back to a group of 19,000 coffee farmers and their extended families in Timor. "They live in very remote areas, which are spread over big big areas in the hills in Timor. What these farmers realised is that they didn't have any sort of health care whatsoever and for them to get into the villages to receive some primary health care was very difficult. Through the fair trade system, they were able to allocate some of those funds they are getting from being paid the fair price for their produce, they took some of those funds and created a mobile health clinic that has a primary doctor and health carer that travel around these big areas on a monthly basis. That's a great example of the benefits of fair trade and what we do."

While other entrepreneurs might start in Australia with visions to go global. Jacqueline has almost reversed this type of expansion. Australians have a long-standing love affair with helping out those less fortunate, so it's only a matter of time before the fair trade and carbon neutral trend integrates mainstream consumerism. República has

been a pioneer of this change. Jacqueline's ethical actions has primed Australia for both social and environmental growth.

"My vision is to build and create the most ethical food brand in Australia. I am thinking about not only fair trade, but what that means to the Australian farmer. Fair trade doesn't only apply to third world farmers, I'd like to see that here in Australia."

Results come from confidence

Without her absolute confidence in her vision, República wouldn't have become the successful organisation it is today. Jacqueline believes that confidence and success go hand in hand.

"If you don't have confidence in yourself you can't expect other people to believe in you."

For women starting out, Jaqueline emphasises the importance of community. "Don't be afraid to pick up the phone because the level of generosity, female or male, to share what they have learnt is incredible. If somebody says no, move onto the next person. The more you talk to more people and allow them to guide you will instill more confidence in you."

What's next for Jacqueline? She has future ambitions to enter the US market as "out of 300 million people there is a high percent that is educated about ethics," and has launched the first biodegradable coffee capsules in Australia. "Currently the capsules made out of aluminum take 200 years to decompose and biodegrade. The ones made out of plastic take anywhere between 400-500 years to biodegrade, the ones we make will take 360 days."

Success looks like "family, children, business and all of those things coming together and are in harmony. It's not just about one side of your life it's across all areas," Jacqueline says.

Jacqueline has made waves and shown her capabilities are limitless as she's recently won over 15 awards including in 2013 Australia's Leading Sustainable Business by Smart Company and the United Nations Business Award for Excellence in Environmental Management in 2014.

"My vision is to build and create the most ethical food brand in Australia. I am thinking about not only fair trade, but what that means to the Australian farmer for example. Fair trade only applies to third world farmers, I'd like to see that here in Australia."

SHELLEY BARRETT

Founder of ModelCo

For ten years Shelley Barrett owned and ran an esteemed modelling agency. In that time she saw professional makeup artists had access to much better products and services than women outside the industry, and was convinced there was a gap in the market.

Identifying the need for innovative, dual-purpose beauty solutions for women on the go, Shelley founded Modelco, one of Australia's most renowned beauty companies, providing award-winning tanning, beauty and sun care solutions for more than a decade. Here she explains how ModelCo uses innovation to drive market trends, but also how she seeks inspiration and harmony.

MODELCO

Founded
2002

Awards
MANY INCLUDING ERNST & YOUNG'S YOUNG ENTREPRENEUR OF THE YEAR

Inspiration
A FORMER MODEL AGENT, SHELLEY SAW A NICHE IN THE MARKET FOR INNOVATIVE, QUICK-FIX, MULTIPURPOSE BEAUTY SOLUTIONS.

Today, ModelCo spans across a full cosmetics, self-tanning and sun care range also including products for the eyes, lips, face, body, nails and tan. In 2014, ModelCo launched a natural skincare line which includes moisturisers, cleansers, facial oils, a booster, an exfoliant and a toner. ModelCo, has enjoyed spectacular global success with the brand now sold in 5 continents, 11 countries and over 3000 retailers including department stores.

From an early age, Shelley always had a strong desire to create her own business. "This was innate in me," she explains. "I knew that I loved that drive to see a project through from start to finish, no matter how big or small."

Her passion to succeed is a driving force behind the idea of ModelCo. Seeing the high demand for quick, smart beauty solutions for women gave Shelley the confidence to pursue her ideas.

"I experienced first hand the limitations of innovative beauty products on the market and the lack of accessibility professional makeup artists had to premium products," she says.

"I create products for women who want to look and feel their best whilst enjoying a busy lifestyle. That's what ModelCo is about – achievable, every day glamour."

From one product – a heated eyelash wand – to a global enterprise, Shelley's success with ModelCo is nothing short of astonishing. "I certainly didn't realise at the time that I was creating a global beauty company!" she admits.

Stay ahead of the curve

Shelley has one very simple yet clever secret to selling good products: "The single most important thing I keep top of mind is to stay ahead of the curve by producing truly unique and innovative products, which are smart beauty solutions, not just a fad or gimmick but which become an essential part of a woman's beauty regime."

While observation and innovation are integral in a product based business with changing market trends, they won't get far without continued development and execution. When Shelley launched the first ModelCo innovation, Turbo Lashwand Heated Eyelash Curler in 2002 she soon saw a gap in the market for other products. Shortly after she launched the world's first aerosol self-tanner Tan Airbrush in a Can, which was an international sell out and drew interest from some of the world's most premium stockists. Myer and David Jones Australia, Collette in Paris, beauty mecca SpaceNK in London and Henri Bendel and Sephora in the USA, all snapped up the product.

A decade after its inception, Shelley Barrett is a household name on equal footing with ModelCo. Having built a brand with such high credibility it has managed to attract the endorsement of Elle Machperson, Danni Minogue, international model and singer Cheyenne Tozzi and former Victoria's Secret model and Vogue cover girl Rosie Huntington Whiteley. Ms Huntington was signed for the face of the 2013/14 summer campaign, which she was extremely happy with.

"I'm so excited to be working with ModelCo. We all want a quicker, smarter way to look and feel glamorous and ModelCo is a trustworthy brand that makes me feel exactly like that!" Ms Huntington said.

Shelley views the signing of Ms Huntington as a key moment for her business. "I believe in organic partnerships; it is important that whoever represents ModelCo loves and identifies with the products and who we are as a brand. I have great respect for strong and empowering women and our ambassadors have all embodied everything we stand for," she says.

ModelCo's success has come from keeping ahead of the market. For Shelley this means the company not only pre-empts the market, but drives trends. But, Shelley recognises that this requires caution as well as boldness. For example, with her international expansion she has taken care not to expand too quickly but rather conquer one market at a time. She also advises that mistakes and small failures should be expected as part of the journey, as they enable "you to re-evaluate your business goals and re-focus on the most important parts of the business."

Seek inspiration and harmony

Seeking inspiration and help from others has been key to Shelley's success. "I like to seek advice from people whom I admire in the business world. I am constantly learning on the job," Shelley explains.

An important inspirer is Shelley's mother. "Mum has always instilled a strong work ethic in me and has been an inspiring mentor. Mum continues to be involved in my business to date. She is a great source of support and works in the business with me."

Balance is essential to making it as a businesswoman. "Personally, I am sure that I speak for all women when I say that success is about achieving that perfect balance between a phenomenal working career, family commitments and personal life," she says. "I strive to work on this every day and feel proud when all aspects of my life are work together in harmony."

Shelley has balance between life and work down to fine form. "I try and keep everyone happy," she says. "I have found that it is essential to plan ahead to keep your sanity. I also strongly believe in taking time out for yourself every week, even if it is just a couple of hours, makes all the difference to managing a hectic schedule."

Working together in harmony has also been important from a team point of view at ModelCo. "ModelCo HQ is a wonderful team environment. I always lead by example and find that my genuine passion and enthusiasm for ModelCo rubs off onto my employees and creates a positive and energetic team," says Shelley.

It is not just the positive team environment, which helps generate ideas for ModelCo, but being surrounded by inspiring people, objects, places and beauty is important.

Her final three pieces of advice for success? "Understand the business that you are going into. Surround yourself with people who have more knowledge than you and who can guide you through the process. Work out the funds you need to start up and then double them!"

LAYNE BEACHLEY

Founder and CEO of Aim For The Stars Foundation

You can't help but feel an overwhelming sense of happiness while in the presence of Layne Beachley. Seven time world surfing champion-cum-social entrepreneur, she has a refreshing self awareness about her you'd struggle to find anywhere else.

Founder of Aim For The Stars (AFTS), a foundation established to offer assistance to help women achieve their ambitions, Layne's positive mentality is contagious. Her ability to build a strong personal brand both in and outside of media is rivalled by few, now her mission is to empower women to take ownership of their lives, to get out of their way and take control of their futures. Through financial and moral support, they can dare to dream and aspire to achieve in all endeavours such as academia, business, arts and sport. But above all, she says, life and love are the two most important things in Layne's world.

AIM FOR THE STARS FOUNDATION

Founded

2003

Achievements

28 WORLD CHAMPIONSHIP TOUR EVENTS
SEVEN TIMES WORLD SURFING CHAMPION

Inspiration

MAKING IT EASIER FOR YOUNG WOMEN TO ACHIEVE THEIR GOALS

I NEVER SPEND TOO MUCH TIME LOOKING BACK, ONLY FORWARD, BECAUSE THE REAR VIEW MIRROR IS A LOT SMALLER THAN THE WINDSCREEN

Proving herself

Layne has always wanted to prove her worth to the world. A beloved and cherished Australian sports star, an icon and household name to many, she is the first woman in history to gain 7 World Surfing Championships, six of them consecutive. It's not surprising she has amounted to such success, as she recounts that from the moment she left school and won her first world title, she was determined to be the best female surfer in the world, even if that meant sacrificing mental and physical health to do it.

Believing an entrepreneur is someone who is living their life according to their truest values and beliefs while pursuing a career path, Layne feels that it is her passion to make an impact that gives her motivation and inspiration to jump out of bed every morning. She says all entrepreneurs have a similar drive. "Sometimes they may not want to jump out of bed, sometimes they may have to roll out of bed involuntarily but they are still doing something that's true and meaningful to them. They are not subordinating themselves to societal beliefs or expectations of them. They are innovative, creative, the life-blood of the economic success of most nations."

As children we are naturally willing to learn and we don't consider falling down as a failure, Layne points out. But, as we get older and wiser, we somehow become so conditioned to fear of consequence, failure and looking "stupid" that we will let someone down when failing to learn is the biggest failure of all. "You have to experience what you don't want, to understand what you do. A lot of us are unwilling to put our hands up and open our hearts just in case it doesn't work out," she says.

The journeys of high achievers, particularly professional athletes, are never easy. Layne has spoken widely in the media about battling depression, chronic fatigue and even suicidal tendencies on the path to achieving her dream. Adopted at birth by the Beachley family, growing up in Manly on Sydney's Northern Beaches, Layne has overcome many obstacles to be in the place she is today. Through her gallant efforts she has defied gender stereotypes and carved a path for the women that have and will continue to follow in her footsteps, not only in sport but all walks of life.

"The memories always come flooding back from my 6th world title and the impact it had on my life. I was so focused, driven and intense. I had such high expectations of myself and of those around me. I had the compassion of a tiger shark; I was on a mission and it almost killed me because I was operating and succeeding on nothing but fear. That's what I learnt to trust in. Shortly after that win I realised that love has to emanate from within first and you can't achieve anything without accepting who and what you are. I grew a lot. I am one of the fortunate few that have done that. I have always been aware of my influence and the consequences of my actions, every path I've chosen, every road I've taken, it's always been a very conscious decision based on the impact it will have on the lives of those around me."

Identity and equality

Layne's journey has been framed by a constant search for identity and a fierce desire to be considered equal, particularly among her male counterparts in the surfing world. In the early stages it was a difficult battle for Layne as there was an overall lack of investment in female surfers, "I needed people to believe in me, I needed financial security, I needed a network of support. I learned very early on that you're as good as the people you surround yourself with. I looked at my career, in 1994, I was number two in the world, earning $8000 a year from my sponsor, I was traveling the world and trying my absolute hardest to claim my first world title and I didn't have the financial means and independence to chase my dreams. That was one of the first times I wanted to quit but the empathy of one of my employers who believed in me sent me $3000 for my next around the world ticket."

Layne has spoken openly about being a child of rape, and also of losing her adoptive mother at the young age of six. It's for these reasons, the tough struggle for so many women, that Layne founded Aim For The Stars. "I remember before I became a world champion, I thought about all of the things I really needed but couldn't manifest without meeting some sort of challenge and adversity. I realised that when I became successful all the things I really needed

were just thrown my way, but I actually needed those things before I became successful."

The kindness shown by her employer prompted Layne to help other women experiencing that same level of financial hardship and challenge. She wanted to become a role model, mentor and provider for these individuals lives by creating tangible change. "There are so many charities out there that help masses but everyone's supporting teams, organisations and movements but no one is really supporting individuals. Having someone tell me that they believed in me increased my own self-confidence and changed my life, that's why I started AFTS."

There's a great deal of red tape and paper work when it comes to establishing a charity; Layne was fortunate to meet Peter Russell from accounting firm KPMG who led the establishment process. Eleven years later, Russell still remains on the board as a financial advisor.

Just like any enterprise AFTS has not been without hiccups. "We haven't been able to clearly articulate or understand our value proposition so we haven't had the confidence to sell ourselves and ask what we need to provide a service in return."

Layne is confident in the momentum of the charity, and wholeheartedly believes in its purpose. "We have just done a strategy in sponsorship and marketing, now we have a much clearer idea of what we have to offer and how much we need, now it's a matter of asking for it and asking the right people, " she says.

The Foundation awards a minimum of $70,000 worth of scholarships each year. Open to girls 12 and up, individuals being granted a $4000 scholarship while groups have access to a $6000 scholarship. Since it's inception, AFTS has supported over 170 girls and women, whom have all been instilled with the value of 'paying it forward'.

"One exciting individual was a young girl we supported, Carolyn Buchanan, she's a world BMX champion and world mountain bike champion. Having been part of the who 'Aim of the stars' and seeing the positive effects we had on her life, she wants to pay it back and forward and she's created this program called 'Buchanan next gen' and it's identifying two future mountain bike or BMX aspiring champions and sourcing sponsorship and support for them, in turn AFTS is supporting that."

Challenges and strategy

With a few struggles in funding and some unfortunate sponsorship losses, in the future, Layne would like to see AFTS become financially sustainable and ultimately become bigger than her and outlive her. "I love the difference it makes but we have not told the story well so that's why this whole redefining our strategy has been so important for the continuation and success of the mission."

Layne has a great deal of life lessons to pass onto these women, believing you should be aware of how you're thinking and how you're feeling. Announcing her retirement from professional surfing in 2008, Layne was confronted by serious internal angst by the transition. "When I retired, I felt lost. I lost my identity, I lost my purpose, my vision, I felt like I lost everything. It was how I identified myself, I identified myself through my career as opposed to wholly. I remember sharing these challenges with people because I didn't want to be in that state for very long. I learnt the difference between frustration and dissatisfaction. When you're frustrated you're in a state of negativity."

MY MISSION IS TO EMPOWER WOMEN TO TAKE OWNERSHIPS OF THEIR LIVES, GET OUT OF THERE WAY AND TAKE CONTROL. THAT'S WHAT I'M ALL ABOUT

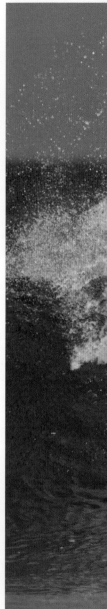

A strong advocate for women, Layne asserts that we often don't want to show our vulnerabilities or weaknesses and because of this we become islands, we ostracise and we isolate, not only ourselves but others. "Don't get stuck in this world and hope that things will change and hope things will move and hope things will be different. Because hope defers satisfaction," she says.

Lessons from Layne:
- If you have to ask yourself why you are doing something, justify and rationalise it to yourself, then your heart's not in it.
- Hope defers satisfaction. Don't hope for change. Make it happen.
  Be aware of how you're thinking and how you're feeling. You know what you're capable of.

Layne knows perseverance like no other. Met with many closed doors, but fueled by winning and achievement, Layne has had to constantly assess what it is she wants from life. "I was the executive director of the women's tour for many years and I made a lot of sacrifices, a lot of compromises and a lot of decisions that were disagreed with. I realised if I have to ask myself why I am doing something, justify, rationalise or reassure myself of something, then my heart's not in it." Always an honest and open leader, Layne admits she's currently not sure what her own future looks like but is certain to continue with positive momentum to help more ambitious women achieve their dreams.

"We are the architects of the future and we have the power to change the world if only we would get the out of our own way. We are the world's worst enemy, we can be so critical and judgmental, hard on each other, hard on ourselves. I see so much potential and power in women and I want that to shine through. That's what I really want. That's become my own personal mission."

JO BURSTON

Founder of Rare Birds

No matter what time of day, whether she's at the beach or skiing down a mountain, Jo Burston is constantly thinking about better ways to do business in order to achieve better outcomes.

The founder of Job Capital, as well as a plethora of tech businesses, Jo now steps purposefully into her future with new venture Rare Birds. She is goal oriented, and her confidence makes a powerful engine to execute the new opportunities uncovered by a curious mind. After several business successes, Jo has learnt many lessons and her new venture, Rare Birds, is fuelled by a passion to share her hard won knowledge with those that need it and encourage others to extend themselves. Her one motto, "If she can, I can".

JOB CAPITAL & RARE BIRDS

Founded
2006
2014

Achievements
SMART COMPANY TOP 30
FEMALE ENTREPRENEURS
2011-2014

NSW PEARCEY AWARDS -
ICT ENTREPRENEUR OF
THE YEAR 2012

Inspiration
TO GIVE EVERY WOMAN
THE OPPORTUNITY TO BECOME
AN ENTREPRENEUR BY CHOICE,
GLOBALLY.

Natural curiosity and leadership

Growing up in Revesby Heights in Sydney's South-West, Jo's father was a fireman and her mother a banker. Jo had an innate thirst for learning that has transferred itself into a passion for achievement. In an era where women were expected to stop working once they had a family, Jo attributes her desire to lead, and her sense of resilience to the strong influence of her mother and grandmother. "The women in my family are the strong ones. We have a lot of matriarchs and very few patriarchs," she admits.

Jo's sense of curiosity and initiative was evident from a young age. Her style of learning was very much about seeing and doing. "I was always very inquisitive as a child and I asked a lot of questions," she remembers. As a kid, she was also interested in money, for the independence it could buy her. Jo found independence very early and was looking after herself financially by the time she was 19.

"I moved out of a very stable, loving home to be totally independent and loved it. I still do. It's a driver. Financial security gives me the freedom and independent pathway I love."

At 25 she left a job in retail to spend two years travelling. "I wanted to see what was around every corner and that remains in me with everything I do. "I want to know why things work the way they do, why others make certain decisions, or why they think in a certain way. I think my natural curiosity lead to wanting to have a lot of travel at a very young age as well."

She came home with a new perspective and desire to step into a new career.

"I fell into a migration (Visas) desk and was to build the sales for the company which I did really, really well. I joined as a junior when I was 28 years old. I was at the bottom of the rung and most of my 30 year old colleagues had finished degrees and had really big incomes." Jo quickly began to even out the ledger, and by the end of her tenure Jo was 32 and had managed to work her way up to the general manager's position.

"I had learnt how to read basic profit and loss statements; I could write and run sales reports, sales meetings and I could get a group of people together and motivate them. I could understand the logistics behind the commercial agreements and the logic behind them as well."

GO OVER, UNDER, AROUND OR SMASH STRAIGHT THROUGH YOUR BARRIERS

I FIND I AM MOST EFFECTIVE AND AM AN EXTRAORDINARY LEADER IN SMALL TEAMS. I ASK PEOPLE TO TRUST ME, WHICH IS REALLY HARD FOR SOME PEOPLE TO DO AND TO TAKE WHAT AN ENTREPRENEUR SAYS AS WORD

Jo was constantly finding ways to improve how the business was operating but having reached the top of the ladder in her business, there was little room to move, and she began to get itchy feet.

A relentless belief

Flying to Melbourne to make a business pitch to a renowned businessman, Jo had what she calls a sliding doors' moment. "I walked in and he was frantically trading on some screens. At that time, the stock market was running in a crazy way, and he said to me 'take a seat where ever you want' and somehow I just became really ballsy and bold. I walked around to his side of the desk and sat in his chair and said to him "I'm going to sit here one day so it may as well be now". I ended up pitching my own business to him and he saw a strength in me that I didn't even realise I had yet. Some weeks later I had an investor and a new business called Job Capital."

Finally, Jo had a mentor - someone who believed in her - someone with an intense background as a serial entrepreneur.

In the first four years, Job Capital hit a turnover of $40 million with 12-13 staff. In its infancy, Jo remembers that they managed to make things work despite a serious lack of infrastructure in the business. "We were trading off MYOB and we actually had no CRM and no website for the first two and a half years of the business which seems really outrageous".

So, how did Job Capital become such a success in such a short period? What Jo did well was sell. "I built and groomed salespeople in the company. It was one of the greatest things I brought to the business. Where did that come from? One of the lessons was that my mentor used to walk into the office everyday and say "Jo what are your sales and what is your cash in the bank?"".

Being cash-flow-positive is essential to not only a sustainable but a robust business, and Jo soon learnt the most important thing about starting her business is sales "because that's the fuel that gets everything else driving".

Negotiating, building and strategy

Jo believes entrepreneurs have an insatiable appetite for achieving, propelled by an 'eye on the prize' mentality. Part of acquiring that high comes through understanding necessary processes, finding the right team to execute and negotiating to get you across the finish line.

"I also had this insatiable thirst for winning the deal, this insatiable thirst for knowing how to sell well, close deals and win big," she says.

Operating in the payroll industry, in a business that was growing quickly, required Jo to manage several outsider parties. "Being a good negotiator was something I had to learn to do very, very quickly and believe in and be strong in that space as well." Her competence soon paid off.

"Some of the greatest things in my journey were the awards we won, the accolades we were able to share as a team, those very first awards. Winning a smart company award getting on the BRW fast starters list three years in a row, the BRW list four years in a row, becoming a female entrepreneur top 30, top 40, top 50, year after year."

Having developed an extraordinary network in Sydney and globally, relationship building has been key for Jo. "I have extraordinary relationships that are built on trust and respect as a foundation. I always deliver on what I say I am going to do."

Every journey has complications and Jo admits hers has had rough patches. Certain of her strengths, she has also become aware of her weaknesses, after making her fair share of mistakes. While an entrepreneur should hire for skills they lack, hiring has not been her strong point. "I have made terrible hiring decisions along the journey. I've interviewed people for an hour or two and made the

wrong decision. I've done more talking than listening when hiring and I've also hired people on credentials rather than attitude."

What works well for her is working in small teams. "I find I am most effective and am an extraordinary leader in small teams. I ask people to trust me, which is really hard for some people to do."

As Job Capital moved into a healthy life cycle, Jo learnt that to create changes in the business, she required strategy. She points out that entrepreneurs should pay particular attention to threats they can't control. "Uncertainty and change taught me to strategise and strategise everyday," she says.

With a balanced understanding of how her business worked, Jo wanted to gain better knowledge of the technological landscape and in pursuit of this goal, built tech ventures Big Data, SignEzy, Cleaning Maid Easy and Candidate Bank among others.

Lessons from Jo:

- Believing in yourself is essential to becoming a good negotiator.
- Relationships are built on trust and respect. Always do what you say you are going to do.
- Be loyal to people who are loyal to you. Surround yourself with people who care for you and believe in your vision.
- If you do nothing, nothing will happen.
- Go over, under, around or smash straight through your barriers.

Inspiration and Rare Birds

Once Job Capital was built Jo wanted to find what would make her happy and fulfilled in more than just financial stability. She found her cause while receiving an award. "I remember standing on a stage accepting a Pearcey award for ICT, Matt Barry had nominated me for, I looked around the room and couldn't see any women".

Plagued by the internal question of 'where are the women?' Jo felt it was her responsibility to be the catalyst for change when it came to women in entrepreneurship.

"I took a film crew in 2013 to my old schools, the University of New South Wales, Revesby South Public school and Picnic Point High School and asked young girls and women what they perceived as being a woman entrepreneur and what being an entrepreneur meant to them in Australia."

The response was deflating for Jo. Not only did they not really know what an entrepreneur was, but they couldn't name an Australian one let alone a female.

"That was an epiphany for me and the place where Rare Birds started. I wanted to establish a company that really focused on what we now call 'profitable smart heart' and the ability to have 'cold passion'; the ability to have your heart and mind working in conjunction with each other.

Jo decided her next year was to be spent aligning her purpose with a financial value proposition. It was going to be about building a business, being highly profitable, but also with a social and economic impact both locally and globally.

"Our mission is to give every woman globally the opportunity to become an entrepreneur by choice. Choice being the key word. Rare Birds will encourage every little girl and boy, every aspiring and every current entrepreneur to be aware that entrepreneurship is a career choice and Rare Birds is a place that nourishes and supports this choice with real tools." Jo says.

Rare Birds is about giving current entrepreneurs a voice. "We want to inspire women. We want to allow them to tell their story and share it with our global community, so that a few years from now, when you ask a young girl what she wants to be when she grows up, it's not so surprising when she says she wants to own her own business or even change the world."

Today, Rare Birds is exactly as she envisioned, inspiring women and creating a safe space for them to learn, act and do in the entrepreneurial world. Making its home in Australia, Rare Birds is beginning to plant seeds in major cities across the globe. But, Jo assures there are far greater things to come.

"Today what you see is one or two steps in the first million women entrepreneurs to be encouraged globally by Inspiring Rare Birds and Rare Birds the business. This is only part of my journey and the rest is to follow. I think I am half way there in life and I can't wait to share the rest with you."

CARDEN CALDER

Founder of BlueChip Communication

Carden, a fiercely funny and astute woman, had a strong sense that she needed to learn from other people first before she stepped out on her own. Carden left home at a young age, setting out to better understand the world.

Going into business was always a possibility for her but she admits, she didn't have the confidence to do it. She wanted experience first and the knowledge that she could achieve exactly what she fixed her mind on. By the time she started Bluechip Communications, she knew how she wanted to impact the world, the problem she wanted to fix, and how. Carden co-founded BlueChip Communication in 2004 with a clear vision to create "a better way" – for clients, for talented consultants, and for her as a working mother to balance work and personal commitments. Since then, BlueChip Communication is Australia's leading financial communication company.

BLUECHIP COMMUNICATION

Founded
2003

Experience
PRESIDENT OF ENTREPRENEURS ORGANISATION, SYDNEY

Inspiration
PASSIONATE ABOUT FINANCIAL SERVICES

Moving out

"I left home at 17 with $35 dollars which was very optimistic of me," she confesses rather wryly.

"There wasn't much else I could do. It took me a really long time to land on what my business purpose was. I thought about my life journey and my relationship with finance and I looked at my situation 20 years later; I had more money, there were things I had done to get myself into that situation, my choices were totally different and by the time I retire, by the time I stop working for money, I want my choices to be even wider. "

As a result of her personal journey she believes having finances under control is the next thing from health that gives us real satisfaction and peace of mind and choice. "If you have your income under control and you're saving, living within your means, you're building wealth for the future or a rainy day, the peace of mind that comes from that, the sense of achievement that comes from that are very different."

With a generous balance of compassion and level-headedness, Carden cherishes the quality relationships she has with people close to her and doesn't shy away from her realistic view that money is an essential part as to how we run our lives.

"My business exists to help people learn more about money, we work for clients in the funding sector and we help them get their messages out to consumers and people they do business with. What drives us when we do that, is this idea that when we represent our clients, when we help them get their message out, we can have real impact in the world by giving them information that allows them to make good choices with their own money."

When moving out at 17 most teenagers aren't fully knowledgeable about allocating their finances and financial skills. To Carden's testament, she admits she made it a priority to work out how to manage her money and fully grasped that when she was 30. "The older I got the more time I got to look at people and could see how their actions translated into good or bad outcomes for them. I also saw the flow on effect of that in their lives."

Bluechip Communications was somewhat born out of trial and error with finances. "I was 36 when my last grandfather died. I have been really fortunate to have that multi-generational connection, but what it also gave me the opportunity to do is look at how my grandparents made their money and then how my parents managed their money."

One of Carden's gifts she was given was her intelligence and the ability to have perspective, which is how her wise choices were made. "I worked out that those people that reached the end of their life in really good shape financially often reached the end of their life in really good shape in other ways as well, because they had more choices."

Carden found a sense of projection. She insists that there are two to three sides of the money equation.

1. Protecting what you have ie. insurance or that pod of money for a rainy day

2. Building for the future so accumulating wealth so you have much more money for the future particularly when you retire and you can fund your own retirement.

3. The day to day of living within your means.

IF I DO A GOOD JOB AS A LEADER IN THIS BUSINESS, I WILL TOUCH THE CAREERS OF MANY PEOPLE AND MAKE THEM RICHER FOR THE EXPERIENCE

Moving forwards

From having years experience within the Communications industry, Carden is a brilliant wordsmith herself. Although mentioning that becoming an entrepreneur was not as natural for her as it has been for others, the thrill came from the challenge. "I just loved corporate life, I was excited by working with big brands in sky scrapers and working with really senior folk and being a part of the cut and thrust of news media everyday. For me, that was really exciting but after a decade I stopped and thought I've done everything I wanted to do. By the time I was 30, I had spent a decade in news organisations and loved a lot of it and hated a lot of it and I had the chance to decide what the next phase of my life was going to be and I decided that it was going to be corporate. I was prepared to take more risk."

As Carden describes, each person will carve their own journey to the end goal and that's not something that can be taught. "I don't think there's a right way, each person has to find their right way. For me I had the opportunity to go into business when I left uni and I chose not to, I had a strong sense I needed to learn from other people. Going into business was always a possibility but I didn't have the confidence to do it, I didn't think I could do it and I felt like I needed to go and learn things from others first. That gave me the confidence to go out and actually do these things," she says.

Moving priorities

Carden's purpose is to live a very full life. Her ultimate happiness comes from firstly her family and dedicating her life to her children whom she hopes to instill solid grounding so they may flourish as adults.

"I think the most important purpose in my life is to have a good impact on other people's lives in everything I do and the people I will have the greatest impact on is my children. The first purpose I have in life is to make sure I set my children up for happiness, confidence and to follow their own path in life well by the time they leave my care and beyond. I have a similar responsibility to the people I work with."

She holds the notion that her life's purpose is about helping people get connected with others and achieving something greater. "If I do a good job in this business, it will have a significant impact on Australian's abilities to make good decisions about their financial futures. If I do a good job as a leader in this business, I will touch the careers of many, many people and make them richer for the experience. As a mum, I have an indelible impact on three people who are going to go out into the world and hopefully make it a better place."

Terms of success can be like a cycle, something we move in and out of. Carden definitely feels there has been some specific wins in her time as an entrepreneur, but she feels she's not yet at her most high achieving.

"There have been high points professionally and personally. There have been points where I have done really well. But I certainly don't think I'm there yet, and what does it mean to me, it means a rich and fulfilling life which is almost always in the final analysis with people about relationships. I partly define my success on the quality of relationships I have around me, particularly the quality of relationships I have with people close to me and I also define it by the impact I have in business".

By now we know that gender most certainly plays a role in business and also for the speed at which women entrepreneurs develop. "The statistics show if you're female you're likely to make it far less to the top. That's a question we have to ask ourselves as a society, why haven't we made progress, we have actually gone backwards." "For me there are things I'd do that I wouldn't do as a guy in this business. One of the things I do is take a very holistic view of my own life and of my colleague's lives. I look at it as less of a production and more as people who have a lot going on in their life. They have a professional story, they have an emotional story, family story, future professional story. I think about all of those stories when I look at my team. My part in their life journey, I need to add value in many ways, not just as the person who is the boss."

Carden mentions we have to be mindful when it comes to gender generalisations. "The more female role models, the better. It shows more people what is possible. When I talk to women, I know it has an impact. They think gee, she's not perfect but look what she has achieved. Women are only likely to put themselves forward when they have 11 out of 10 for the selection criteria. We need to be honest about our journey, warts and all, so they can see the ups and downs and so they can see real people are doing well. We are not such 'rare birds' we are ordinary people who chose to go down a certain path and often we have just stuck with it long enough."

Moving on up

When it comes to fostering the next generation of women entrepreneurs, it's about strength, confronting the brutal facts and identifying positive input for Carden. "I value frank feedback and welcome it, I ask my team to give it to me and in my close relationships and friends. And it hurts, often. But we also need to keep ourselves strong enough so we can hear that and take it onboard, understand that everybody has strengths and weaknesses and move forward without it paralysing us."

"What I have come to understand is that emotions are like seasons. It's windy and cold today, tomorrow might be rainy and the day after that it might be 30 degrees. Regardless what the weather is like, I still need to go to work and do my job. Regardless of what my emotional weather is like, I still need to go to work and do my job," Carden expresses.

Lessons from Carden:
- Life is about helping people get connected with others and achieving something greater.
- There's no right way, or one set path for being an entrepreneur.
- It's worth taking the time to figure out what you're going to do, so you can do it really hard.

Learning to manage that and to stay, calm, confident and productive without the emotional weather, is a tough one for anyone. Having an outlet is important and one of Carden's is running. She aims to complete a marathon in the future and her determination will get her there.

With the future always on the mind and moving forward positively, Carden would also like to dedicate more time for herself and community. "I'd like to be there more for my kids. The next 10 years for them are pivotal. I still want to be working, and I still want to have more from a community point of view."

In terms of her hopes for women and the entrepreneurial landscape, she'd like to see a change of approach. "What I've learnt is that equal outcomes, don't result from equal treatment. They need different sorts of support from different groups to reach the end goal. Programs that target women will help women achieve much more. Women are more prone to be less self-confident and take fewer risks. They take less risks because they are not self confident. We do things that are quite self-defeating. I do think there's an opportunity to educate women in particular about what the special needs of a female entrepreneur are."

THE MORE FEMALE ROLE MODELS, THE BETTER. IT SHOWS MORE PEOPLE WHAT IS POSSIBLE. WHEN I TALK TO WOMEN, I KNOW IT HAS AN IMPACT

REBEKAH CAMPBELL

———

Founder and CEO of Posse

A prominent face in the tech community, Rebekah Campbell is the type of person that will make you believe in dreaming big. She has a talent for raising capital, ambition to take on the world, and has developed her entrepreneurial skills and confidence through trial, action and learning.

Her most recent venture, Posse, founded in 2013, was born off the back of a string of successful businesses, which Rebekah, with an enduring thirst to go global, knew innately were never going to be her "billion dollar business". She backs Posse though, the end goal of which is to host a massive network of engaged merchants and consumers, globally. A dream that, with Rebekah at the helm, seems entirely achievable.

POSSE

———

Founded

2012

———

Awards

MANY INCLUDING APEC YOUNG WOMAN INNOVATOR OF THE YEAR

———

Inspiration

DECIDING TO BECOME AN ENTREPRENEUR AT AGE 9

BE HONEST WITH YOURSELF AND WHAT KIND OF BUSINESS YOU'RE TRYING TO BUILD. I KNOW I WANT TO BUILD A BILLION DOLLAR BUSINESS

Not your average entrepreneur

Rebekah is touted as one of the most fascinating entrepreneurs around and her peers and the greater Australian entrepreneurial community is keenly attentive to her progress. Having raised over $4.5million in funding and attracting investment from the likes of Google Maps' Lars Rasmussen and notable venture capitalist, Bill Tai, it's no wonder she has been pegged as 'one to watch'. At the end of 2014, Posse also merged with e-commerce heavyweight Beat the Q in the hopes of creating one all-encompassing retail consumer app.

Affectionately known as Bek, she grew up in Wellington, New Zealand with a strong sense of the power of ideas. "I think I always remember having ideas as a kid, I was an only child so I spent a lot of time by myself and I thought about things and made up my own games and started my own businesses at a very young age. That drive to execute my ideas carried on to my adult life and has always outweighed things like a salary or a job. At the age of nine, when my mum was working for an entrepreneur in time share, I thought entrepreneur was a cool word. It stuck with me as someone who has a vision and goes ahead and does it. I knew that was what I want to do, to be," says Bek.

Like most entrepreneurs, Bek was unprepared to settled into the role of passive observer when she saw a problem. While in University, she was plagued by Wellington's high youth suicide rate and in the attempts to raise awareness and see it put on the political agenda, Bek undertook a venture that would be indicative of her future as an entrepreneur, the Levi's Life Festival. The festival saw 15,000 young people come to watch twelve of New Zealand's music artists perform across two stages; an operation that required a clear vision, raising sponsorship money, securing artists and working the media to publicise the event and cause. Bek self describes it as "a turning point" in her life. Pulling off such a large-scale event cemented the idea that "anything was possible".

Raising capital and confidence

Possibly one of the most apparent discrepancies between male and female entrepreneurs is the ability to ask and ask big, particularly when it comes to investment. Bek is not shy about what she wants and needs for her business, understanding that if we want to go global then women need to think bigger about the potential of their businesses and the markets they can potentially tap into.

"It's hard to raise money unless you can be very big. It depends on the class and person you're going to and the objective. Figure out people's objectives and what kinds of people you want to go to. Be honest with yourself and what kind of business you're trying to build. I know I want to build a billion dollar business."

"What's important is looking at what kind of business you want to build and finding the right investors for it. If you're trying to build a focus business and you're raising it for a 2 million dollar evaluation and could eventually sell it for 10 million dollars, that's a very different kind of investor to someone who is only interested in a billion dollar exit and is doing it for totally different reasons.

"Raising money is obviously a huge challenge, but it's also a huge opportunity to learn.

People aren't going to put money into you unless you really know what you are doing, so you have to figure things out during that process. I see loads of startups fail because they don't look at the metrics. They will choose the best metrics report and go, "Oh, okay we can drive that, we can keep raising money." But people aren't using the actual fundamentals of the products, so it's important to be really honest with yourself and your team and address those fundamental issues."

Bek attests that she really worked on confidence this year. Seeing it was holding her back, even though she may have appeared to be confident, "it was almost a bit of a front I think and inside I didn't feel that confident".

"I started to read a bit on body language in the summer holidays and there was a study by Masschusetts Institute of Technology done that you can predict the outcome of a sales meeting without hearing any of the dialogue with 85 percent accuracy. So I was like well, if I am feeling like this then what is my body language saying, that's something I can't control, so I started reading all these things about the way you can change your body language and doing things like victory position before going into meetings. It was mainly focusing on my body language and that changed the way that after a while, the way I felt about myself, and that self doubt, is honestly gone. I've recently closed a bunch of pretty big deals and I don't think I would have gotten that

done unless I was completely confident even though I can pretend to be confident, it's never really the same thing as being confident."

Mentorship and womanhood

When it comes to development as an entrepreneur, role models and mentors are hugely helpful but for women they seemed to be few and far in between, Bek claims. "It doesn't seem that there any many role models out there. Naomi Simson is definitely a role model for me, I remember watching her on Kochie's business builders while she was running a tech company and I was running my music company and I was like, "wow that's so awesome", and I thought I could do that, that was definitely an inspiration for me. I think it's great to highlight other role models for women coming through. I don't think necessarily getting together and having champagne and nibbles really helps; women mentoring really helps. I don't think any smart entrepreneur will have trouble creating a network. I have so many people who have given me so much time for nothing."

On Posse, Bek notes that they are the only company to have built a two sided network that engages with stores and consumers. "We are building a network of shops and consumers for Posse, and then we are going to start putting other things through the network. We have 50,000 merchants using the platform and so we want to put things like mobile payments through it and a whole lot of other things, so you can use Posse to do a lot more than just find places."

While the merger with Beat The Q may more tightly align Bek's dream towards Posse becoming that 'billion dollar business', Bek laments that she couldn't have gotten to where she is today without the tenacity and resilience that ultimately drives her. But, she admits that she hasn't been saved from the gender discrepancies that exist within this world. A type of experience which can lead to serious self exploration.

"I've been through this experience and I always thought I was really ambitious and driven and didn't really have any limit to what I thought was possible. But, then I was sitting in these business meetings and they were talking about that "this is going to be huge and we're going to IPO". I can feel myself saying "can I really do that?". I think that's self-doubt, and that feeling of impostor syndrome."

Working hard, thinking big

Bek won't sugarcoat the journey either, she'll tell you it's hard, you have to work hard, anyone that's made it somewhere has. However, she indicates that women have this advantage of always questioning themselves, which she believes is really important. "Constantly ask yourself what it is you are doing, can you improve anything and then take responsibility for answering and executing on those objectives and goals?"

IF YOU'RE GOING TO START SOMETHING JUST BE REALLY CONFIDENT WITH YOUR VISION AND YOUR ABILITY TO PULL IT OFF. DON'T SECOND GUESS YOURSELF

Lessons from Bek:
- Be confident with your vision and your ability.
- Listen to your instincts.
- Don't be afraid to ask.
- Be honest with yourself and what kind of business you're trying to build. Don't settle for less.

"I think we are quite good at looking at things and taking responsibility and balancing that with self confidence. Don't lose that ability to self reflect and take responsibility for everything that goes wrong, and learn that you've got to be really confident and be confident in your vision. I've wasted a lot of time in my journey, and at the beginning I wasn't confident at all in my ability to design a product and there were all these guys that had more experience than me. They said it should look like this and it wasn't what I had in my head and what I thought it should look like. And, then I did it their way and it turned out that no one understood it. I wasted time because I didn't listen to my gut, and that's our strength as women, our intuition.

Finally, her advice to aspiring women entrepreneurs, "If you're going to start something just be really confident with your vision and your ability to pull it off. Don't second guess yourself. Listen keenly to your instincts, I have and always will. A dream will always be a dream until you make it a reality".

KAREN CARISS

———

Founder of PageUp People

PAGEUP PEOPLE

Founded
1997

———

Awards
MANY INCLUDING BRW'S
TOP 50 FEMALE
ENTREPRENEURS

———

Inspiration
TO MAKE HIRING EASIER
FOR BUSINESSES

Karen Cariss constantly aims to remain passionately committed, focused and driven with her ears open and on an always forward path. Karen was Ernst & Young's 2008 Young Entrepreneur of the Year and also won the 2009 Victorian Telstra Women's Business Award. An accomplished tech entrepreneur with a heart for making the world a better place every day, Karen is chief executive officer of PageUp People while Simon, her husband is senior vice-president in charge of innovation.

The power couple established their company in 1997, after finding themselves sorting through a myriad of job applications for a web-developer role. PageUp People provides both software and consulting services to help companies recruit staff and manage performance, mainly to blue-chip clients such as BHP Billiton, Coles, National Australia Bank and Origin.

Kicking goals early on

As CEO, Karen is a key driving force behind the success of PageUp, setting the strategic direction of the company as well as overseeing internal activities to ensure synergy of all divisions. Simon exerts his expertise in innovation as the senior vice president. His passion for the company and innovative new technology has been publicly acknowledged with PageUp receiving the B3000 Innovation Award in 2006 and frequently delivering first to market innovative solutions. Karen's commitment to the company is evident in her work and attitude, which has been publicly acknowledged by being listed as 28th on BRW's Top 50 Female Entrepreneurs in June 2006. Today, her vision and mission for the business is admirable. "I want to connect the careers of 100 million people by building technology that people love to use," a huge aspiration she admits. But with her sheer tenacity and unshakeable confidence, it is surely a sight she is set on reaching. Originally the goal of PageUp was to become the market leader in the Australian enterprise market, which she defined as working with the Top 100 ASX companies.

"We now work with 34 of the Top 100 ASX companies and are a strong market leader of this segment. We are now focused on continuing to strengthen our position in the Australian market while growing our global footprint. As part of our new goals I have relocated to Singapore as we drive significant growth across the Southeast Asian markets."

Now based in Singapore, entering into new global markets has proven particularly challenging. "We first entered the US market in 2009 and it is only now, some 6 years later that we have designed an approach that is providing us with momentum in the market. We have spent millions of dollars over the course of those years trying to get the formula right. This has distracted us in other areas of the business and as a consequence it has slowed our overall growth down. So, although we have now designed a good business model for that market, we have had many failed attempts along the way.

Courageous culture

Still enthusiastic about new concepts and entrepreneurship in general, Karen sees herself as an effective entrepreneur because she has, "identified a problem, designed a solution and delivered that to a market that values it.

She is insistent that upskilling and self development to stay ahead of the curve is vital to her role as CEO of PageUp.

"I learn every day through a range of different mechanisms. Reading books/blogs/ezines, asking questions, observing and listening to people, through to more formal learning such as conferences or courses. There is quite a lot of trial and error learning involved in areas where we are doing something completely new or experimenting.

But, she also concludes that the learning should never start and stop at the head of the business, there needs to be a trickle down effect in order to create a culture that moves with a fast changing market.

"In terms of company alignment, one of our company goals is 'Everyone Developing', where each employee is encouraged and measured against their regular development. To underpin our company's growth we need to make sure our people are also growing so they can deal with the new challenges a bigger company brings. We also have another company goal called 'Courageous Culture' which is about encouraging people to give things a go. Experimenting can be a great way to learn."

For women entrepreneurs, Karen feels diversity can lead to developing better solutions quicker.

"People's different approaches and their ability to identify problems in a market can lead to significantly richer lives for a greater percent of the population. So having a base of women entrepreneurs that reflects the demographics of the Australian population is important to help create a diversity of businesses that can enrich the lives of a greater percentage of the population."

IF YOU WANT TO DO IT, THEN VALIDATE YOUR IDEAS WITH THE MARKET, REFINE YOUR PLAN, QUIT YOUR DAY JOB AND BACK YOURSELF

As someone that has felt both the hardships and triumphs of her own entrepreneurial journey, Karen's advice to those on the cusp of their own journey is to just go ahead and do it.

"There's never a perfect time and always a million excuses you can find not to take the step, but if you want to do it, then validate your ideas with the market, refine your plan, quit your day job and back yourself. Most entrepreneurs love to help other entrepreneurs and you should develop some mentoring relationships with people that have been through some of what lies ahead of you so that you have some support during the difficult moments, which are very frequent in the early days."

Lessons from Karen:
- Diversity can lead to developing better solutions quicker.
- Create something people love.
- Develop a learning culture that moves with a fast changing market.

For herself, success means contributing to delivering the business's mission everyday.

"It is not a destination that I will arrive at, but a way of life that allows me to challenge myself each day to continue to contribute and to stretch the boundaries of how I'm doing that and of course have some fun along the way."

THIS BOOK IS SO OVERDUE NOT ONLY IN AUSTRALIA, BUT GLOBALLY. I READ HUNDREDS OF BOOKS ABOUT BUSINESS AND HAVE PUBLISHED MANY MYSELF, THIS IS ONE THAT CUTS THROUGH MOST I HAVE READ, SIMPLY BECAUSE OF THE FOCUS ON WOMEN ENTREPRENEURS AND THEIR UNTOLD STORIES.

───────

Chris Gray, CEO - Your Empire
Media and property commentator - Sky Business News, Australia

NAHJI CHU

Founder and CEO of MissChu

Slightly unorthodox and wildly unpredictable are just a couple of ways to describe the queen of rice paper rolls, Nga Chu, more commonly known as 'Nahji' or as her namesake, MissChu.

With public foot-traffic engaged in Nahji's catering kitchen in Sydney, the first MissChu tuckshop was opened in 2009. Peering out through the service window, was where Nahji became the Queen of the Rice Paper Roll. Nahji is the creative and marketing communications director of the company. She is also responsible for directing the contributions of a large array of creative talents.

MISSCHU

Founded
2007

Achievements
PROMINENT KEYNOTE SPEAKER: TEDX AND VIVID FESTIVAL

Inspiration
LOVE FOR HER HERITAGE COMBINED WITH FOOD CUSTOMERS ENJOYED

I HAVE MADE MISTAKES BUT I AM VERY GOOD AT COMING BACK TO THE PATH

Arduous path to success

Originally from Laos, Nahji escaped the 1975 Pathet Laos Regime with her immediate family, inhabiting various Thai refugee camps over a four-year period. Not long after, the Australian government made them one of the first Vietnamese/Laotian refugees to settle in Australia.

It is this history, which Nahji acknowledges every day with her brand Misschu. She admits there is a fair amount of ego involved in it.

"I'm very proud of my culture, very proud to be a Vietnamese refugee who has made it in this country, she says. "I wanted to say to Australia, 'I want to celebrate what it is that is Australian – and that is refugees and migrants'."

Nahji's approach to gourmet fast food is aggressively and unashamedly political, unlike anything Sydney's e astern suburbs have seen. The enterprise is the fusion of an entire life existence: from the menu, to the interior design and decoration. All of it

reflects the rich and complex history of Nahji's life including her experiences at school and struggling to learn a new language and culture.

Nahji is no stranger to starting from scratch. From moving across country, to arriving in Australia and learning a new language, Nahji and her family's history shows just how hard they worked to make a new life time and time again.

Nahji's grandparents and her parents before her went through the same experiences of 'moving through circumstances for survival,' as Nahji puts it. She recalls how strange and new Australia was to her and her family. "Everything's really polished and shiny to refugees."

Nahji is one of six children. "Three boys and three girls. We were all one year apart." All of them attended different schools, which were yet another culture shock for Nahji and her siblings. "We were the first

Asians in school and no one liked it. All the Australians were like 'I hate you' and they were the looks we would get. It was full on hatred. We were kicked and it was really like the Asian invasion back then."

Language was another barrier, Nahji adds. "Things like I had to go to the toilet in class but you didn't know how to say it. I had to learn the ABCs from scratch. Even though I was bright I used to always use cheat cards. I was desperate to catch up with everyone else."

It wasn't until Nahji and her family moved to Melbourne to reunite with an aunt living in Richmond, they received the first gestures of welcome.

"The people were more accommodating," says Nahji. We hit the local papers, as we were the first Vietnamese to hit that area of Australia. The story read, 'let's help the refugees,' so the whole community came with tins of food, crockery, furniture, clothing... our whole house was decked out with community gifts. It was really welcoming."

Nahji is the first to bring a nostalgic school feel to the high-design hospitality experience and it has resulted in friendly, chatty, fun and fast spaces. The design themes for MissChu came straight from her refugee history.

"I thought about the refugee visa I had, it was always exotic looking and I was very proud of that. For me it was a visual piece that you could frame and put on the wall, it would be the first thing that could be drawn to go just look at it in amazement, it has so much history about it, there is so much storytelling behind the three faces as well."

Nahji says it was then that she started to use the faces as part of the menu design. "I made it into a postcard and then I put a chopstick on it and then I put my business card on it. I gave it to my staff and said, 'put it in everyone's letter boxes' and printed about 5,000."

Soon, people came and said, "Are you Miss Chu? You're a genius!" I wanted everyone to see my visa; most people just loved the chopsticks. Most people don't even know that that logo is the girl in the refugee camp. It was my way of saying, 'I know you're going to love my food because my grandmother did it since 1978,' and I wanted to contextualise the Vietnamese identity."

Dreams lead to ambition

So what of her identity as a businessperson? "I knew I was a business person and ambitious, I didn't know I was an entrepreneur until I started Miss Chu and until I had multiple stores then people started calling me an entrepreneur. I didn't call myself an entrepreneur at all. I was a business owner.

I was a sole trader then made money and my accountant said, 'you need to form a company as you have employees,' then it wasn't until I became a brand, quite recently, 2-3 years ago...and then people started saying, 'so you're an entrepreneur' and I took it on board because I created something from scratch, it was original, I didn't copy cat anyone."

Nahji is well aware she has created something special with her MissChu brand. "I knew I created a frontier out of this. I looked at myself as the first person in the world doing this...this was my grandmother that was doing this and if she were alive she'd be so proud today."

Her advice to aspiring entrepreneurs is, "listen to your instinct because it's always going to be designed for you. It's different for everyone and it comes down to what you can do for yourself is how you get the gut instinct."

Nahji explains she is instinctual herself. "I have made mistakes but I am very good at coming back to the path. I partied and took drugs but I came back. It's a part of my journey and what makes me the person I am. A lot of Vietnamese women are not allowed to party. It's not ladylike, it's disrespectful. Mum would say, 'It's not what we do in our culture.' She was worried about what people were going to say about me but I was like, 'they will say things, but not to you, you've done a great job with me.'"

Nahji says happiness is also essential. "True happiness is important to me. Being myself completely makes me happiest. I get out of bed and I'm Miss Chu, feeding people is a nobel science. It's the biggest job in the world. Miss Chu is like an ingenious business. You have drivers, you are feeding people, it's like a hospital or an airport, and you're dealing with people's stomachs and dealing with the masses." She says her staff are 'really proud' representing the Vietnamese culture in Australian context. "We work with career trackers and Blue Dragon - children's foundation, and various little groups that come to me along the way."

Proud of her achievements, Nahji has come a long way from being the refugee without a single word of English and selling simple rice paper rolls. She is proud of aiming high for her dreams.

"I've dared to dream hard. Before I became Miss Chu, I dreamt to be wealthy and independent. I dreamt and said to my mum, 'I am going to make it big, I know it.' The brand is good food at a low price and I want respect. I'm giving you really good food and we are only charging $6. That's been in my blood since day one, making money is important but making money and a difference is what I want to do."

TOPAZ CONWAY

———

Chairman of PAFtec, Springboard Enterprises, and Biothoughts

BIOTHOUGHTS

—

Founded
2010

—

Awards
SEVERAL INCLUDING TOP 100
AUSTRALIAN BUSINESS WOMEN

—

Inspiration
ADVOCACY TO THE CREATION
OF A STRONGER AUSTRALIAN
INNOVATION CULTURE.

An initial verve for negotiation and future thinking developed in a chaotic but loving childhood has evolved for Topaz Conway into a passion for reinventing and reinvigorating businesses.

For Topaz, the corporate culture meant doing what you were told and not rocking the boat. She just kept seeing ways to make a better boat. Now the chairman of Biothoughts, Topaz is shaping both her industry and the world. Topaz has over 20 years experience working with early stage companies across a number of industries. Today she is an investor, is Chairman of PAFtec and Springboard Enterprises, and consults to Accelerating Commercialisation (formerly Commercialisation Australia) helping entrepreneurs achieve commercial success. She has Founded, and sold two of her own companies – both in the US – and her commitment is to 'give back' the support she experienced as an entrepreneur.

Roughhousing and high ceilings

From a young age, Topaz learned the skills of negotiation and delegation. Being the only girl in a house full with three brothers, two older and one younger meant it was typically hard to find ways of escaping the taunts and terrorising. As a line of defence Topaz would negotiate her safety by offering deals to ensure she wouldn't get the pointy end of the roughhousing with her 'band of brothers'. That early start helped Topaz develop her lateral thinking, quick analysis, and eye for win-win opportunity. Topaz grew with optimism and began to see situations in a unique way.

When she entered the business world, her focus was on developing ways of doing things better: how could she better sell, better market or do deals better. This approach ran with her for life. Through her education to every job she ever had, she would always push the envelope, looking at ways of making things run better.

In 1990, Topaz moved to Australia from the United States and entered the corporate life. As a single mother having to support young children she needed consistent and regular pay and the corporate life was the direction to go. In 1992, she began working as a general manager at the State Chamber of Commerce New South Wales where she was in charge of a team of thirty-four employees. She took care of business services including, commercial memberships, business, export, and corporate policy advisories. Topaz found herself at the heart of business in Australia, and it began her Australian journey with women in business.

At the Chamber of Commerce Topaz worked with the federal government and a group of like-minded professional women to establish the Australian Council of Businesswomen in 1994. The move to form the Australian Council of Businesswomen meant that women in business were finally given a voice at the Federal policy level, something that had never been achieved prior. This body was specifically designed to offer advice around problems relating to the 'glass ceiling', finance, corporate and small business owners .

After some time, Topaz left her role at the Chamber of Commerce and moved into another general manager/CEO role in 1996 at the Garvan Institute of Medical Research in Sydney. Her KPI's in this role were to build the Garvan brand and create a sustainable strategy for bringing funding into all programs within the research Institute. The Garvan brand grew and thrived under her leadership, and in 1999, the Garvan won the 'Arthur Anderson International Award for Best NFP Ad Campaign'.

For Topaz, the years spent in corporate life helped her realise that her strengths and skills lay in more entrepreneurial pursuits, she couldn't help but challenge the status quo. This was not always appreciated or encouraged in the corporate setting in the 1990's. So, when Topaz had the opportunity to work more autonomously, it seemed like the natural thing to make a shift.

"I returned to the US to start my businesses since entrepreneurism was not a culturally supported path in Australia at that time. I don't think most people realise that it was not that long ago when that term wasn't even used."

Finding a place

So in 2000, Topaz moved back to the United States to explore the dot com boom as a partner in a US firm, which suffered and closed after the crash in 2000. In 2002, she took an advisor role with Pacific Horizon Ventures, a Seattle-based venture capital firm focused on early stage biotechnology. There, she worked with several companies, including Illumigen BioSciences, which later exited to a large Pharmaceutical.

From there, Topaz became CEO at Cytopeia, a bioengineering company that had developed the first benchtop cell sorter. The three-year-old company was just about ready to launch their new product, but was in trouble from poor management and a loss of primary development funding. Around threats of mutiny by the team, Topaz was thrown into a rescue mission to get the company back on track. Over the next 2 years, she launched the product globally, secured funding, and retained the team. It was a good outcome for all and the company sold two years later to the target acquirer.

Next, Topaz decided to try building her own company, and started Vine Tales in 2005, an internet-based wine sales and wine club portal that offered high quality, boutique and value wines. The problem she was solving was her own, she had a love of wine but did not know how to pick the good wines so found it time consuming and expensive. Vine Tales offered a monthly shipment of personally selected boutique wines that weren't available in bottle shops. She used her creative flair and wrote about the wines in a fun and entertaining way so you knew what you were drinking, why you liked it, where it was from, a little bit about the winemaker and what food pairings were best. Her logo and artwork were inspired from old pin up girl artwork from the twenties and thirties, communicating the lightness and fun in her idea. Topaz built the company and then sold it in 2007 to return to Australia.

Upon returning to Australia Topaz decided to address the cultural void she found for entrepreneurs in Australia. It bothered her that entrepreneurs did not experience the support and celebration of entrepreneurs as she had experienced in the US and she was committed to working to build this with like-minded people. Today, besides the time she freely gives to entrepreneurs, she serves as, chair with PAFtec Pty Ltd (one of her investments), chair of Springboard Enterprises Australia (a program to assist women-led companies to raise growth capital), was a case manager at Commercialisation Australia, now Commercialisation advisor for Accelerating Commercialisation, and chairs her own company, Biothoughts, Pty Ltd.

Being an entrepreneur

Having worked with many founders, and being a founder herself, Topaz has a strong sense of the hitch-moments that a founder goes through when building a company. Topaz says it is very difficult to go through the transitions of a growing company and you have to learn to let go of the control and ownership of all things.

"I think letting go is the hardest thing to do as an entrepreneur. When do you let go? When do you trust someone else? When do you not get in the way of growing your company? The most important thing is when your company needs skills beyond your experience, look outside, you want someone who brings different skills to the table but who has the same commitment and passion for what you are doing."

Topaz says that as a founder you must seek good advice. And if there are signs that things are not going well look inside yourself as much as you are looking outside. Everyone needs to take counsel and that is one thing that women have not traditionally been comfortable doing. Topaz says entrepreneurs, especially women, should start talking about their challenges running a company, talking about the hard stuff.

"In Australia, culturally people don't talk about failure. As women we feel we're judged in a "man's world" when it comes to business, by standards men have set as far as what success should look like. Women think we need to be flawless, continually strong, continually smart, continually without hiccups.

This is where we run into trouble because we don't share these things, we don't talk openly about those problems or share how to help each other- share our stories."

Topaz's 'secret sauce' is her insight into people. "I really like people and I understand people. But mostly, I like to help people. That's a very strong motivator for me and if I think I can help, I will try. I believe in 'giving back'."

Lessons from Topaz:
- Topaz says that Australia has not been good at saying. "How can we do things better?" We tend to be followers and while we have great ideas there is not the focus on striving for improvement in all things. This is what an innovation economy is about.
- Support innovation – support each other – support challenging the status quo.

Over the next five years, Topaz hopes to continue to work more with early stage companies. She loves startups, the journey, the challenge and the up and downs, but would like to see more women in the spotlight.

"I would like to see women on the front cover, not under the cover, in the business section of the media. I would like to see women celebrated and recognised more in Australia, paving the way to ensuring equal access to capital to make it."

Topaz lived through the eighties and even nineties watching successful women climb the ladder, and pulling it up behind them. Sadly we still experience some of this exclusion by women themselves, but she would love to see women representing themselves better and start thinking bigger. Nobody is wildly successful without help, and women need to help each other achieve whatever successes they pursue, with their male counterparts taking a strong lead to promote women in their worlds..

"Women should rally around each other more –develop the 'mate' network. And as we succeed, we are obliged to give back whatever support we can offer to ensure we shift this paradigm more quickly."

CAROLYN CRESWELL

———

Founder of Carmen's

CARMEN'S

———

Founded
1992

———

Awards
MANY INCLUDING TELSTRA
AUSTRALIAN BUSINESS WOMAN
OF THE YEAR

———

Inspiration
TO PROVIDE HEALTHY
PRODUCTS FOR A NATION.

At the age of 18, Carolyn Creswell bought a business for $1,000 and with tenacity and determination, built that small investment into giant food manufacturer Carman's.

The company is famous for its high quality food products, exporting muesli and other food products to over 32 countries. What began as first steps at a very young age, can now be viewed as the realisation of a very big dream.

Carman's product range includes muesli, muesli bars and oats. As a proud mother to four children, Carolyn understands the importance of producing nourishing foods for her family and applies this to every Carman's product. Only 22 years from cottage industry to a multinational, Carman's is a trusted Australian brand.

The drive to succeed

Carolyn Creswell believes she was born with the drive to succeed. "I do think there are certain parts of your personality that are innate," she says. "My parents never gave me any pocket money as a kid, so I was always looking at ways to earn money. I had lots of part-time jobs and that was how I came into Carman's."

A small business, which made artisanal muesli for cafes and delis in and around Melbourne, Carolyn worked one day a week at Carman's while studying at Uni. "I loved it," she adds. When the owners put the business up for sale, 18-year-old Carolyn offered them $1,000, which they at first dismissed out of hand. "And then finally, they took up my offer," Carolyn says.

Thinking outside the box has lead Carolyn down some interesting avenues. She was featured in the second series of Recipe to Riches, a Network Ten reality TV show that sought to uncover budding food entrepreneurs. She remains an ongoing cast member. She was also involved in an entrepreneurial think tank led by Richard Branson.

Best known for its muesli products, Carman's is 100 percent owned by Carolyn and run with a small team of 25 employees. The company has developed several new products, including a range of protein bars. "We have heaps in the pipeline for the next 12 months and are looking forward to entering into some different supermarket categories," says Carolyn.

The growth of Carman's has been cited as an almost overnight success, though Carolyn points out that she has been "chipping away" for about 20 years. In that time though, Carman's has grown from a cottage industry into a multinational Australian brand. It has been named as one of BRW's Fastest 100 Growing Companies. There seem to be no indication of Carman's growth slowing, with the company shipping products to over 32 countries.

But Carolyn believes it's no excuse to relax on the job. "I have always lived with a healthy concern about the business, its liability and competitors," says Carolyn, "so I never really sat back and thought, 'Great, this is fantastic!' It's not part of my DNA; I'm always on my toes."

Fear and passion.

Carolyn admits she didn't foresee just how successful Carman's would come to be.

"I never had any idea it would be this big and for a long time, I was trying to work out how to get out of it because I was earning no money and my friends had gone on these great new vacations. I could never do anything like that because I had the responsibility of this business."

Carolyn adds that the option of leaving the business was one of many challenges while building Carman's into a reputable food manufacturer. "It's just a lot harder to get out of a small business because I was in debt, there was overdraft, I had to ask my parents for money to help fund my business so there were a lot obstacles in that way."

When reflecting on what it means to be an entrepreneur, Carolyn says it comes down to seizing opportunities. "To me, I think an entrepreneur is someone who can see an opportunity and then bring it to a commercial reality. They can actually make it happen. Being able to go 'right, that's my idea, I'm going to make it happen,' that's my instance on being an entrepreneur and that's how I've been able to think and bring to fruition, I just don't ever see the word 'no' or think, 'I can't do it.'"

Carolyn adds that while she thinks of the word as "just a kind of label," she is inspired by multiple-business entrepreneurs. "They are the ones that I really admire," she says.

IF YOU LOOK INTO THE CONSUMERS AND UNDERSTAND WHAT THEY ARE LOOKING FOR, YOU DELIVER TO THEIR NEEDS

Carolyn's can-do attitude is one of the keys to Carman's success as is the small team working behind the scenes. The achievements they make are extremely rewarding. "We make healthy food, but we feel extremely proud of it and the reach...the little difference we have of enriching the lives of people every day."

Carolyn's team of 25 employees are just as passionate about Carman's as she is. To her, having a love for what they do is important. "I want people to love what they do so much, even if they want to do part time. I want to work with passionate, strong people who feed off each other. It's your choice what attitude you bring through the door each morning and you really want that to be a team-focused, positive, smart, savvy, switched on attitude."

Lessons from Carolyn:
- Look into the consumers and understand what they are looking for
- Always think about what's next.
- Work with passionate, strong people.

As for Carolyn's own passion, "I care about what I give, I care about the impact we have, so I don't do things for my own personal brand." But the real secret to her success, Carolyn says, is her 'street smarts.' "I can see what people are looking for and what is going to work with consumers."

She also believes that being product-focused is essential. "If you look into the consumers and understand what they are looking for, you deliver to their needs. You will get the loyalty and the brand obsession by delivering something amazing that people will just be blown away by."

In 2012, Carolyn won the Telstra Australian Business Woman of the Year Award. the 2009 InStyle Women of Style Award, the 2008 Veuve Clicquot Award and the 2007 Ernst & Young's 'Young Entrepreneur of the Year' Award. Carolyn is a graduate member of the Australian Institute of Company Directors. She has four young children and is proud of the balance she keeps between her career and growing family. She is also an active board member for Stephanie Alexander's Kitchen Garden Foundation, which works to get kids into the garden and the kitchen, so they appreciate the origins of fresh food.

ANDREA CULLIGAN

Founder of HartEffect

Andrea stands barefoot by the water on her property's edge in Birchgrove. Charlie, a cheeky cocker spaniel bounces around her ankles while a lovely hybrid of city and coast sets the scene behind her. It is the perfect prelude to her story. A Canadian from a small town in Northern Alberta who became the CEO and founder of Harteffect, a Sydney based branding agency. As a connector, an adventurer, singer, sportswoman, and leader, Andrea Culligan is a wonderful dichotomy of complementary opposites; all of which make her the high functioning entrepreneur she is today.

Harteffect is an integrated branding agency that helps companies develop, transform and execute brands. Andrea and her group of talented creatives "thrive on making you look good." Andrea's passion is in helping companies tell authentic stories to attract the right people to their business.

HARTEFFECT

Founded
2000

Awards
OVER 10 INCLUDING TELSTRA SMALL BUSINESS OF THE YEAR

Inspiration
TO REBOUND BACK FROM ADVERSITY AND USE HER HARDWORKING NATURE TOWARDS A BIGGER LIFE PROJECT

Unveiling love and loss

"Talking about myself isn't really something I like to do," she says with an infectious chuckle echoing across the harbour. As Andrea's job is to help others tell stories about themselves, it's hard to believe this lively communicator doesn't take joy in telling her own.

Across her entrepreneurial journey, Andrea has received more than 30 awards but is particularly proud of being named 2009 Telstra Young Business Woman of the Year while also holding the 2009 Telstra Small Business of the Year Award. She is testament to the fact that lucrative global businesses aren't built overnight; they take resilience, strategic vision and the ability to see opportunities where others don't. Her views on living life as an entrepreneur are simple, "Creating a business is one thing, creating many businesses is another. It is about being able to see opportunity and act on it. You can have lots of ideas but if you're not putting them into action, you're a dreamer."

The daughter of a customer centric car salesman, Andrea moved sixteen times as a child and started working full time after leaving school at the age of 14. She is a self-proclaimed doer, someone that gains more from experience than books. "I don't learn from listening, I learn from doing. I have to have a really kinetic and auditory approach; I'm very much hands-on, I like to ask questions so I can twist the content into how I see it."

Her strong work ethic lead her into employment from a young age, often holding down three to four jobs at one time. That constant is something she looks at as a way of making connections with new and varied people. At one time, she was employed at her father's car dealership carrying out receptionist work while also pumping gas. At times she worked in a -40 degree Fahrenheit climate, in a neighbourhood not quite conducive to a young girl serving strangers through their car windows. But Andrea has been steadfast in her pursuit of achievement, and, has never limited her actions according to what she 'should or shouldn't' do.

"It's funny because up until eight, maybe nine years ago I always held a minimum of two jobs. I worked the markets and was making great money, I had time on weekends and just felt like someone needed someone else to help out, then the next thing I'm working every Saturday and Sunday. Just like the way when I was younger I used to work a day job, followed by two hours of rugby training, then I'd head to working at the bar where I might play the piano and sing after my shift. Usually I'd get home at 2am and get up at 6am to do it all again. I just always felt like there was time." Hard work, in particular physical challenge, is something Andrea embraces with gusto.

Andrea is adamant that her entrepreneurialism was born from a kind of opportunism, and love of

CREATING A BUSINESS IS ONE THING, CREATING MANY BUSINESSES IS ANOTHER. IT IS ABOUT BEING ABLE TO SEE OPPORTUNITY AND ACT ON IT. YOU CAN HAVE LOTS OF IDEAS BUT IF YOU'RE NOT PUTTING THEM INTO ACTION, YOU'RE A DREAMER

work done well. "When people ask me, and have asked me for a long time, why do you have so many businesses, my response is because I can, because the opportunity presented itself and I grabbed it with both hands. I saw something that could be done better and so I did it better. It's the only thing I've ever known," she says.

Andrea has not always made good choices. Before she turned 20 she had a phase of becoming what she called a "...deadbeat, mixed up in drugs and all sorts of bad things." She also became dependent on Ephedrine stacks to sustain an elite level of performance while playing rugby. She needed to change her life.

"I had a serious look at myself and decided that there was a big issue and so I spoke to one of my best friends about going to Australia. I have dual citizenship because my dad's Australian, but she was scared so I made a decision to go alone. I hadn't bought a ticket, but I knew if I worked at the pub every night that week I'd have enough money. Three weeks later I

arrived in Brisbane with all of my belongings in garbage bags because I didn't own suitcases".

Charisma

She would spend the next few years travelling across Australia's diverse landscape, from Bunbury, to Perth, to Hervey Bay and all the way to Sydney, capitalising on opportunities, making friends and landing jobs without any real experience along the way. Her now husband and colleague Roger attributes much of her success to her amazing capacity to build rapport.

"Andrea has a fantastic ability to connect with people at a sincere and deep level which builds trust and mutual respect to foster really genuine relationships. Her tenacity is what carries her forward; with a relentless ability to face the music and get stuff done, she takes a lot of pressure and stress in her job, which although it takes its toll (because she's human), she will always get back up with composure and keep going".

After nomadically traversing the country in her formative years, finding work and even brief love interests in strange places, Andrea ended up in Sydney. With some time in project and sales coordination Andrea was recruited by Unimail in 1999 to head up their business development. At the time Unimail was a pioneer, offering students free uni inboxes with the ability

THINK VERY BIG, COMMUNICATE ON ALL LEVELS, ARTICULATE A VISION TO PEOPLE ABOUT SOMETHING THAT DOESN'T EVEN EXIST

to use their own name as the email and also connect with other students via the platform.

Andrea spent 13 years growing Unimail, now Harteffect, from a two person dot-com to a global business and knows personally that being an entrepreneur means rolling up your sleeves and wearing all the hats.

Culturally savvy, Andrea has a profound awareness of her environment and a sensitivity to what does and doesn't work contextually. From Unimail, Andrea developed complementary businesses that fed cash back into its core. She met challenges her clients faced and answered them with new ventures. Over time, Unimail developed into a three pronged business; a jobs directory for university students, a distribution business that distributes, assembles and stores events material for career events on campus and lastly an employer branding agency that builds and develops brands for employers, that want people to want to work for them.

"We would sit down with clients and ask, what challenges are you facing, and then we would

literally take on their challenges. We started the first ever Association of Australian Magazine for Graduate Recruiters and we helped connect the suppliers and the association of the members with content they weren't getting anywhere else, we also bought a magazine to inject cash flow into the business while we were setting up the company further".

Andrea's contribution to the industry has been well recognised. The Australian Association of Graduate Employers has presented her with the award for Most Contribution to the Graduate industry three times. In addition, unimail has thrice been awarded winner of the Supplier to the Industry by the same association.

Andrea bought out her business partner in 2011 and proceeded to focus her energies on the branding side of the company. But, life and business is never without its trouble, and while Unimail experienced positive growth for a number of years, long term fast growth suffered from structural issues in the business. As a result, in 2013 the company spent time adapting systems, financial processes, structure and business strategy to find a new focus and

company vision with a solid growth plan to invest in the future of the business. In 2014, after selling a number of the businesses within the Unimail Group, Andrea rebranded the branding arm of the business, launching Harteffect with its motto "Building Brands that Get People".

Stand up and stand out

Andrea finds calm amongst the trees or fishing by a lake in natural landscapes. There she gets to recharge and reflect. As her husband points out, "Some of Andrea's best boardroom decisions are conceived way off the beaten track deep in the wilderness somewhere around the world! Her motto on meeting her goals in both business and life even when you might be unsure is to "Always think big".

"Think very big, communicate on all levels, articulate a vision to people about something that doesn't even exist. These things have to be innate. You can go to as many presentations as you want but the passion for being able to stand in a room and engage people, to get them to believe in what you do, that takes thinking big and thinking big with passion."

Lessons from Andrea:
- You can have lots of ideas but if you're not putting them into action, you're a dreamer.
- Sit down with clients and ask, what challenges are you facing. Find a solution.
- Always think big.

In the early days, success used to be about growth for Andrea, now that's changed, now success is about safety and purpose.

"When you go through tough times you realise how important safety is. Safety is about profitability and it's about allowing me to exit from day-to-day business and focus on other things and then success is purpose. I'm looking at how I can connect that back to my business. Then there is authenticity, passion, stage and singing. I'm trying to figure

out how they all connect… I feel I need to have a bigger impact on the world. I've been through all these experiences and so I feel it only right that I use them to give back."

Andrea admits she finds it easier to see other people's purposes before her own but finally feels its time to become the narrator of her own story.

"I want more humility, strength, silence and listening. I've become much more in tune with a deeper and in depth way of thinking. I always thought there was only one way of doing things and one way to be, but now because of my peers and other inspiring women I look up to, I know everyone's path can be different and still lead to something great."

Andrea ruffles Charlie's golden tresses and throws his ball across the yard. "I am on a journey of purpose now, I am looking for another phase. I'm not sure what that looks like exactly, but I do want to get to that point, that point where I can see my own story more clearly".

NICOLE ECKELS

—

Founder of Glasshouse Fragrances

GLASSHOUSE FRAGRANCES

Founded
2006

Aspiration
FOCUSING ON CREATING
THE BEST PRODUCT AND
BRAND IN THE WORLD

Witty, charismatic and positively full of life, Nicole Eckels is the product of a quirky and inventive mother.

Growing up in New York, with a mother who was constantly generating "zany business ideas", it's no wonder Nicole has become so commercially creative, now based in Sydney as founder of Glasshouse Fragrances. Glasshouse produces thousands of candles a day with a strong independent retailer focus. A powerful presence and a rare ability to communicate honestly and openly, Nicole has a knack for knowing what people want in the cosmetics industry. A truly inspiring Rare Bird with the desire to make the very best product in the world, Nicole found a gap and she owned it.

The journey

Nicole's mum, a stay at home mother with four children, planted a seed in Nicole's growing mind during one summer break from school. "My mom once read this article about Mrs Fields cookies, before they were big in America, and she said to me, "I have this great idea, you can make cookies and sell them to the office workers after lunch". So, my mom convinced me to start this cookie business - I would stay up all night long baking cookies, I must have been 13 years old. I then hired all these pre-teens and we'd fill baskets with cookies and when people had finished their lunch we'd sell them a cookie for fifty cents. We had to obtain a license from the city to be able to walk around selling these cookies because we kept getting fines. It was very funny." Nicole's resourcefulness and ability to see potential in a problem was evident early on. "I discovered how to make money and I thought well, if there's a will there's a way. After the summer break ended, I needed a way to

YOU'RE GOING TO HAVE DO THE HARD YARDS, SO BE ETERNALLY OPTIMISTIC, BE RESILIENT AND ABOVE ALL, BE DETERMINED

make some money during the school year, so I bought boxes of candy (because the school didn't have vending machines) and I'd tell the kids to come to my locker to buy candy. I was always getting in trouble, but it didn't matter...I was always selling something."

Fast forward to 20, Nicole had her first child and a marketing degree, but wasn't enthused by the idea of life confined to an advertising agency. A self-confessed make-up addict, Nicole went to work in cosmetics. "I worked for Chanel at Saks Fifth Avenue and shortly after was offered the resident makeup artist position. I loved makeup and everything about cosmetics, makeup and fragrance. I found it deeply satisfying to transform someone so that they felt and looked great. To this day I am still in that business and that is what I love the most. Making someone feel incredible."

Nicole found an industry that fit her, in more ways than one. "Being a 5'9" and voluptuous woman, makeup always fits, shoes always fit, purses always fit. I loved the industry, absolutely loved it. I made great groups of friends with people who were really passionate about what the best products were," she remembers.

Wanting to earn a better income, Nicole left the cosmetics industry for an account executive role at Primedia, and then onto the gym chain, Equinox as the director of corporate sales, selling employee benefit programs to big corporates. They offered her a position in California.

"My son was 11 at the time and I was always worried about life as a single parent in New York City. I worked long hours and I was concerned that my son lacked supervision. So, I accepted the company's

offer to move to California but I knew that living in California wasn't sustainable."

Nicole moved to Sydney in the winter of 2005 and fell in love. "I had this tiny, crappy studio on Victoria Street in Potts Point but I had the most beautiful view of the Opera House. I used up the candle I had brought with me from the USA, and I went to David Jones to buy another one and they had nothing I wanted to purchase. It was either very high end, or poor quality and overpriced. It was in that moment that I had my next big idea and my excuse to stay in Australia."

Meeting challenges and learning lessons

Nicole knew she needed capital to begin making candles, and was able to secure the investment required to begin Glasshouse Fragrances. But money wasn't the only

I BELIEVE THAT IF YOU FOCUS ON MAKING WORLD CLASS AMAZING PRODUCT AS WELL AS CREATING A POWERFUL BRAND, CONSUMERS WILL NOTICE AND THE REWARDS WILL COME. OF COURSE, ANY BUSINESS NEEDS TO FOCUS ON PROFIT AND GM AND SO FORTH, WE HAVE GREAT ADVISORS AND A FINANCE TEAM THAT CREATE MILESTONES, BUT I HAVE NEVER FOCUSED ON SHEER PROFIT AND THAT'S REALLY HELPED US STAY FOCUSED ON THE BIG PICTURE

problem. No one in Australia knew how to make candles at the calibre she required. She met this challenge with a clear vision. "We didn't know how to make candles either at that stage, but we definitely knew what our candles needed to look like and more importantly how they needed to perform."

Glasshouse started with a complete business plan that allowed for a range of salaried positions and building a factory. We hired the best people from big brand backgrounds and because of that philosophy, we have a dream team at Sapphire Group. "I was not going in

this to fluff around. I have big dreams and I was in a global frame of mind," she recounts.

Nicole acknowledges the nature of her particular industry is tough to navigate. "It is one of the most closed industries in the world and getting information is almost impossible. Candle makers do not seem to change companies very often, and if they move they get picked up by another company instantly. Candle companies aren't caring and sharing sort of people. It takes years of investment, trial and error and expertise to perfect candle making and no one wants to share that

information. Now that we have lived through that process at Sapphire Group, I can certainly understand where they are coming from."

For the first five years Nicole and the team at Sapphire Group struggled through trying to perfect a product with little technical advice. But, as Nicole indicates, becoming an entrepreneur is not for the weak of heart. It is an everyday, every hour slog, of course Nicole does it all with a wonderful sense of humour. "If someone's looking for work life balance and quality of life, it will not happen if you want to be a global entrepreneur, that's for sure!"

DON'T CONSTANTLY LOOK OVER YOUR SHOULDER AT WHAT OTHER BRANDS ARE DOING. HAVE A CLEAR VISION, BLAZE YOUR OWN PATH AND BE AWARE OF WHAT'S HAPPENING BUT DON'T LET IT DISTRACT YOU

Glasshouse was the first brand and Circa Home, which produces soy wax candles and diffusers, came later, both of which sit under the Sapphire Group umbrella. Nicole sent product to all the independent retailers she could find in magazines like Home Beautiful, and three years ago, Glasshouse landed David Jones as their first department store retailer, "sure enough, as soon as Glasshouse launched in David Jones it just went nuts. We were immediately one of the top selling brands and during gift periods we outsold big established global brands, it was crazy," she says.

Nicole admits the life of an entrepreneur without the right community can be very closed and lonely. Often the wider perception is that only the strongest survive, which can be true particularly for women, but Nicole identifies the need for better resources and referrals to make the transition from startup to a sustained business more achievable and accessible.

Lessons from Nicole:
- You have to do something that is different from everybody else.
- Have a clear vision, blaze your own path and be aware of what's happening.
- Plan and reach out for support, particularly to other women.
- Be eternally optimistic, be resilient and above all, be determined.

Having a strong support network, is vital to your success, Nicole says. You have to surround yourself with people who know something you don't or can teach you what you want to learn. "You need the right support network to keep you sane throughout the journey."

"You have to do something that is different from everybody else. You have to. Don't constantly look over your shoulder at what other brands are doing, have a clear vision, blaze your own path and be aware of what's happening but don't let it distract you. Plan and reach out for support, particularly to other women, there are organisations you can get involved with right from the get go. Don't feel you have to do this alone."

AUDETTE EXEL (AO)

—

Founder of ADARA Group

ADARA GROUP

—

Founded
1997

—

Awards
SEVERAL INCLUDING
ECONOMIC JUSTICE AWARD
YPO INTERNATIONAL SOCIAL
ENTERPRISE

—

Inspiration
BUSINESS FOR PURPOSE

—

Money raised/funded
US$6.5 MILLION

Audette Exel is well known and loved in the entrepreneurial and philanthropic communities. As an optimist, she holds the underpinning belief that people want to do good in the world, even when it comes to the financial services community. Audette cultivated the idea of business for purpose, using her business skills to apply real change.

She applies a complete package of skills and knowledge, she creates businesses that work on both financial and positive social impact measures. Audette is renowned and respected as a social entrepreneur and founder of the Adara Group (formerly known as the ISIS Group), which is made up of Adara Advisors, a corporate finance for-purpose business that funds the core support costs of Adara Development, an international development organisation with the intent of alleviating poverty.

Passion and drive

Audette is one of the youngest women in the world to have run a publicly-traded bank. As the former managing director of Bermuda Commercial Bank and Chair of the Bermuda Stock Exchange, Audette was a fierce and thorough negotiator and calls herself a "calculated risk taker".

She believes success relies on a mixture of passion and grit. "We have had to have courage; we try to always think outside the box. If nothing else, I am tenacious, because nothing drives me more than social justice. There were times when I've been afraid, exhausted, times when the size of the responsibility weighed heavily on my shoulders, but there was never a time where I got out of bed thinking I don't want to do this anymore."

Businesses have increasingly become motivated by a sense of compassionate self-interest; a movement mixing the best of the old ideologies of capitalism and socialism, to solve some of the worlds' most prevalent problems. The Adara Group works for commercial reward, which it uses to fund public good. It makes money by advising and making investments for some of the world's most iconic companies, and 100 percent of its profits then fund Adara Development. Through the business for purpose model, the

Adara Group has changed the way people think about the role of business, and the power of business and not for profit partnerships.

Designed to work side by side with communities and children in remote areas in Nepal and Uganda, Adara Development improves the quality of life in these communities through health, education and other development projects. Projects have included alternative technology, remote mobile-healthcare services and anti-trafficking initiatives in Humla. They also have projects in Kathmandu focused on the emergency relief, rescue and care of trafficked children, and health care for disadvantaged communities.

To avoid one of the perennial problems of charities and assistance programs, Adara is also committed to conducting detailed research, which allows them to give help that's actually needed, and will make real change.

Problems and missteps on the way to achievement

While Audette has managed to achieve a great deal with the Adara Group, she admits much has been trial and error. "I remember a pivotal moment not long after we got our first project started in the remote Nepali Himalayas. I received a call from some

American nurses, who were based in Humla, which at that point was 25 days walk from the nearest road. It was when the political unrest in Nepal was just starting. These poor nurses were stopped by a group of people holding machine guns. They were terrified, as there had already been violence against our Nepali team. They rang me crying, saying "get us out of here" and we had no idea what to do. We had no evacuation plan or any way to get them out."

However stressful, Audette highlights that it's often the most difficult circumstances that produce some of the best entrepreneurs. "If you can survive without electricity, without rule of law in place and you can

WE HAVE HAD TO HAVE COURAGE; WE TRY TO ALWAYS THINK OUTSIDE THE BOX. IF NOTHING ELSE, I AM TENACIOUS, BECAUSE NOTHING DRIVES ME MORE THAN SOCIAL JUSTICE

still build something and support your community, you are a true entrepreneur."

Audette acknowledges that running a social enterprise, and being an entrepreneur in general, can be a rollercoaster ride. "Being a CEO or a leader can be lonely, you can't ring up your competitor and say "What do I do?" You can't burden your team, who are relying on you to do the right thing. I'm not saying you should pretend that you have all the answers, but you need to carry a sense of, "we will be fine, I know what to do". Then you need to go home and fully collapse into a bottle of wine, or into the arms of your family or close friends."

Now 17 years on, the Adara Group has grown into an esteemed enterprise, something Audette attributes closely to the ingrained culture of the business. "We talk about the 'Adara family'; it's a family all around the world. When you create that culture, where people love the

people they work with, great things happen. If you create a family structure where people cry, laugh, socialise and stand together it's great. It's got this heart and soul. It's a bigger picture, a bigger motivation and purpose."

For Audette, founding a business, particularly a business for purpose has been a very special experience. 17 years in, it is important I am still focused on the business, but Adara Development is an amazing organisation led by an incredible team. I would stand it against any non-profit around the world. It's amazing. My role now is simple. I am the keeper of the stories. I am the one who has the memories of when we began. 17 years ago, I drove up the drive of where the hospital we support in Uganda now stands. Back then, there were only two doctors, going on to the ward was like fighting a war. Today, the neonatal intensive care unit and maternity ward now take thousands of women and

babies a year. I think, wow. I remember what it used to be like and this is what it is now."

Many people come to philanthropy late in their career, when capitalist success begins to seem hollow, but Audette wanted to bring the richest and poorest sides of the world together from the start. She does not see capitalist outcomes and social goals as naturally opposed. "We cannot make change if we stand in corners throwing stones at each other. We have to bridge together. I decided to pull two parts of my life together in a way that other's before me possibly hadn't thought of doing."

In 1995, Audette was elected a "Global Leader for Tomorrow" by The World Economic Forum. She was the recipient of the Economic Justice and Community Impact Award from the Young Presidents Organisation Social Enterprise Networks in 2010. In 2012, Audette won the Telstra 2012 NSW Commonwealth Bank Business Owner Award, and was the winner of

IF YOU CREATE A FAMILY STRUCTURE WHERE PEOPLE CRY, LAUGH, SOCIALISE AND STAND TOGETHER IT'S GREAT. IT'S GOT THIS HEART AND SOUL

the 2012 NSW Telstra Business Woman of the Year Award. She is also one of The Australian Financial Review's 100 Women of Influence in Australia in 2012. In 2013, Audette was awarded an honorary Order of Australia for service to humanity and in 2014 was recognised by Forbes as a "Hero of Philanthropy".

Women and entrepreneurship

In terms of entrepreneurship, Audette believes women are absolutely suited to be entrepreneurs. "We are well suited as we are multi-skilled. There are still significant obstacles for women rising to leadership in accepted power structures. Women generally are fantastic multi-taskers and entrepreneurship gives you huge flexibility for what you can create, so I think it's an obvious place for women. I think we need more women running companies, big and small." As someone that sees innovation come out of the most impoverished countries, Audette's advice to women in developed and first-world countries is to make great choices. "Women like us have the choice every day to get up and survive. Why would you not make the greatest choice you can and step out of that cage you built yourself?"

"We have the freedom to do almost anything compared to other women on the planet. Dream big and don't let anyone stop you... There is a lovely saying, would all the people that say it can't be done please get out of the way of the people who are doing it."

Undertaking and driving a social enterprise takes wild ambition, resilience and perhaps even, as Audette mentions, just a little bit of naivety. "I think the reason I thought it was going to work was because I had no idea how big what I was going to do really was. It's an interesting mixture of short sightedness, and big dreams," she admits.

Lessons from Audette:

- Have courage
- Try to always think outside the box
- Project a sense of, "we will be fine, I know what to do". Then go home and collapse.
- Ignore the voice that tells you not to do it. Don't let anyone stop you.

Truly an inspiration, Audette is proud to be a female entrepreneur, hopeful that by telling her story, she might help other young women to believe they can do anything if they have the will.

SIMONE EYLES

Founder of 365cups.com

365CUPS.COM

Achievements

WINNER BEST APP FOOD &
DRINK 2012 - 2013 AUSTRALIAN
MOBILE AWARDS

WINNER EXCELLENCE IN
INNOVATION MURRAY-RIVERINA
BUSINESS AWARDS - NSW
BUSINESS CHAMBER

MORE THAN 45,000 APP USERS

OVER 150 CLIENTS ACROSS
AUSTRALIA AND NEW ZEALAND

Inspiration

TO FOLLOW HER DREAMS

For Simone Eyles her journey began in the big smoke of
Sydney where she was born and spent her childhood,
teen years and early adulthood. Finding herself working
within the walls of an advertising agency in Leichardt for
several years was stimulating, however not satisfying.

Doing the unthinkable, Simone's boss encouraged her to
"follow her dreams" and go to university to study graphic
design. What happened next was where a useful and
valuable creation began. Today she's the co-founder
of leading smart ordering company 365cups.com (365cups).
A mobile ordering platform that changes the way you order,
breakfast, lunch, coffee and tea, also winner of Best App
Food and Drink at the 2013 Australian Mobile Awards.

Small town, big idea

The supporting reassurance from her boss was what Simone needed to truly kickstart her career, so she heeded the wise words and started out on the path towards her dreams. That path lead her 500 kilometers away from Sydney to a country town called Wagga Wagga.

Wagga became the town where her company, 365cups, came to fruition in January 2011 and also where Simone met her husband. Simone proves that not all businesses that are thriving and successful have to be located in a major metropolis like that of Syndey. Country towns, she believes, can provide the nourishing environment for a digital company to grow sustainably. She proves, that with the insurgence of online, you can be an entrepreneur from anywhere. There are no boundaries.

Simone says that "having an idea and making it happen" is what makes someone an entrepreneur. She also says that certain aspects such as her love for people is what enables her to be a better entrepreneur. "We may work in a global tech company but everything we do is about people and some good old fashioned customer service," Simon mentions.

What is 365cups? The idea came about when she was having coffee with her friend, ironically, and they were chatting about "how great it would be to order your coffee from your mobile and have it ready, waiting for you when you got to the café".

With that passing idea and solution to fix a problem, it soon became a concept and reality. "We now co-own a business that is experiencing rapid growth. Since going live in January 2011, the business has gone from strength to strength, and we are now sharing our proven mobile ordering technology with other retail and hospitality businesses," Simone says.

Entrepreneur and mother

So how does one become an entrepreneur? It's simple, just start.

Lessons from Simone:
- You become an entrepreneur by just starting.
- Start researching, start planning, start dreaming, start doing all those things that you need to do and before you know it you will be in the market and have customers.
- Know what funding is available to you.

In saying that, it's important not to jump into deep waters with limited knowledge. The expectation of any forerunning business is to have a clear mission and purpose to steer the product around. "My mission is to help people understand how technology can work for them. From ordering a coffee to your phone, to a business being able to streamline and improve their work flow and increase their sales by using technology," Simone expresses.

The burning topic for many startups and individuals establishing a company is around funding. The education surrounding this is limited and also half the reason why failure is a common thread. Often, startups don't have enough funding to get their idea off the ground or the company is either self-funded for six months and then the pool of available capital dries up causing the business to close.

For young entrepreneurs in need of capital support, the importance of knowing the types of funding that are out there such as bootstrapping, equity funding or debt funding and becoming familiar with industry words is a crucial tool.

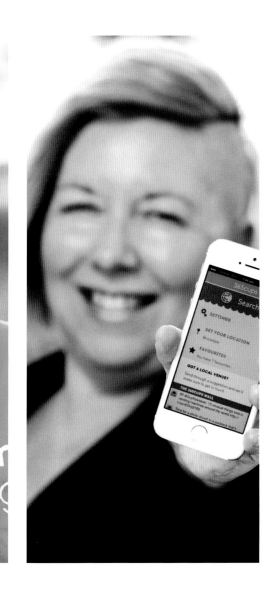

Simone shares her perspective on money and the significance of understanding it's importance and value to a robust business,"money is important but isn't everything. As a startup money is scarce so you have to have a big dream and a lot of passion to keep you going. Paying customers is the best money you can have."

Know the goal constantly changes and uncertainty is part of the process. "We didn't know if anyone would ever use our system or pay for it. Once the product was ready we took it to market and within two days were live with a paying client. We have stuck to our original plan which was to build a solid foundation to grow a solid business. Our business has grown and evolved but we are still true to our core goals," Simone says.

At the core of this brilliant mind lies a caring and conscious heart. Simone has been honoured as a recipient of Kidney Health Australia's Operation Angel Awards Program after an obstacle confronted her and her husband when her child, Joshua, was born with a rare kidney disease.

"He had a kidney transplant, he is now two years post transplant and we've had a lot of hurdles including 9 months of hemodialysis before his transplant as he became very sick." In effort to find out more about the disease and life with the condition, Simone devoted two years to write a book, that compiled the stories of other Australian families with children living with kidney disease.

365cups has won numerous awards including the 'Best App Food and Drink' by Australian Mobile Awards in 2012 and 'Excellence in Innovation' by the Murray-Riverina Business Awards in 2013. To Simone, success looks like "creative freedom and being free to have wild ideas".

Simone still has dreams of having more of a presence globally in the United States and United Kingdom. However, where ever her future journey takes her, it started in a country town away from a big city with an idea and ambition to create.

JODIE FOX

Founder of Shoes of Prey

It's no secret that Jodie Fox has become one of Australia's most loved and talked about entrepreneurs.

Founder of Shoes of Prey, a custom shoe retailer, the Lawyer-turned-advertiser and two-time entrepreneur is a pioneer of customisation in women's fashion. She knows her talents, she knows herself, and she knows a thing or two about innovation as well. Shoes of Prey is a global, multi-channel retail brand that enables shoppers to design their own shoes online. The company is changing the way women shop for shoes, and is on track to become a significant international retailer over the next five years. Having gained global recognition, Shoes of Prey has recently expanded to the US after sealing a six store roll out with Nordstrom.

SHOES OF PREY

Founded
2009

Awards
MANY INCLUDING
TOP 30 MOST INFLUENTIAL
WOMEN IN RETAIL 2014

Inspiration
WANTING TO CREATE HER
OWN SHOES THAT WERE
COMFORTABLE

INNOVATION ISN'T THAT COMPLICATED, IT'S SOMETHING THAT WE DO PRETTY NATURALLY AS HUMANS, BUT MAYBE IT'S MORE CONDUCIVE IN AN ENTREPRENEURIAL ENVIRONMENT

Being and doing

Jodie is an unassuming luminary in the best style. She enters a room and commands your attention not because she's extreme or autocratic, but rather, reassuring through her calm and harmonious manner. The saying rings true; the loudest person is not always the one most clearly heard, and when Jodie opens her mouth to speak, you can be sure she has something worth listening to. She'll make you laugh, think, and care deeply all in one sitting.

Half Sicilian and half Australian, Jodie has always had a love of beautiful things, and an interest in fashioned leather. But, it wasn't until after two changes of career that she would really engage with the idea of starting her own business. Constantly torn between creative and intellectual pursuits, in her final year of schooling she was struck with the decision to either take on a law degree or pursue her other love, becoming a professional ballerina.

"I was thinking about the fact that I had been so involved in creative endeavors that when

I sat down to watch the news or read the newspaper, it didn't really make that much sense to me. I didn't understand how the world really worked. I always imagined being involved in an international business and doing great things, so I thought if I really wanted to get in there and make my life something bigger and better, I really needed to know how the world actually works. I ended up deciding to take a dual degree of international business and law".

If we can draw any parallels here, it's that entrepreneurship often requires encompassing skills and abilities that other occupations do not always cultivate. Jodie knew that if she wanted an interesting and well rounded future she needed to build a depth of knowledge and practical skill. Her creative side was robust and flourishing, but the analytical and discerning side needed development. Jodie threw herself into the challenge, and equipped herself with some of the tools that would be necessary to make her the award winning entrepreneur she is today.

A Gritty reboot

Originating in Lismore, in the far north east corner of NSW, Jodie found her start as a banking and finance lawyer before hopping over to the advertising industry to reintegrate the creative side of her personality. Her love of beautiful things began to find direction, at first fulfilling her own desires, and then discovering through friends that those desires were the seeds of a rich market.

"I used to travel a lot and when I heard about this person you could commission shoe designs with I went and saw him about making my own shoes. Now every time I would go to Europe I would zip through Hong Kong just to see him and on one of my most epic journeys I had a five hour stop over. I ran out of the airport, designed 14 pairs of shoes, came back to the airplane and he would then have them delivered to me, so as I was doing that my girlfriends were like "oh they are cool shoes, where are they from?" One thing lead to another and I started commissioning shoe designs for friends".

Shoes of Prey was established in 2009 with then husband Michael Fox and business partner Mike Knapp, who she met while studying law and international business at university. Both partners are ex-Google, giving the stamp of the innovation goliath to her initially small business. Today the young, dynamic business has won multiple awards, has a strong global presence and is now venturing into omni-channel retail with brick-and-mortar stores located around the city, a move towards a more comprehensive retail offering and brand experience.

While people may have predicted the rise of mass customisation for some time now, even Jodie admits that she never thought about turning it into a business, let alone a global one. Essentially, customisation started as a return to old service giving somewhat bespoke style businesses a chance for some new appreciation and greater customer reach. When explaining the business to her Nonna, Jodie collected various leather swatches and placed them in front of her while they went back and forth on their personal preferences and Jodie clarified the process. Not surprisingly, her Sicilian grandmother responded, "Jodie this is how I used to buy shoes" and then described how she would take her designs and chosen leather down to the cobbler to be made into a most fitting pair of shoes.

But, mass customisation is something entirely different. More sophisticated technology and a pursuit of the international customer has given way to a whole new market. "We were the first people to do this globally, so it was totally a brand new idea and we were the pioneers of the movement," says Jodie.

Innovation, observation and extension

Jodie is an innovator at her core, and while that word might often be thrown around casually, particularly in the entrepreneurial space, it's not one Jodie uses lightly.

"I think that innovation is such a sexy buzz thing. I think that it's a real misnomer and it's about solving the problem without manufactured insights but by doing those really human things you'd normally do to solve a problem, observation".

For Shoes of Prey, observation is about looking at the tools and resources they have to more effectively meet the changing needs of their customer. They look at data, they look at how people interact with their website, they sit down as a team and take a holistic approach to solving problems.

"We use our imaginations and throw away the barriers of self-editing. We just imagine what the best possible plans would be regardless of what currently exists in the world and then work back from there to deliver it. I think innovation isn't that complicated, it's something that we do pretty naturally as humans, but maybe it's more conducive in an entrepreneurial environment because we have that environment of creativity where we have minimal budgets and multiple problems to solve and so then are quite forced into that mindset."

And so, observing and understanding is integral to Jodie's success. Like many visionaries, gathering knowledge of the environment surrounding her, as well as a sensitivity to what works and what doesn't, allows her to capitalise on whatever opportunities might present themselves. In 2011, Sneaking Duck was born and catered to a customer looking for 'cool prescription glasses for every mood'. Jodie and partners, Mike and Michael would frequently purchase numerous pairs of glasses when they travelled. They could buy interesting, inexpensive glasses, which meant they could build up collections to match their outfits, rather than only having one conservative pair. The company has moved through startup phase successfully and Jodie mentions they are now looking at new strategies to better target growth.

Failing and learning

Achieving entrepreneurial success requires an acceptance that not all progress is linear. Adamant about being realistic and action orientated, Jodie acknowledges that these are lessons she has had to learn the hard way. "I learnt that failure is ok, but it's not ok to stand by and just accept it as a learning experience. I ask myself "If we fail, should we fail fast?" So sometimes, fast failure is important and sometimes failure is not an option, so we need to understand the distinction between those two. Then I look at what the breadth of my capability is and whether I need to open my mouth and go and speak to people to help me get through."

Her advice to others when building a business is to be certain on what kind of business

you intend to have. Particularly in terms of product, Jodie turns her attention to scaling. "Scaling requires you to build relationships with suppliers. It's looking at how you're going to target the market segment by segment and not just targeting for growth. Target by doing a little test in a certain area so that if that test really bombs you've only affected a small part of the market not the entire thing. It's just really critical to remember if you burn people because you haven't scaled properly you'll lose them for life".

Lessons from Jodie:
- Do it for yourself, and trust that you're not the only one.
- Find good partners, and know yourself – how you contribute and where you need help.
- Be transparent and work through your emotions. They don't need to be a liability; well-honed emotional intelligence is an asset.

Though Jodie appears charming, bubbly and fun, she also exhibits a high degree of self-trust, emotional balance and an acknowledgement that challenges will be significant. Encountering a myriad of problems and at times huge handbrakes is a natural part of the journey, but Jodie's transparency and ability to work through her emotions during those tough times has been a virtue.

"I've struggled with anxiety. When things happen in business there are definite triggers that will push things and there have been challenges in my life that took me to a dark place but it's important to realise that optimism and positivity is a critical part of being an

entrepreneur. It doesn't mean you're immune to these things. There needs to be lots more conversation around that and we carry so many typical traits that feed into that set easily, so it's important to say no you're not going crazy, it's just something that's happened to you, chin up".

Emotions are traditionally a female failing, but Jodie points out that if you're capable of articulating and processing your emotions, it can be an asset for business.

"I experience things from a very emotion based perspective and so for me in an environment when it's not a job it's a life, it's a really interesting thing to work with. It's been about and still is about, learning to take emotion and processing it in order to give your brain clarity to move. I think it will be an ongoing lesson for my life."

As the chief creative officer at Shoes of Prey, Jodie's intellectual and creative sides have finally come together in harmonious equilibrium. She's fuelled by her love of a satisfied customer and genuinely cares about the personal experience. "I want you to feel that wow experience when you open up the box of shoes you designed yourself. The whole idea comes from the fact that we care about giving you what you're looking for and making that special for you."

Jodie's authenticity and ability to execute business practicalities while building a busy media profile, are just a few traits that make her one to watch. Her honesty, ambition and love of the game are the qualities she hopes to take from Australian success to global market domination.

LAUREN FRIED

Founder of Pulse Marketing

PULSE MARKETING

Founded

2003

Awards

OVER 9 INCLUDING TELSTRA
NSW YOUNG BUSINESS
WOMEN'S AWARD 2010

Inspiration

INITIALLY FROM BEING
A FIERCE COMPETITOR

Nationally recognised marketing expert Lauren Fried remembers initially misunderstanding what an entrepreneur actually was, believing it to be "someone who ran a business and had lots of money".

Now 12 years into running Pulse Marketing Group with another marketing tech startup, Joule, under her belt, Lauren sees an entrepreneur as "the brains that turn an idea into a business" and a high functioning entrepreneur as one that can turn an idea into an accessibly large, global business. It wasn't up until two years ago, that Lauren truly felt herself to be an entrepreneur.

The Adventurous Type

Lauren is a lover of life and experience. Her greatest fear is looking back on her life and seeing the person she could have been but didn't have the guts to be. Growing up in Sydney, she has always been impulsive, a frequent traveller and explorer, and particularly the type of person adept at communicating a message, be it persuasive or organic.

"I love going into lots of different businesses and I love dealing with business owners. I just get it. It's like a language, one I speak well, and clients trust me because of that. I love the feeling of that."

Constantly driven to achieve, Lauren has a love for challenges and a tremendous ability to perform well under pressure. Winner of numerous awards including Telstra NSW Young Business Woman of the Year Award, it is no wonder she has built Pulse Marketing Group to be the A grade business it is today. She is the kind of person who can implement a new or significantly improved product or process, and talk people into adopting it enthusiastically

Lauren credits a great deal of her learning in her early years to the training she received while working in the marketing department for McDonalds. She remembers it taught her about team culture and ambition to achieve great results. In the business of building brands, as the Managing Director of Pulse, she chooses to engage with like minded people that have both the respect and spirit for a great idea. An essential ingredient to her own growth is surrounding herself with other entrepreneurs. She admits that it's vital to her learning and success to be in the company of extraordinary people.

IF YOU DON'T HAVE AN ONLINE BUSINESS IN FIVE YEARS TIME YOU DON'T HAVE A BUSINESS

"The people in my circle seem to all share the same qualities: extreme loyalty, deep thinkers, don't give me advice and clearly don't judge me, they are highly intelligent, authentic, tolerant, they don't see minorities, and they see everyone from a different angle. I have an amazing group of women around me who are extraordinary, that makes me want to be extraordinary. They make me believe there is no limit to what can be done."

Back to her beginnings, Lauren described that she had a privileged upbringing. With a dad as a pilot, Lauren equates her childhood as to "one of those families that went to Disneyland". She is very appreciative of the fact that she never went without.

While she had accumulated a great deal of knowledge and skills at McDonalds, founding Pulse at the age of 23 was a whole new ball game to Lauren. She began consulting and soon needed to bring on employees to manage the incoming work. "I was so young. I was just a baby. I didn't know how to recruit, I remember printing all these applicants' resumes out and taking them over to a friends house going, okay what do I do, what do I ask them?"

Culture and Investments

As someone that owns both a service business and a tech startup, Lauren confides that she enjoys the nature and culture that the size of Pulse brings. "I want this business to be the business I love working in and that we retain a very close team, that's so important to me. It's a service business and I just love the functionality of it now. I love that we can all fit in the board room, all do things together and that we all care for each other. Organically we will grow without me stretching us thinner."

Joule and Pule Marketing work in the same realm, with some Pulse employees keenly invested in what Lauren has set out to achieve. In the future, Lauren sees Pulse expanding off shore. "We had a new team member who has started in Frankfurt. There's also another employee who is going to move to Jakarta. It's such a treat for these guys to ask me, can I go over and train the team in this country? I love their involvement."

While the discrepancy between the confidence of male and female entrepreneurs is highly apparent, Lauren indicates that launching Joule has given her a sense of entrepreneurship she didn't have while first founding Pulse. Joule, a platform that offers high quality, low cost creative solutions to large scale e-commerce companies, has ignited Lauren's true inner abilities as an innovator and executor. "There are concepts within pulse that are entrepreneurial and very much everyone in the team has that spirit about them, but when I launched Joule, I finally felt very happy to call myself an entrepreneur."

The concept for Joule came about after Lauren heard Freelance.com founder, Matt Barry speak at an event to which he told the crowd, "if you don't have an online business in five years time you don't have a business". From this, Lauren felt the need to develop an online platform that both filled a gap but wasn't a far stretch from what she was already doing with Pulse.

"I am not developing a market, it's a market that exists but I found key advisors and some other people to assist me and we tested the concepts and found it to be really sound. We did some online experiments and not long after we were getting client inquiries from the UK, US, Berlin and even a professor from Cambridge. I couldn't believe it."

Lauren is inspired by entrepreneurs who execute brilliant business plans outside their fields of expertise. "I am a marketer and the new business is in the marketing space, so I am not moving away from my skill set. When people aren't working in their technically skill, I am blown away. I would like to think if someone said to me Lauren, here's a hairdresser, make her successful, that I could. I am not technically a hairdresser but I could look at that business, make it grow and hopefully expand and get franchise, go global, get sponsors...do it with an edge. That's where the entrepreneur comes in where they can look at something from a very different perspective or try something new for the first time."

Womanhood and Risk Taking

Across her journey, Lauren feels one of the biggest obstacles has been being a woman in business and letting her own insecurities around that dictate her demeanor. "If I could do it all over again I would say calm down. I thought I was being judged every meeting I went into, I had no authority, not enough experience, I would walk into meetings with a chip on my shoulder. I remembered every conversation I had to have laser focus. I actually employed my mentor into the business who was an older guy and people would assume he was the doer."

Lessons from Lauren:
- Take the risk, it's worth it.
- Engage with like-minded people that have both the respect and spirit for a great idea.
- Look at things from a different perspective or try something new for the first time.

Excited for the future of women in entrepreneurship, Lauren's advice is to absolutely own what you're doing. "Believe in it, because your success is so much based around how you frame yourself as an entrepreneur as opposed to how other people see you. Set yourself up for a win and others will see you in that same light."

While you might encounter obstacles, Lauren indicates that while the journey can be long and hard, it's all very much worth it.

"The biggest risk is leaving a full time job and doing your own thing, it's still the biggest decision I have had to make. All I can say is, if you are truly talented and you do your own thing and it doesn't work, don't worry, you'll get snapped back up into a business pretty quickly because you are truly talented. Take the risk, it's worth it."

KYLIE GREEN

Founder of Dentsu Aegis Network

Having built, sold and exited three companies, now working as the managing director of Activations Aust & NZ - Dentsu Aegis, Kylie Green is a recognised advertising guru. The group specialises in brand activations including promotional, experiential and shopper marketing, working with some of Australia and New Zealand's largest and best-loved brands.

She understands the privilege of growing up in an entrepreneurial family where self-empowerment was instilled at the dinner table. Today, a solo mother of one, Kylie has a career which has spanned over 25 years in entrepreneurial, marketing and senior management roles. Kylie admits that despite talent, drive and charisma the glass ceiling has been a constant along her entrepreneurial journey. Luckily, she's not afraid to invest in herself, making choices that have seen her build and exit three companies to date.

DENTSU AEGIS NETWORK

Awards

APMA - STAR AWARDS 1999 - 2010 - GOLD, SILVER & BRONZE

APMA LIFETIME ACHIEVEMENT AWARD 2013

CREATIVE SUMMIT AWARDS 2003 - 2010 - SILVER & BRONZE

WHO'S WHO WOMEN IN BUSINESS IN AUSTRALIA 2004 - 2009

Building the businesswoman

"From a very young age, I remember having conversations around the dinner table to do with business and money. My parents always spoke to me and my siblings like we were all equals, they were directed their questions to me about pocket money and saving like they would to someone else investing in property. That was a type of accelerated learning, invaluable to someone wanting to run a business," she says.

Kylie's first venture, Kaleidoscope began as a brand activation agency founded in 1998, which she sold to the Photon Group of companies in 2005, remaining as CEO till 2010. During her time as CEO, Kylie managed to attract the engagement and work of blue-chip clients such as Emirates, Panasonic, The Good Guys, GSK, Campbell Arnott's, Jurlique and many more.

Before founding she took 12 months and wrote myself a business plan. From there she worked her "butt off" and in the first year turned over $1million.

After selling, with time to focus on the business' output, Kylie felt she really found her feet. "The agency just boomed. It grew from zero base to an annual turnover in excess of $15million, with three offices in Sydney, Melbourne and Brisbane."

Kylie often comes back to her upbringing. She talks about how they taught her that success was a matter of choosing your priorities and making investments of work into achieving the future of your vision. "My parents always reminded me that it was all hard work and that success was not handed on a silver platter," she remembers and describes how even her father mostly learnt through tough work and trial and error. Her father instilled the motto of 'the harder you work the more you get' and Kylie has adopted that work ethic since.

Kylie and her siblings were also guided by their parents when it came to investing in property early, and from this, her ability to pick 'winners' was born. "We were told from a very young age by our parents that they would like us to invest in property at 18." Since then, I've never gone wrong in property and have become an entrepreneur in property investment, to some degree. Having a father who has worked in property development has definitely helped."

Life choices

From 2010 through to 2012, Kylie founded and ran two businesses The Oven and Adland Jobs, then took some time out from starting businesses to start a family, joining the Board of Directors for Layne Beachley's Aim for the Stars Foundation and working as an industry mentor to several industry business owners in BTL marketing, creative services and PR.

Kylie joined the Dentsu Aegis Network as managing director of Activations for Australia and New Zealand in September 2013, managing the ApolloNation activations businesses in Sydney, Melbourne and Auckland as well as Synergy Brand Experience in NZ. She is extremely well respected by her colleagues and peers, who hold her in the highest esteem.

Fellow Rare Bird and friend, Layne Beachley sees Kylie as a massive inspiration.

"Kylie is Incredibly organised, efficient, connected and hard working, if you ever need a job done, Kylie is the woman to achieve it! I'm proud to have her join the Board of the Aim For The Stars Foundation

PUT YOUR SPIN ON IT. BELIEVE IN YOURSELF, BELIEVE WITH REAL CONVICTION AND THINGS WILL COME. THAT'S MY KEY WORD, BELIEVE

and appreciate the endless amount of effort she invests into every role she choses to sink her teeth in to," says Layne.

As an entrepreneur, Kylie sees her own strengths as networking and identifying opportunity. "I'm here for the long term, my brain, heart and gut is on fire, I'm excited and the opportunities are endless," she says.

Her advice to aspiring entrepreneurs? Kylie sees that anyone with passion can make things happen. "Have love for what you're doing, that's number one. Number two is to not let limiting beliefs and other people tell you you can't do it, because you can, just have a go. Number three, the same rule doesn't always apply to everyone. Someone might have

needed $100,000 to start a company but I've known people who started with $1,000 and $50. I started with $0. Break the mould and be the exception to the rule," she expresses.

Ambitions and advice

While she says it's important to be realistic, she also believes in thinking big. "In my business plan I said at year ten I want to sell this business to a multi-national. If I've done it, you can do it. Often we've got ideas in our head that we say I can do it differently or I can do it my way. I'm not university educated, I'm street smart. Anybody can be an entrepreneur and there is no rule book around who can and who can't be an entrepreneur. Too many women look at their past and feel more comfortable sitting

there with the past or present and not looking to the future at how they might change things."

"Put your spin on it. Believe in yourself, believe with real conviction and things will come. That's my key word, believe," she says.

Lessons from Kylie:

- Don't ask for special permission. Do what you want to do.
- Anybody can be an entrepreneur. There is no rule book around who can and who can't be an entrepreneur.
- Invest in yourself.

One of Kylie's most treasured and greatest achievements was choosing to go out on her own, often against the advice of friends and family, and have her daughter Addison. "I made a very big decision to have a baby on my own."

"I became an inspiration to all these women who wanted to have a child on their own and they all started contacting me via social media so I was also mentoring them in my year off. I just juggle a lot of balls and keep them up in the air. I don't ask for special permission to hand something in later than usual because I'm a single parent. Any woman can do it, women are naturally very resilient"

INSPIRATION, AND A BELIEF THAT
SOMETHING IS POSSIBLE, ARE THE
FIRST STEPS IN REALISING YOUR
DREAMS AS AN ENTREPRENEUR.
I URGE YOU TO READ THIS BOOK
TO GET THE MOTIVATION TO
MAKE YOUR NEXT BUSINESS AND
ENTREPRENEURIAL MOVE!

––––––––

Verne Harnish, founder of the world-renowned Entrepreneurs' Organization (EO);
CEO of Gazelles; and author of Scaling Up: How a Few Make It...and Why the Rest Don't

DONNA GUEST

Founder of Blue Illusion

Donna Guest is truly a seasoned entrepreneur. Vibrant and tenacious, she, with partner and husband Danny, have formed a powerful complementary partnership, and forged a formidable path in the retail world.

With boutiques in every state in Australia, stores in over six cities in New Zealand and three stores in the United States, their success is due to a slick combination of innovation, intuition and mutual support. Founded in 1998, Blue Illusion has become an evolving story of success and adaptation Blue Illusion offers everything from women's clothing to the latest fashion accessories and footwear. Customers can also find books and home ware items too such as candles, books on fashion and styling, beauty products, vases and their personally created aromatherapy oil that customers love.

BLUE ILLUSION

Founded
1991

Boutiques
109 STAND-ALONE STORES

Inspiration
PASSIONATE ABOUT CLOTHES
AND BUSINESS

Journey

The evolution of many successful businesses often comes down to a series of iterations; where several processes are repeated and changed to achieve a desired goal. Rapid change is essential to the iterative process, and a keen, intuitive awareness of what's working and what's not is the only way to guide that change. Cemented as a leader in mature women's fashion in Australia, Blue Illusion, which now boasts over 127 stores across three countries. Danny and Donna's business catered to their interests in its early stages, flexing around their needs with a newborn baby and their love of the active lifestyle. Keen skiers, they spent a great deal of time at Mount Hotham in Victoria and started producing après ski wear as wholesalers.

Donna acknowledges the type of motivation and work ethic needed to get your business from an embryonic vision with no startup capital, to the next phase. For her and Danny, that meant embracing a multitude of roles in the business, with little regard for status or norms. "We were so small to begin with, it was really just a handful of us. I remember taking my baby daughter in the car and driving around and dropping garments off at the dye house. Then I'd go and have garments embroidered, I'd come back to the factory/ office at the end of the day and I'd help lay up a table of garments and while I was doing all that, Danny was managing sales but if needed would be sitting sewing on the machine. Every day we would just do what we had to do to get the product out the door," says Donna.

The entrepreneurial journey isn't the same for everyone, but Blue Illusion possibly wouldn't be both the online and the bricks and mortar retail powerhouse it is today without Danny and Donna's grit, and willingness to work through failure to an outcome. "You have the person who gives up and folds up because they've run out of cash, and then you have the others that don't believe it and keep going and turn it around. There's not a lot that go through that turn around. So, you can start off, have an idea and start a business and get to years three and four and crash and burn. Then some people start another idea, we didn't have anything to begin with so everything seemed like we had nothing to lose."

Innovation

Donna is a self-described clotheshorse, confident in her ability to pick and see things her customers would really love. Complementing her intuitive sense of fashion was Danny's charisma and innate ability to work with people. Their relationship perfectly nurtured and supported a growing business. After wholesaling for 10 years, the Guests saw the potential to move across into retail. Donna was heavily involved in the production side of things and arrows began to point towards female fashion. It was a natural progression for the dynamic duo.

A visionary and outcome driven duo, Danny and Donna saw a niche in the market, and their avenue to success. "We saw a hole in the marketplace that didn't cater for the customer we wanted to produce garments for," Donna shares. In 1998, the world saw the first Blue Illusion boutique.

Donna is product focused, and includes in her remit the design of the concept stores, as well as keeping a thumb on the pulse of the company. She feels that her strength lies particularly when it comes to making changes and improvements, but insists she could not provide for all the needs of the company without her husband. The two don't sugarcoat each other's strengths and weaknesses, and this realism keeps the business grounded.

Intuition

Positioning has been essential to the success of Blue Illusion, not only in terms of market but also location. Store placement was vital to reaching the market Donna sought to woo; an older female age-group whom she felt was disregarded by the industry but knew were viable customers in terms of disposable income. Positioning their boutiques in community-centric regional areas, airports and holiday destinations has been a key strategy in customer acquisition and brand positioning, as was creating a brand that spoke both fashion and comfort. "While everyone else was concentrating on the Gen Y market and trying to get the newest thing on the floor, I was looking at a market who was stable, who loved fashion and but also wanted to buy comfortable items that made them feel fabulous."

Donna's intuition and knowledge of fashion history was an asset in identifying the needs of an older market. "I was in my mid 30s then, so I was dressing someone 15 years older and I thought why should woman at that age not feel good in what they wear? And, why is the fashion industry disregarding you when you were part of the fashion era of the sixties and seventies, which changed everything! Which is where we continue to bring back as inspiration for every season ... why would we want to cover you up or make you feel drab at that age? Lets make a fashion statement!" Recently, Blue Illusion have announced French actress Juliette Binoche their Ambassador for the brand, given her strong public image, clear self-determination and confidence. Binoche makes being fifty sexy, and that's the confidence Donna wants to supply through her brand.

Diehard entrepreneurs think globally and for Donna and Danny expansion came as they hit a geographical stalemate with growth. "About four years ago we really understood our business. We could only grow the business to a certain point in Australia and New Zealand so what were we going to do then? A part from new concepts, the other option was to expand overseas and I had been saying it for a long time as all the internationals had been coming to Australia. I thought New Zealand retailers were already onto it years ago, they were expanding overseas in retail and I said well how hard could it be? We could really only see it as opportunity." Placing boutiques in airports was vital to this international expansion. "No one beyond our local customers really knew the brand before we started going into shopping centres and airports. The brand was like a secret to our ladies. But now, we've got a very strong brand recognition because we've been able to represent a woman who wasn't necessarily acknowledged before."

Challenges and growth

Donna acknowledges that particularly during the tough transition from wholesale to retail, the Guest's mentor relationship

with Just Jeans founder, Craig Kimberley was key critical success factor.

"At first, Craig was seeing Danny every three months and a year later he wanted to meet me. It was a three-hour conversation and he structured us into a board, and then said 'you can't just have your head in product, you need to understand the numbers.'

Then he recommended some other experts in different fields to teach me how to run design meetings and in particular the importance of asking questions because I was a decision maker". According to Donna, it was this advice that really moved Blue Illusion forward.

As an entrepreneur, Donna also has a strong social heart and now sits on the board of the not-for-profit organisation Dress For Success in the USA. Under Donna's leadership, Blue Illusion is also known for generous philanthropy, from local to top tier with weighty involvement in World Vision, National Breast Cancer Foundation and The Smith Family, amongst other community driven charities. To date, the company has donated in excess of $732,000 annually to charities, a real life testament to the core values of the brand.

In the beginning, Donna was reserved about integrating her contributions and alignment with charity into the business, until she realised the potential she had to create real positive change by including her customers in the experience of giving - something that's remained a strong value throughout the growth of Blue Illusion. "It became very organic and we started having in store events for all sorts of charities, from nurturing local change in places like kindergartens to aged care. Each

boutique takes ownership in nominating a local organisation and in doing that, there is a wonderful sense of empowerment."

Lessons from Donna:
- Mentorship can be a key critical success factor. Find a mentor who suits your style.
- Work through failure to an outcome. You're not beaten til you think you are.
- Pivot, if you see a niche that fits your desires. Think about the core of your business.

While the Blue Illusion journey has been a long and winding one, Donna seems to infer the secret ingredient to their success and future potential revolves around the partnership of her and Danny.

"Being a husband and wife team we know what's going on, we are sweating it out together. If you're a one-person show, you take a whole lot of pressure on to your own shoulders. We make things happen, quicker and much more smartly because we're in it together and there's something that happens when more than one person believes in something, something great."

MANDI GUNSBERGER

Founder of Babyology

Who thought that cross-checking a market of baby accessories could lead to the creation of a global company?

After collating large amounts of data around the types of products used for her daughters, Mandi Gunsberger decided the information would be useful for other mums. First creating a blog and registering it as Babyology, Mandi has built a business and online platform viewed by thousands daily. Described as "a lifestyle website keeping hip parents and their bubs up to date with the world of baby-related design". Babyology is essentially a directory that is constantly evolving to meet changing consumer trends while staying abreast of the 'baby' market. Mandi's staff is made up of women all over Australia working from home in various capacities and experienced professional women who also want to have flexibility in their lives to juggle work and family.

BABYOLOGY

Founded
2006

Achievements
ONE OF THE BEST BLOGS IN THE WORLD BY THE INTERNATIONAL WEBLOG AWARDS

Inspiration
FAMILY HAS ALWAYS BEEN HER NUMBER ONE PRIORITY. MANDI DECIDED ALL THE OVER-RESEARCHING SHE DID WOULD BE USEFUL TO OTHER PARENTS.

WE HAVE A VERY STRONG AND ENGAGED AUDIENCE OF OVER 550,000 FACEBOOK FANS AND 750,000 UNIQUE VISITORS PER MONTH

Juggle street

History tells us women have traditionally had run businesses or careers before stepping into motherhood. To do it the other way around, where a business is born from babies, seems an anomaly, but in today's digital landscape it appears an entrepreneur can begin wherever, whenever and in whatever stage of their life they choose. Mandi is the perfect example of creating a high turnover business whilst wearing the full time 'mum hat'. Since December 2006, she has been running and growing a business while juggling the demanding needs of her three young children at the same time. But, funnily enough, without them Babyology would not have been born.

"For my first child, I did so much research on products that I had built a database

of prams, cots and high chairs available all over the world with different colours, weights and dimensions," Mandi retells.

Consequently, Babyology attracted a large audience and Mandi decided to register it as a business. "This is how Babyology was born, with no business plan or funding. After living in San Francisco where blogging was taking off, I decided to register the name and start writing about products each day as well as setting up the section with all prams, cots and highchairs. I wanted to work from home as I was pregnant with my second child and was about to have two children 18 months apart," Mandi says.

Babyology represents a shift in the types of career options for women. "I always thought I would work my way up to management levels in large corporations,

but now I would never even consider going back to corporate world," she says.

Mandi is not only disrupting antiquated conventions, but she's creating an online space for others to follow. She leads her team of stay-at-home mums who are scattered across every state in Australia and internationally, communicating via online avenues.

"Our staff are made up of women all over Australia working from home in various capacities. They are all amazing, experienced professional women who also want to have flexibility in their lives to juggle work and family," Mandi says.

How does she hire them? Mandi bases employment behind personality and "fitting in with the team". Mandi explains she would

rather hire mothers that don't have the right skill level but who are enthusiastic and will fit in with the team. She adds that those women can easily be trained, nurtured and accelerated to high positions.

Driving the business pram

The goal for Mandi when she set out was far from the course Babyology has now taken. Babyology is positioned within an untapped niche market "we had a fantastic product that people wanted to connect with, both the wider parenting community and the brands," Mandi says, and uniquely has an advertising based business model.

This means that income is solely generated by newsletters and banner advertising. To attract the masses to the blog and website, the flow of traffic has to be constant in order to attract this revenue.

"Our team of writers put together three to four articles daily and we have a very strong and engaged audience of over 550,000 Facebook fans and 750,000 unique visitors per month. We sell advertising on the website including display advertising, social media ads, native advertising through editorial, newsletters, competitions and in 2014 we launched Baby Shower events in Melbourne and Sydney and sell sponsorship for these," Mandi explains.

Mandi has a bachelors degree from the University of New South Wales in commerce and spent eight years in the hotel industry in the marketing and public relations area. "My first job out of University was at Menzies Hotel as a sales coordinator for a year, then I moved onto the Hilton as marketing & PR coordinator," Mandi says.

With this marketing background and a sound business model, Mandi built Babyology off a meagre budget of $5000. Of course, with a background in computer science, Mandi's husband assisted in getting the site off the ground. "My husband is the COO of the business and while we have our specific business roles and are very complimentary in our skills, we work together on most aspects of the business and it's wonderful having someone as passionate about the business to go over plans and ideas."

So, what makes this mother-of-three an entrepreneur? Mandi says it's her intuition. "We have always gone with what we believe is right when making small or large business decisions. This also lets us make decisions quickly, which is critical when you're making so many every day. People often talk about entrepreneurs taking risks and I am not a huge risk taker. It has also taken six years to take the plunge with three kids and a mortgage for my husband to leave his full-time role and join the business."

Mandi's mission and purpose surrounds the branches of family. Visibly, family has been at the core for Mandi and always her number one priority. "Babyology only exists because I wanted a way to be more present in my family's lives. I also have to be doing something I'm passionate about," which streams into Mandi's perspective on money, she believes the experience of her staff, readers and clients is the most important part.

After that "the money will come, I don't believe in maximising profits at any cost. I'm constantly faced with decisions where we could make more money at the expense of one of these, so it's important to stay focused on this principle," Mandi says.

While juggling Babyology and her children, one of Mandy's goals is to mentor women who are just starting out. "I want to share my knowledge and experiences. This also includes mentoring and talking to girls still at school about career choices and helping educate them on a path that allows them to design their own careers."

Success comes in many forms, shapes and colours and is different to each individual. For Mandy she already feels it through the flexibility Babyology allows her to have. "I do feel successful already as I am present in each of my children's lives on a daily basis. The business can support my family's lifestyle and allow me and my husband to work from home on something that we love. This allows me to have the flexibility to work when needed, mostly more hours than necessary, and gives me the ability to be fluid in my daily life if children are sick, if there are school concerts or if there is work travel."

An underlying reason why Mandi set out on the journey with Babyology was because of her father, who was a great part of Mandi's life, and died suddenly in 2010. This was a personal hurdle, one that impacted her greatly, "I was very close to him and he was the reason I started Babyology. He was very entrepreneurial and taught me I could do anything I wanted to do. When I had my first baby and was unsure what I wanted to do next, he took me to a one day course on building a website and this is where I came up with the Babyology concept and soon after launched."

Mandi has achieved amazing things from the comfort of her own home. Her four important factors to being an entrepreneur:

- Inspiration.
- Determination.
- Flexibility.
- Passion.

Finally, her advice for starting a business is to "Just do it. There's always a reason to not do something. You're too young, too old, too busy, etc. It's never been easier to get something off the ground. We use over 20 cloud-based systems to run Babyology. You don't need expensive offices and hundreds of people to do amazing things."

JANET HAMILTON

———

Founder of The Shed Company

Janet Hamilton is a woman who's motivation and determination to succeed has come from a childhood of 'unpleasantness' and growing up in an environment with little support. Her sheer tenacity blossomed as Janet decided her future was going to be far different from her past.

"Government Housing in a family which was not only poor but broken and shattered this certainly was the catalyst for me wanting to make a difference in my life," Janet tells. With many years of experience across several business sectors and many roles Janet found her niche when the concept for THE Shed Company was born. Her desire to make a difference within the industry, the network and her team gave her the drive to succeed. THE Shed Compnay offers Australian consumers the very best Australian made and engineered buildings solutions.

THE SHED COMPANY

———

Founded
2005

———

Awards
SEVERAL INCLUDING FINANCIAL REVIEW'S SMART INVESTOR MAGAZINE IN 2007, 2009 AND 2010 IN THE TOP 8 FRANCHISE GROUPS IN AUSTRALIA.

———

Inspiration
TO MAKE A DIFFERENCE AND INSPIRE PEOPLE TO LEARN AND ACHIEVE

NEW ERA, NEW BUSINESS NEW FOCUS

Early stages of the journey

When exposed to adversity, many business owners have greater chance of succeeding. Janet says "knowing that I would have to fight to survive and to change my life gave me a doggered determination and can do attitude." By using challenges for self growth it makes future hardships more tolerable. Janet utilised her ability to overcome adversity to begin her first company in 1978.

Janet's sister helped her open her first business in Tweed Heads, New South Wales. "We sold the business however it still trades today (2014) which is amazing for a small business. It was started with $2000 and two women who had a gutsy determination to be a success," says Janet.

Fast forward ten years later Janet's second venture began in Yagoona, New South Wales when she had a desire to have flexibility to work her own hours after having three kids. "I created a business that would see many changes, as the need grew the business changed".

For any mother, working and parenting can be a juggling act, trying to keep the balls in the air is a common topic of discussion as women begin to compromise their careers in place for a family, "I sold the business and this also continues to trade again amazing in the climate of today's world," tells Janet.

However the biggest development Janet was to create and work on came in 2005. "The business was started firstly to sure up our own small business and to ensure that our business could grow, the model was to offer Australian consumers the very best Australian made and engineered buildings solutions," says Janet and it was to be called THE Shed Company.

Janet had clear foresight for the businesses mission and purpose "making a difference, to do more than anyone else around me, to provide my team, clients, suppliers and family with a no nonsense environment but one that we can all learn and grow from." She also sought a company culture with values that became a solid part of the company DNA.

"For me it is about the culture of the business. The same values, determination, grit and most definitely a can do attitude with a total focus on customer service. Ensuring the team, no matter what their role, understand that they are part of the big picture and everyone has a part to play, and at some point will need support".

Broken childhood bright legacy

Janet thought that if THE Shed Company was successful, she and the team would franchise, which in the end, they did. "We wanted to make a difference in the industry, hence the caption 'Discover THE Shed Company Difference'," Janet discusses.

However different, the concept of success differs for every individual. Success for Janet is personal, "achieve your goals and see growth in the business. Yes I have achieved that with recently selling THE Shed Company Group and now ready for the next challenge. I don't think we should ever 'settle' and say it is enough there is always more to do and more to achieve."

Janet has seen her own challenges within work, "whilst we are all busy in our day-to-day, businesses do long hours and have many pressures, time out is very important". Enforcing a landing pad for when the tough gets going reset and refueled her. For Janet, family was an essential part of her downtime along with getting away and sitting by the pool with a book.

A lesson from Janet:

- You become an entrepreneur by sheer grit and determination, if you don't have that will, you will not survive. You can never accept no.
- Excellent culture drives growth and learning.

From a broken childhood to manifesting a bright legacy, Janet has overcome many obstacles

proving that determination is at the heart of success. Not only did this inspiring woman achieve her business goals of: "obtaining an engineer, a software package to enable the business, the hope of having 12 franchisees and distributors and to provide them with service that has not been seen in the shed industry previously," she restored belief that she can be her own hero in the story she's telling. Janet also saw THE Shed Company grow to over 70 outlets across Australia.

A more significant end to a milestone was in 2014 when Janet sold THE Shed Company, making way for the next adventure in growing and expanding a range of e-commerece sites. "Selling the Group in 2014 was one of the most difficult things I have done in my professional life, however I watch with interest to see the group grow from strength to strength," Janet discloses.

Janet's support system was a contributing factor in the success of THE Shed Company. "My team at THE Shed Company Group were amazing, all dedicated and driven people whilst everyone understanding the family

values that the Company provided. It took many years to create this but ultimately it worked very well again as it is a team environment that grows great companies."

Following through with what she sets out to do is integral to Janet's future. Janet admits that she asks other entrepreneurs and uses her other support networks, which is incredibly beneficial for up-skilling. "I ask them what their success is, what they can teach me and what can they teach others," she tells.

Now free of all ties, Janet has left with three final words: "New era, new business new focus."

AVRIL HENRY

Founder of Avril Henry & Associates

AVRIL HENRY & ASSOCIATES

Founded
2003

Honours/Awards
SEVERAL INCLUDING WINNER
OF THE LIFETIME ACHIEVEMENT
IN HR AWARD 2006

Keynote speeches
OVER 1,000

Avril Henry is filled with a type of relentless passion that moves those around her to action.

Avril Henry & Associates was found in 2003 which focuses on keynote speaking, consulting and executive coaching in the areas of leadership, people and performance strategies. Avril has countless clientele and works with senior leadership teams from organisations such as IBM, Commonwealth Departments of Defence, Education and State Health Departments NSW.

Women in business: Knowing your history, forging a future

Frequently featured on radio and TV, Avril has delivered hundreds of keynote addresses and workshops to over 100,000 people in Australia, New Zealand and Asia to companies and industries. She is a strong advocate for access to education and the opportunity to do meaningful work, she believes that the definition of an entrepreneur is someone with the courage and boldness to create something or do something that may not have been done effectively before.

Avril thinks about entrepreneurship as arising from a couple of essential qualities, including passion and tenacity. "For me, it's the things that I am really passionate about and have been for over two decades. It's the core value of who I am and what makes me tick," she says.

Avril also indicates that women can be held back from entrepreneurship because of a desire to conform. Women tend to fight against being different and that means instead of taking a risk when they see one to be taken, they might try to fit in. She identifies this as one reason why so many women with the talent and vision for innovative business remain in corporate jobs.

Identifying the importance of support in breaking out of those social and genetic norms, Avril looks at mentorship as key to an entrepreneur's journey. Attributing much of her success to the guidance of prominent business woman, Anne Sherry, known for her roles as

WE OWE IT TO THE WENDY MCCARTHY'S AND THE ANNE SOMERS OF THIS WORLD WHO FOUGHT LONG AND HARD FOR WOMEN TO HAVE GREATER EQUALITY IN SOCIETY, POLITICS AND BUSINESS AND THAT WE DON'T MINIMISE THE EXPERIENCES OF OTHER WOMEN

CEO of the Bank of Melbourne and Westpac New Zealand, Avril feels she would not be where she is today without Anne's mentorship. Their tight knit relationship now spans over 20 years.

"Anne asked me to come and work for her in HR when I was working in finance but she gave me a job no one wanted to do, head of diversity of Westpac. That was about the gender diversity, paid maternity leave and sexual harassment investigations and bullying. It was probably the hardest job I did but it was like I had come home." She notes that being pushed out of her comfort zone, and out of the gravitic pull of the career railroad helped her to find her passion.

"If I hadn't been given that opportunity by Anne I would have continued up the ranks and become a finance director and CEO because I had the technical ability to do that but I was never passionate about that. Anne fostered my inner entrepreneurial abilities."

One of Avril's key messages, when we speak of advice for emerging entrepreneurs in practical terms, is finding the person that believes in you and is willing to mentor and open doors for you.

"Anne Cherry still opens doors for me 20 years later. She recommended me to the chairman of the international Women's Global Summit to speak at the conference," she says still in appreciation.

Some would say Avril was made to be an entrepreneur, constantly disrupting and questioning. Growing up in South Africa during the time of Apartheid, she was naturally anti-authoritarian and as a result labelled a problem child at school. "Wherever I've gone in life, I have been a very vocal advocate for fairness and justice and that has meant I have been a very vocal advocate for women and people from migrant backgrounds. They together with people with disabilities have bared the brunt of discriminatory practices and we continue to experience those discriminating practices right now. I also believe that you shouldn't complain about things without doing anything. If you do you're just an empty vessel so if you care enough about something go and do something about it."

Avril began in investment banking. "Making more money in investment banking for wealthy institutional investors to me wasn't making a difference. But I didn't know what I was supposed to do, then I was fortunate enough to work it out," she recalls.

She left corporate life eleven years ago and believes her official entrepreneurial journey began there, but believes her time in corporate life set her up for success. "I think all that time in corporate life of working in New York, Australia and London was simply giving me skills that will enable me to successfully execute my ideas. A lot of people have big dreams, who want to have their own business and to be entrepreneurs but what they lack is execution."

But, Avril indicates that where she really succeeded was they way she transitioned from corporate work to running her own business.

"I had already spent a year of corporate life thinking and planning, so when I left corporate life I had already set up my Australian Company Number and shelf company. I sorted out my logo and I had started working on my website."

Planning ahead: Success and failure

"I think what happens is people leave a job and go 'I'm going to go and do my own thing' but they haven't planned for it. I say to anybody who goes out on their own, be prepared that you won't pay yourself for 12 months. The other thing I had done is putting money away for a 12 month time frame because people give up their idea when they run out of money. Often either at the point they give up, at that tipping point which is exactly the time not to give up."

It's also about self belief, she says, and knowing your market and services while having financial backing.

Avril's wish for everyone, male or female, is that they find what it is they are supposed to do and that they are passionate about, "If you're an entrepreneur you are different and what you have to do is embrace that difference and be proud of it," she encourages

Lessons from Avril:

- Mentorship is important. Find that person that believes in you and is willing to open doors for you.
- Don't minimise the experiences of other women. A rising tide lifts all boats.
- Consolidate your skills and experience, but make sure you take a risk on an opportunity when you see one you believe in.

Forming Avril Henry and Associates as a way to consolidate all her experience and skills under one identity, Avril has taken her organisation to the next level by working with senior leadership teams and employees from organisations such as IBM, Commonwealth Departments of Defence, Education, State Health Departments NSW, Queensland, Victoria, Optus, BHP Billiton, Commonwealth Bank, NAB, IBM, Astra Zeneca, University of Western Sydney and many more.

Avril contributes her success to something she believes is very important for entrepreneurs, being a prolific researcher.

"I am always looking at what other people are doing in my field, I am always looking at the latest surveys, the latest research, I call it doing your homework. You have to be doing your homework everyday".

Finally, in terms of women in entrepreneurship, Avril compels us not to forget what we call the 'history of gender'.

"We look at men in society as having potential and we look at women in society as having to prove themselves for us to believe in them which means before we will invest in them. We owe it to the Wendy McCarthy's and the Anne Somers of this world who fought long and hard for women to have greater equality in society, politics and business and that we don't minimise the experiences of other women. I don't think we should dwell on it either but we need to make sure that we encourage young women, and we even encourage women of my generation."

JO HORGAN

—

Founder of Mecca Cosmetica, KIT Cosmetics and Mecca Maxima

MECCA COSMETICA, KIT COSMETICS AND MECCA MAXIMA

—

Founded
1997

—

Stores
36 MECCA COSMETICA,
17 MECCA MAXIMA,
AND 8 KIT COSMETICS

—

Inspiration
FOUND A NICHE IN THE
MARKET AND CAME FROM A
BACKGROUND IN BEAUTY
AND COSMETICS

Jo Horgan is an ideas machine, full of astronomical potential. A pioneer in the market of beauty and cosmetics, she has a history of putting the right idea into practice at the right time, Mecca Cosmetica, founded in 1997, is a clear example of that.

Jo has the right qualities of insight and application to implement new and significantly improved organisational methods in all her business practices. Her passionate goal is to bring the best in global beauty to her customers, across three labels: Mecca Cosmetica, Mecca Maxima and Kit. Jo is a game changer.

Background and growth

Jo's childhood was spent in the United Kingdom, and soon after Jo became a teenager, Jo's parents who are both self-employed, decided to move to Australia. "Australia was a real land of opportunity and it appealed to my parents." Her father worked in clothing and owned clothing factories in Europe, and her entrepreneurial mother had established her own mail order business, for handmade kids clothes before starting her own interior design company. Having parents with drive and initiative really stimulated horizontal thinking early on for Jo.

"It was fascinating, I got to watch both of my parents. My mum had incredible taste with interiors and I'd have discussions at the table with my father on different articles and books".

For Jo, "everything seemed possible". After her parents moved to Perth in Australia, Jo undertook and completed a Bachelor of Arts in English Literature at the University of Western Australia, and a Masters Degree in Science; majoring in Mass Communications at Boston University in the US. She briefly returned to the UK, and there, while interviewing for L'Oréal Paris, met a woman who would become a business role model and inspiration.

"I met this amazing woman, one of the most senior women. She was very dynamic, very direct, it seemed like a simple conversation, one where you know where you stand. She asked good questions, some challenging, but I understood the context of them. I thought, this is amazing, you're amazing, I looked at her and realised she was the sort of woman I could see myself working with, so I took the job at L'Oréal Paris in the marketing division as a product manager and was there for two years".

Venturing back to Australia after her time at L'Oreal Paris, Jo had a stronger idea of her strengths, and of the shape of the cosmetics market. She approached some brands with her idea. At that time, she laughs, "I didn't have a lease, didn't have a location, didn't have any staff." All Jo had was a dream, a business plan and her own skills. With those resources alone, she convinced all the brands she approached to sign up.

Palette of ideas

Jo has ideas. The challenge for her is picking which ones to run with, and the process of taking an idea from a seed to a full grown concept is what makes or breaks an entrepreneur. "My ideation flows around: what do customers want, what do I want, how do we do this," Jo says. "I am a creative thinker. I have this mind that keeps ticking over. Ideas are never the problem. The challenge from the ideas is which ones do you run with, and that's the difficult for most." Jo has the crucial ability to pick and choose, and the confidence in which ideas will find successful fruition and which won't. Execution is crucial. With millions of products and hundreds of thousands of suppliers around the world, the choices are abundant, exponentially increasing with the growth of online competition. Being confident in your choices and executing them cleanly once

I AM A CREATIVE THINKER. I HAVE THIS MIND THAT KEEPS TICKING OVER... EXECUTION IS CRUCIAL. IT'S THE DIFFERENCE BETWEEN FLOUNDERING AND FLOURISHING

a decision has been made is the difference between floundering and flourishing.

The industry has changed since Jo broke into it, "I think as a rule you get better at it as you go. When I first started my business there weren't that many brands. I targeted 20 and they all said yes. From that I chose seven which were the absolute bulls-eye of what we were looking for," she reveals.

Along with her natural strength in ideation and execution, Jo points out that there is a lot to be learned from experience and failure, if only in developing greater perspective for the next project.

Following the launch of Mecca Cosmetica, Jo launched her second unique beauty destination, Kit Cosmetics in May 2005. Jo waxes lyrical about the rule-breaking model she pioneered,

"A retail concept that took the stereotype of a 'beauty store' and threw it well and truly on its head. It's a beauty lifestyle store with no false promises, no hype, no rules. Kit has since become a destination for hard-to-find, indie beauty brands," and Kit Cosmetics now has eight stores throughout Australia.

In October 2010, Jo launched her third beauty destination, Mecca Maxima which is described as 'a democratic beauty playground within a shopping centre environment. Maxima brings together a mix of over 70 prestige and niche beauty brands from YSL, Lancome, Bobbi Brown to Nars and Smashbox'. Similar to the high service Mecca Cosmetica environment, Mecca Maxima has both options of utilising the attentive customer service or browsing individually. By the end of 2014 Maxima will have 17 locations throughout Australia.

Keeping it together

To have a solid business model is only one part of a successful company. A strong team, and good customer relationships are also necessary for any retail business. Jo emphasises excellent customer service as integral to brand image and customer loyalty. "The customers are all about the brand and what we do," says Lucinda, Jo's right hand communications strategist. Lucinda also explains that the Mecca Group highly values knowledge and competence in its employees, spending 3 percent of its turnover on education, which is very high for a retail business. Most companies spend less than 2 percent on training overall.

Jo describes the Mecca company culture as "collaborative", "passionately goal orientated" and "a positive environment". It's not just her. The company runs an annual survey, and over the last ten years the number one consecutive key factor that has stood out among employees has been "I feel proud for working with this company." Lucinda has known Jo for over ten years and offers another perspective on her and the business. "Jo is very supportive to her staff. Most of the people have kids and have been in the company for years so they come back on days that they can do. That's why people are so loyal to her because she gets it and gives them the flexibility they need."

"That's one thing about Jo, is that she doesn't rush things. Ultimately with web and digital innovation she knew that for her customers she had to prioritise that experience," Lucinda says.

Distinctive edge: relationships

One of the contributing factors to Mecca's success is the unique business model that Jo has strategically established. As a vendor, every brand that is in Mecca, the team provides internal support from the brand marketing, public relations, warehousing and shipping.

This added service strengthens brand relationships and propels Mecca past other international competitors such as Sephora and local stores like David Jones. "That's one of the things Jo has done differently. She goes to the brands and says, give us your brand, we will nurture, love and grow your brand and you can trust us. The brand is like an extended family member," Lucinda says.

"That's why we only take about 70 brands with Mecca Cosmetica. We have a whole brands and buying team upstairs just dedicated purely to brand relationships. The model has been a huge part of the success".

Lessons from Jo:
- You get better as you go, so if you have the confidence to begin, you can learn from there.
- Relationships are at the core of any successful business.
- Know your own mind – cultivate your ideas, and identify which ones are worth backing.
- Investing heavily into training and culture will set you apart from competitors.

Another strategic move Jo made was hiring her husband who proved crucial in the development of Mecca. She says, "[my husband] was a management consultant, it was an incredibly important time for the business, we were growing fast, we had 12 stores and we were just beginning to be at that point. He has a meticulous approach and he sat there doing boring foundation-building".

More than just a business success, Jo has thrown herself into numerous philanthropic commitments, sitting on the board of the National Gallery of Victoria Foundation, acting as a Governor of the St George Foundation which donates more than $2 million to charities to support women and children, and acting as a proud supporter of The Hunger Project.

Compassion and forward thinking is at the core of Jo's many accomplishments and the balance of this forms her unique entrepreneurial blend.

EMMA ISAACS

———

Founder of Business Chicks

BUSINESS CHICKS

Founded
2006

Employees
25

Memberships
47,000
(SEPTEMBER 2014)

Inspiration
HAD AN ENTREPRENEURIAL URGE
TO TRY SOMETHING NEW

Emma Isaacs is a 'natural' entrepreneur – bringing people together for business goals since childhood. Tenacious and socially perceptive, she escaped the corporate ladder by creating and leading businesses from the earliest stages of her career.

Now the CEO of Business Chicks, Emma has cultivated this community of businesswomen from a meagre 250 to a still expanding 47,000 members over just eight years. Emma has successfully shown that she knows how to build a brand and how to be agile; adapting to changing member preferences and variable economic conditions. Business Chicks produces over 60 events each year and also publishes a quarterly magazine called Latte.

Emma Isaacs first began to show entrepreneurial flair when she was just seven years old, gathering neighbouring children together to borrow money from their parents, which she would use to bulk-buy sweets to package and resell, "I'd go and buy lollies and we'd distribute them into smaller packages and sell them back to the parents at an inflated price. It was a great lesson in bringing people together and making a profit at the same time."

Emma has sustained that driving personality, and the sense that working with others provides market capability that could never be achieved alone. She is the driving force behind the burgeoning growth of Business Chicks, a network driven by the prospect of women forming business connections and fuelled by large scale national events. The network attracts more than 60 individual events annually.

At 18, Emma set her professional life rolling as the sole shareholder and director of recruitment consultancy Staff It, which she ran for the next 7 years. She says it was important that she didn't hesitate to take on the company structure and turn it into something great.

I LIKE BUSINESSES WITH MULTIPLE REVENUE STREAMS AND BUSINESSES THAT HAVE LEVERAGE BUILT IN TO THEM, WHERE THE EFFORT EXPENDED DOESN'T NECESSARILY EQUAL THE OUTCOMES ACHIEVED

"I just saw a job that needed to be done," she explains, "I didn't wallow or give time to whether I'd be able to do it or not – I just gave it a shot. I don't think I consciously knew I could make it a huge success, but I must have had some subconscious thinking that led me to keep going."

Emma notes that it was important to sustain focus on the 'people' aspect of Staff It, both her team and all customers. "I focused on building a strong brand and culture and not apologising for asking for excellence. I asked my team to keep trying to do better, and I promised them I'd do the same in return." In later years, the development of skills in building and leadership would prove vital for Emma's success as an entrepreneur.

Becoming an entrepreneur

The word 'entrepreneur' did not at first characterise Emma's idea of herself. "I suppose I just called myself 'self-employed' or a 'business owner.'" Encountering the Entrepreneurs Organisation at age 24, Emma recognised her affinity for this tribe, registering it as an important moment in forming her identity. "I went along to an event and thought immediately, "Ah, these are my people! We're facing exactly the same challenges and have exactly the same goals. I must be an entrepreneur."

"To be successful as an entrepreneur I believe you need to have a fair amount of knowledge about yourself, and what makes you tick. For me, I need a degree of uncertainty in business, and I need to know that if I'm willing to stretch myself, the rewards will be there."

At 25, Emma sold Staff It and not long after attended a Business Chicks event, which "blew her away". The marketing director at the time announced the business was up for sale. Emma put herself forward for the role, but not

THE WHOLE IDEA OF HAVING A BUSINESS IS THAT YOU DON'T BUY YOURSELF A JOB

without challenge. "There were twelve other parties who expressed interest in the business and we had to really tender for it," she says. Emma managed to get the sale, the rights for the company and agreed further to fundraise for the Kids Help Line charity for three years. Business Chicks has since raised over half a million dollars for the Kids Help Line charity and an additional $850,000 for other charities.

The Business of Business Chicks

The business that Emma bought has been entirely remade. "I saw great potential, taking what's good and making it great." Business Chicks now has 25 full-time employees and a large group of volunteers. It is one of Australia's largest business groups for women and is dedicated to "uplifting women and encouraging them to think that they can do" says Emma. "I won't settle for anything small.' Business Chicks is now in Sydney, Brisbane, Melbourne, Adelaide and Perth."

Emma's aspirational attitude has lead her into good relationships with international businesses and political leaders, including ex-Prime Minister Julia Gillard. Business Chicks launched Ms. Gillard's memoirs in October 2014.

With access to a diverse and growing network of thought leaders, influentials and consumers, Business Chicks has managed to attract the likes of Ita Buttrose, Michelle Bridges, US fashion designer Diane von Furstenberg and Arianna Huffington. The company has also attracted Sir Richard Branson, Olivia Newton-John, Napoleon Perdis, Layne Beachley and Julia Ross make appearances. Other notable people include Australian of the Year winners, Bloom Cosmetics founder Natalie Bloom and Boost Juice Bars founder Janine Allis.

"We recently secured an exclusive deal to bring marketing guru and author Seth Godin to Australia," adds Emma, "A feat that hundreds of businesses have attempted and failed. I always knew we could do it!"

The key to success

Emma believes the key to being a successful entrepreneur is self-understanding and knowing what works well for you. "I've never worked for anyone else before. I've always made my own way, and somehow come up with solutions and made decisions, which have led to strong businesses, great financial independence, and a fantastic life. I feel blessed that I've been able to live the truly entrepreneurial experience and I'm not sure I could do anything but that these days – I think I'd be pretty much unemployable."

She has a continued enthusiasm and appreciation for Business Chicks and the tremendous effect it has had on the wider community. "To meet the people I have...the conversations I've had is an immeasurable blessing and a gift I don't take lightly," Emma states on the business' About Us webpage. "I want everyone to get this bit of magic – we're building it so we can share it with the world." The focus for Emma is on the business, what it can achieve for its customers and its expansion, not on her own job security.

"The whole idea of having a business is not to buy yourself a job," says Emma, "If you want a job, you're better off going to work for someone else, where you can earn way more and enjoy greater benefits."

During her time as an entrepreneur, Emma has sold four businesses, including selling her first business for 15 times more than she invested in it at the age of 18. Now, at 32, she has no plans to stop building the Business Chicks Empire.

Balancing

Emma's focus now is to continue to develop the business into other niche markets domestically and internationally while retaining a realistic approach to her career, family and social time. She admits that some things must fall by the wayside in the entrepreneurial life. "I've never strived for balance. I know I have none and that's the way life just is for now. We can have it all, but just not at the same time. While my business is at this stage of growth, I can't always have the social life I'd like. For now, it's about growing the business and spending time with my family. Everything else fades into the background for now, but I don't beat myself up about it – I just try and enjoy it all."

She says she has learned to "let go of striving for perfection and feeling guilty" and tries to do her best and be kind to herself. "My secret is outsourcing everything," she says.

Lessons from Emma:
- Have self-understanding and know what works well for you.
- Put yourself in uncertain situations where you have to think your way to creative solutions
- Take risks and try new things.

Inspirations

Looking at the success and goals she has achieved over the past 14 years, Emma's tireless efforts are inspiring. But where does her inspiration come from?

"People who take risks. People who try new things. People who have a clear vision of who they are and where they're going and don't care too much about what others think, so strong is their determination to reach their goals. High profile leaders inspire me, such as Hillary Clinton, Nelson Mandela, Mahatma Gandhi etc, but I draw inspiration from everyday leaders too."

ADINA JACOBS

Co-founder of STM

After foreseeing a niche in the market in 1998, Adina co-founded STM - an Australian based company that designs, manufactures and distributes tech accessories.

With co-founder, Ethan Nyholm, Adina envisages the company as a lifestyle brand, part of a gadget revolution which separates them from other pure technology manufacturers. Creative to her core, she attributes her success to remaining agile in a competitive market, a product of partnering her creative qualities with Ethan's commercial nous.

STM

Founded
1998

Achievements
IN 2012 ADINA WAS SELECTED AS AN AUSTRALIAN DELEGATE FOR THE G20 YOUNG ENTREPRENEUR SUMMIT IN MEXICO CITY. IN CONJUNCTION STM BAGS WAS ALSO APPLE ACCESSORY MANUFACTURER OF THE YEAR BY iLOUNGE.COM

Commercial meets creative

Ethan, who first used a padded envelope tucked into a hiking bag to carry around his laptop was sure there had to be a better way. He quickly realised there was an opportunity to deliver a product to market that fit the demands of the growing tech accessories industry. Knowing Adina's background in merchandising, marketing and product development, and aware that she had worked as a buyer for several years, Ethan suggested they go into business together. "Ethan said 'you know about accessories, you know about offshore development and importing, lets do something with it'," says Adina.

Though Ethan had a great deal of experience in the IT industry, and Adina had just come from swimwear giant Seafolly, starting out wasn't easy. They needed to iterate a number of times to find exactly how they were going to fit into the market. The initial backpack offerings met with little interest. The tech accessory market was new – both untapped and untested.

"We happened to channel the Apple users and that's what changed everything. People that were happy to buy Apple didn't mind buying accessories, they didn't get a free black briefcase with their laptop, they were more aesthetically driven and they cared about the protection of their laptop. It was by chance, but it was the next step after the luggage stores that didn't want a bar of us." Today STM have developed efficient systems for product development that help them make choices in the face of fluctuating trends.

STM got its first big break when Adina reached out to the OH&S department of PricewaterhouseCoopers after learning that their staff members were complaining of aches and sore backs from carrying heavy shoulder bags. With that connection, STM Bags found it's first big corporate customer.

As the creative head of the business, Sydney-born Adina has indeed spent most of her life refining products. "I'm good at product development, I'm good at the fine detail, that special ingredient that brings a product together that people want, that's useful, that's functional and of good quality," she explains.

Concentrating on these aspects, STM starts with a simple thought process: what's the need and how the product is going to be used, then they work backwards and develop a platform around that. While the tech accessories industry has become extremely saturated, Adina says it's about, "knowing what your market can handle and pushing them that extra little bit. We've kept up with what's happening in the tech space, which is a bit behind what's happening in the fashion space. I know we have a good reputation and I know we build great product."

Ethan seemingly "runs the show" as the CEO of the business, he makes "commercial sense" of Adina's ideas. The value their partnership brings to the business is essential to its sustainability and growth. "I'm more of a creative and tactile person - he's the business guy". Ethan manages the incomings and outgoings of the business, "Having a business partner that's really numbers oriented has been imperative. It allows you to plan for things as best as you can," says Adina.

As a partnership, their individual assets complete the equation. "We have completely different skillsets and that's always worked really well for us. We try and communicate as openly and honestly as we can, we don't always agree. But that's fine, what ends up trumping is what's best for the business, it's not about us personally or about our egos."

Since inception, Adina has had a family of three children with husband, Marc. Without complete trust between Ethan and Adina, it would have been very hard for her to take her hands out of the business while having children. But she waxes lyrical about Ethan's understanding. "Ethan's been unbelievably supportive over the years while I've taken a bit of time out."

"It's not easy to be away from the business. It's frustrating. In the past I've always kept a hand in the business because we didn't have the people to sustain it without me. I had to be involved or things just stopped. Now we have a bigger team and Ethan manages them seamlessly."

THE VALUE OUR PARTNERSHIP BRINGS TO THE BUSINESS IS ESSENTIAL TO ITS SUSTAINABILITY AND GROWTH

Be agile and pivot on point

STM was born with the intent of producing accessories to make 'your digital day easier'. This kind of business goal helps to shape their product offerings, without limiting their ability to remain flexible in a rapidly moving industry. Currently their product range includes bags and cases, but in the future, as Adina says, it could be anything. "We are looking at how we can expand our product offering to keep abreast of the digital market. That's our focus, we want to move into new sales territories and get into new categories."

They've never had investors. Ethan and Adina started with $15k and with the help of a few bank and family loans have kept the business moving from there. However, Adina admits she began with little idea of how to run a business. "How to be in a business, how to be a boss, how to manage a team, run training, I didn't know anything about that, but being involved in an entrepreneurial community and being exposed to other types of entrepreneurs has opened my mind to different ways of doing things".

With time and experience along the way Adina and Ethan learnt that being agile in business is more important than being perfect. "You need to be able to make smart business decisions and not hang on to something because it's sentimental, you need to be agile and change so that you can grow."

Lessons from Adina:
- Being agile in business is more important than being perfect.
- If you don't like what's happened, you can't change it. Just do things differently the next time.
- Change so you can grow.
- Find the need, and build a product to meet it.

Finding like-minded people

The trials and tribulations of having your own business can be daunting. There are many highs and lows to sift through and because of this it's important to find a tribe that understands the many facets of life as an entrepreneur. Adina lost her dad suddenly and her sister was diagnosed with cancer dying 18 months later.

"I was just barely hanging on. I pulled away from what would have been entrepreneurial for a couple of years and sometimes I didn't even come in to the office," she recalls.

It wasn't until Adina was invited to be an Australian delegate for the G20 Young Entrepreneur Summit in Mexico City in 2012, surrounded by like-minded entrepreneurs, that she began to feel inspired again.

"In my personal life I don't often get the chance to have a conversation with people that get where I'm coming from. The Mexico opportunity came up six months after my sister died and it was the first time I felt like I could breath. Surrounding myself with people that are on the same kind of path as I am, a community of entrepreneurs, has opened my eyes. I have people to go to and discuss issues in full confidentiality with. It helps me think of different ways of doing things in my own backyard. They are people that are smart and switched on and people that I respect. It's opened up a part of my brain that wasn't working properly before."

The support of her husband Marc, who also has his own business, has been invaluable to the livelihood of STM and the time Adina can give. "Without him I wouldn't be able to do what I do. The assurance that he holds up the parental end of our family makes it all possible," explains Adina.

Success for Adina is all about enjoying what she does while growing a sustainable business along the way. "I love being challenged everyday by what I do at work – collaborating with smart people while developing clever and unique products are aspects of my job that I find truly gratifying. I am incredibly fortunate to have the flexibility to be a Mum, wife and businesswoman. In each of these roles I am looking forward to finding as much success and fulfillment as I can.

Ethan and Adina's balanced partnership has allowed them to remain flexible in a changing market, without losing sight of their business' needs or their personal values. That bodes well for the long term future of STM, and of Adina as a businesswoman and innovator.

PIP JAMIESON

Founder and CEO of The Dots

Pip Jamieson's gentle and light disposition as an entrepreneur is framed perfectly by her ability to grasp the big picture. Living on a houseboat with her husband in London, Pip's never been shy of doing things differently, or even a little bit out of her comfort zone. Her persistence and thirst for innovation are a few of her enduring entrepreneurial traits. Known for successfully disrupting creative recruitment with her first venture The Loop, a creative networking platform founded in Australia in 2009, Pip now has her eyes set on Europe.

Loving the industry she revolves in, Pip took a step and exited The Loop and parting ways with co-founder Matt Fayle, Pip fulfilled her aspirations and acquired the international rights to the technology. Pip is now the founder of The Dots which was born in late 2014. The Dots is based in the UK and has attracted some of the most profound brands in the European market.

THE DOTS

Founded
2014

Awards
MANY INCLUDING AIMIA AWARDS BEST ENTERPRISE

Inspiration
BUILDING COMMERCIAL BUSINESSES WITH A SOCIAL AGENDA.

A thirst for discovery

Pip is an Antipodean, being born in New Zealand but educated in the UK. She was very dyslexic as a child, but as she says, thanks to some amazing teachers at school, a supportive mum and talented tutors at university, she ended up with a first class honours degree in Economics from Edinburgh University. Moving around the world with her father's work meant a sense of adventure became a part of her DNA.

"We spent much time travelling and experiencing all the amazing things that goes with discovering new cultures and people. That sense of adventure and a love of new places, people and challenges, has stayed with me."

Pip worked as a fast stream economist for the British Government but became quickly disillusioned with politics and governmental bureaucracy, and instead chose to pursue her passion and dream of working in the creative industries. Her strong sense of ingenuity saw her working with the BRIT Awards in London, then as strategy and development manager for MTV Networks Australia, then taking the reins as head of marketing for MTV New Zealand in 2006. "It was an incredible experience helping launch a channel into a new region, in many ways it was a lot like running a start-up, and I'll always be eternally grateful to MTV for giving me such an amazing opportunity at the tender age of 26."

In 2009, with co-founder Matt Fayle, Pip founded The Loop, which she likens to, "a beautifully designed, content rich and more creative version of Linkedin".

"We hit the market at just the right time and The Loop grew into the leading professional networking and recruitment site for creatives in the region, with over 65 percent of all Australian creative professionals registered to the site. This highly engaged community enabled us to secure two rounds of investment, a Commercialisation Australia Grant and over 10,000 corporate clients."

The Loop business model works off a free subscription to creatives while revenue streams come through company listing fees, an engaged community is built off the back of this. But, as all entrepreneurs can attest to, this cemented model doesn't just happen overnight. Back at The Loop it took Pip and Matt two years before they really worked out the businesses core value proposition. "As with many fledgling businesses, in the early days we struggled to clearly articulate what we did. We were a platform that helped people and companies in the creative sector to promote themselves online, find inspiration, network, collaborate and connect with talent, jobs, clients, courses and workspaces. All well and good, but when you do so many things, how do you measure success and where do you focus limited time and resources to maximise return?"

WE FINALLY WORKED OUT OUR CONCEPT, WHICH WAS CONNECTING CREATIVES TO COMMERCIAL OUTCOMES, AND AS SOON AS WE DID, IT CHANGED EVERYTHING

After reading Good to Great, Pip realised she needed to focus the business on a single, measurable goal that aligns three questions: What can we be the best at?, What best drives our economic engine?, What are our core people deeply passionate about? "We finally worked out our concept, which was connecting creatives to commercial outcomes, and as soon as we did, it changed everything," says Pip

While it has experienced great success in Australia, Pip had that same gnawing feeling often attributed to diehard entrepreneurs, one of vision, one that was global, one that said, 'I can go bigger'.

Breaking boarders and new markets

Once again Pip combined her creative flair with her entrepreneurial ability and The Dots was born. Her vision for the business continues to be to become the leading professional networking platform for the creative sector globally. "I got part-way there with The Loop, by helping build it into the leading site for creatives in that region, but success will be taking The Dots the whole nine yards," she says excitedly.

Only in its infancy, Pip relays The Dots has experienced overwhelming initial growth. "We already have tens of thousands of incredible creatives on board."

Within weeks of it's launch in the UK, The Dots had been identified as one of the top 100 companies in 2014 redefining the digital space in the UK by Tech City Insider with over one thousand clients. The Dots has connected talent and drawn the credibility of brands and companies including the likes of: BBC, Net-a-Porter, Spotify, Condé Nast, Sony Music, Facebook, Virgin Group, among other notable entities.

Pip knew there was certainly a market for it in the UK after learning the creative sector was growing vigorously. A recent Government report highlighted that the UK's creative industries are worth £71.4bn to the local economy, generating just over £8m an hour. The plan is to launch The Dots in the UK first before branching out within Europe and then the US and beyond.

Similar to The Loop, The Dots works off a freemium basis, it's free for individuals and companies to join and set up a profile. Users can then either choose to pay to headhunt talent or advertise jobs, workspaces and courses on the site, or earn free credit by inviting new individuals and companies to join the platform. This cost varies depending on the opportunity, but typically an advert for a full-time job will be around £150.

Back in startup mode, this is where Pip flourishes. "I've worn so many hats while starting a business: strategist, negotiator, marketer, product manager, salesperson and finance manager. It's been a never-ending learning curve."

Not shying away from her disruptive tendencies, Pip aims to be at the forefront of change in the creative industry. In the UK, The Dots mission is to connect one million creatives and freelancers to commercial opportunities by 2018 - helping build a stronger, more profitable and diverse creative sector.

"The next couple of years will be incredibly exciting for The Dots. Now that we have launched in the UK, we will continue to develop the platform, including mobile, and plan to expand in Europe and the US. This will open up further opportunities for creative professionals and freelancers looking to work overseas and will also widen the talent pool for companies."

Naturally, with this recipe for seeing a two sided online community move from establishment to actual monetisation, Pip's core strength is business development and isn't afraid to pronounce herself an all-rounder. "I love meeting amazing new people and getting them excited about The Dots. I must admit that it never really feels like work. Having a background in economics has also been incredibly useful from a business/financial perspective."

Mentorship and lessons

Mentorship has also been key to Pip's success, "I have a number of mentors who specialise in areas such as venture funding, business process, start-ups etc. I never really went on the hunt for mentors but rather met amazing people at events and along the journey, invited them for a coffee and if there's a connection, suddenly you end up catching up regularly."

A role model herself, Pip is excited for the current landscape of female entrepreneurs, "It's very hard to influence positive change for women within existing corporations, whose

SUCCESS WILL BE TAKING THE DOTS THE WHOLE NINE YARDS

habits and practices have been shaped by men over the centuries. But with more and more women building successful businesses from the grassroots, collectively we can shape the corporations of the future, making not only our investors happy, but our staff, their families and society as a whole."

Entrepreneurs often become intrinsically tied to their businesses, feeling the highs and the lows more heavily than any other. While it's now all smooth 'boating', Pip says leaving The Loop was a tough separation for her. "Exiting The Loop was one of the toughest

decisions and hardest negotiations of my life. I can't begin to tell you how difficult it is to leave a successful business you put your heart, body and soul into. But it was the best decision I've ever made. I now wholly own The Dots and the world is our oyster."

Lessons from Pip:
- Spend time on finding the right business model and honing in on that.
- Never stop learning, ask questions everywhere you go.
- Every step counts, no matter how small, don't lose sight of the bigger picture.

Quirky and unconventional to her core, the future for Pip and The Dots is certainly exciting. As she continues to work towards being positive, accountable, focusing on solutions not problems and addressing all key issues head on, she's sure to achieve her dreams for connecting one million creatives with commercial opportunities by 2018. There's no doubt we'll all be watching on with admiration.

KRISTINA KARLSSON

Founder of kikki.K

Kristina Karlsson has the type of entrepreneurial acumen desired by many. Growing up in Falkenberg, Sweden, before coming to Australia she always had a love of beautiful, well designed and useful objects.

With a desire to follow her passion, Kristina turned an idea into world renowned design and retail business kikki.K. Now, with boutiques across Australia, New Zealand and Singapore, they also reach their global customers, in over 70 countries, through their online store.

By combining her appreciation of design with her love of stationery, devotees from around the world delight in kikki.K's range of delicious stationery, gorgeous gifts and Swedish design. In 2001, Kristina opened her first boutique in Melbourne CBD.

KIKKI.K

Founded
2001

Awards
MANY INCLUDING BEING INDUCTED INTO THE BUSINESSWOMEN'S HALL OF FAME

Inspiration
TO RECONNECT WITH HER HOME COUNTRY INTEGRATING IT INTO A STATIONARY BUSINESS

A Late night light bulb

Kristina often refers to kikki.K as her '3am business'. Prior to its conception, Kristina lay restlessly awake one night thinking about what she was going to do with her life. Her partner, Paul, encouraged her to take out a pen and paper to make a list of all the things that were important to her. "On that list, I included things like; I want to do something I am excited and happy to drive to work for on a Monday morning, I want to do something where I'm surrounded by beautiful Swedish design, I want to do something that always connects me to my family and friends in Sweden, I want to have a business of my own and I want to make $500 a week. I'm so happy and grateful to have ticked all of those off that 3am list now."

From that original list, a goal setter emerged, and after that a formidable achiever was born. The high level goal at kikki.K became, 'having something kikki.K in every stylish life the world over and to become a world class, enduring and meaningful business in every sense' and today, it has not changed substantially.

Kristina started small. She borrowed $3000 to create a sample range, showed samples to somewhere around 40 focus groups of 10 or more people and received an overwhelmingly positive response along with a surprising amount of orders. This was the catalyst for a buying trip around the world.

Since the day Kristina had her late night light bulb moment, she has been passionate about building something more than just a traditional business. "Since crystallising that dream and making the incredibly exciting journey to where we are today, we've worked relentlessly to build an organisation with a compelling and crystal clear vision and 'meaning' at its core. A meaningful purpose."

Dark moments, brilliant opportunities

Anyone who starts a business knows that there are many mistakes made along the way. For Kristina, she always welcomed failing or making mistakes and held them as important learning opportunities. Kristina has a refreshing and productive take on

challenges, "Genuinely, my instinct is to always reframe problems as opportunities and mistakes as brilliant learning opportunities".

In its beginning, Kristina was short of the business skills required to launch this now high functioning company. She often refers to kikki.K as the MBA she never did. With no formal business training she hit many knowledge barriers including: bookkeeping, getting distribution, briefing suppliers and not knowing the general aspects of how to grow a business.

The things that helped her overcome these challenges included: having a clear vision, passion and determination, continually asking questions, networking, making mistakes and learning.

Lack of capital and difficulty sourcing capital in order to scale the company was a significant obstacle for Kristina. "Initially I just had to work two to three jobs to make money so I could build kikki.K. I worked in a hotel doing breakfast shift starting at 5am – then I'd work on kikki.K during the day – and then go off to work as a

MY INSTINCT IS TO ALWAYS REFRAME PROBLEMS AS OPPORTUNITIES AND MISTAKES AS BRILLIANT LEARNING OPPORTUNITIES

waitress at night and on weekends. Then as the business needed big chunks of capital to grow I convinced my partner Paul to sell his house – which got our first store open. From there we had many landlords wanting us to open stores so they contributed some cash to our fit-outs which helped and we convinced our shop-fit supplier to give us long payment terms so we could pay for stores from the store revenue."

Kristina has since been able to attract bank and investor support which has supplemented their earnings to provide the capital needed for rapid growth. "Looking back I think it was a blessing to have little cash because it forced me to work hard, be industrious and just find ways to get things done," she says.

Ever grateful, Kristina and her partner Paul have always shared the twin aims of kikki.K, "'leaving the world a better place for us being part of it' and of 'creating something that

wonderful people would be excited to be part of and feel meaningfully engaged in and inspired by'," she asserts that these values are absolutely vital to the ongoing kikki.k culture.

Kristina believes the success of kikki.K is really built off the following: having a crystal clear vision and sharing it widely to align all stakeholders, a great team at all levels - and creating a brilliant culture, treating everyone with respect, being tenacious, being self-aware and very honest about what you don't know, having a thirst for knowledge and learning, systemising learnings, aligning the team to a shared plan and shared priorities, creating beautiful products that people love, being innovative always and quick to change and evolve, and above everything - keeping their customers at the centre of every decision they make to ensure the company's relevance.

Spreading the light

"My natural instinct and love of learning in many and varied ways has without doubt just become part of the kikki.K culture. It has led to coaching and learning being at the core of the way we do things every day, aligning everyone in the team. Without doubt that's a key contributor to us having an extraordinarily high engagement with our team, which resulted in us being named one of BRW's Top 11 Great Places to Work in 2014."

While Kristina constantly celebrates her journey, she sees the need for more entrepreneurs not only in Australia, but the world over. "The world needs entrepreneurs. Restless spirits who dream big, follow their dreams and in the process bring value to the world in many and varied ways – driving economies, creating innovative new solutions, creating employment, inspiring others, spreading optimism, solving problems, assisting communities and leaving the world a better place more often than not," she encourages.

Lessons from Kristina:

- Make a '3am' list. The things that you know late at night in your heart will make you happy.
- Leave the world a better place for you being part of it.
- Study and model what other entrepreneurs you relate to have done. Commit yourself to lifelong learning.

As someone with a great deal of heart invested in her business, Kristina prompts aspiring entrepreneurs to really love what they do.

"If you absolutely love what you do, you'll get through anything and be likely to find more joy in life more often. Study and model what other entrepreneurs you relate to have done. Commit yourself to lifelong learning. Think very hard about whether it really is right for you – because it will be incredibly challenging at times while it may also be incredibly rewarding. And after all that, if you're really up for it - just do it. Find a way."

IF YOU ABSOLUTELY LOVE WHAT YOU DO, YOU'LL GET THROUGH ANYTHING AND BE LIKELY TO FIND MORE JOY IN LIFE MORE OFTEN

THERESE KERR

Founder of Divine by Therese Kerr

Being the mother of Miranda Kerr, one of the world's most successful supermodels is not Therese Kerr's one achievement.

Through ThereseKerr.com Therese freely shares her knowledge, runs life changing empowerment programs and retreats engaging like minded health professionals. Therese also shares wellness information and arms people with knowledge to make informed choices for their health. Divine By Therese Kerr is Therese's certified organic personal care line and offers products that compliment her daughter's brand, KORA Organics, a certified organic skincare range.

DIVINE BY THERESE KERR

Founded
2014

Awards
WINNER OF THE JOHN LAWS/ TOYOTA "KEEPING THE DREAM ALIVE" BUSINESS OF THE YEAR AWARD. HEALTH AND WELLNESS AMBASSADOR FOR THE MIND FOUNDATION AND THE HEALTH AND WELLNESS AMBASSADOR FOR AUSTRALIAN CERTIFIED ORGANIC

Inspiration
TO EDUCATE AND INFORM OTHERS AS TO THE HARMFUL EFFECTS OF CHEMICALS USED IN EVERYDAY, CONVENTIONAL PRODUCTS AND TO PROVIDE CONSUMERS WITH A CHEMICAL- FREE, CERTIFIED ORGANIC OPTION.

Integrity meets opportunity

An impressive business woman and accountant by profession, Therese has worked in senior management roles for both domestic and international companies. She was the CEO of Kora Organics, and has, in conjunction with her husband of 32 years, owned and operated many of her own businesses and won countless business awards. Married at the age of 17 Therese still refers to her husband and business partner as her 'childhood sweetheart'.

Therese has integrity and a drive is that is undeniable, measurable in the trust given her by every employer she's had. "Every company I have worked for has asked me to become a partner in their firm or become an equity partner. I give my heart and soul to everything I do and now I am living my passion and it's so beautiful when you find that passion."

In 2001, Therese discovered she had tumors in her spleen. This was the catalyst for her and her family to develop a keen interest in health and nutrition. Over the last decade, Therese has become a sponge for information on all things relating to health, nutrition and spirituality. Through Divine and her own personal brand, Therese believes she's providing healthy alternatives by a way of certified organic products and also by way of education.

"It's not about preaching, but providing information and education so they can make informed choices. Whether customers choose to access the information is entirely up to them but I want to hopefully make a massive difference to mums, generations moving forward and also to our environment."

The cosmetics industry in Australia is not well regulated when it comes to chemical use in products. Since the inception of Divine, Therese has been working with researchers, professors and other international educators around chemicals and their impacts. "I realised there was a serious complacency in the overuse of chemicals in everyday products and the fact that none of them or very few of them are tested for safety."

The goal for Divine is to reach the Australian audience, not through pharmacies but through health and wellness practitioners, stores and innovative medical doctors to change the mindset around product usage. "We have been working with a holistic dental appreciation centre to actually create an oral care range that's based on certified organic." Therese is

WE WANT TO BE A GLOBAL BUSINESS THAT IS IMPACTING PEOPLE IN THE MOST POSITIVE AND BEAUTIFUL WAY IN THE WAY OF EDUCATION AND BY WAY OF OFFERING HEALTHY ALTERNATIVES THAT THEY CAN USE

also ambitious, expressing a vision that spans the globe. "We want to be a global business that is impacting people in the most positive and beautiful way in terms of education and by way of offering healthy alternatives that they can use appropriately." She has a step-by-step plan for this global domination, taking advantage of an online-to-retail business model which takes into account the exigencies of the modern market. "We will grow our online business, we'd love it to be about 80 percent of our business but maintain a retail presence so customers can go and try the products. We plan on expanding internationally into the US and Hong Kong, the United Arab Emirates, the UK and eventually NZ."

In order to grow into this global business Therese she admits that they have to really embrace the online space. "It's the way of the future, you have to share information and have your customer become a part of the business you are creating," she says.

Beyond the business savvy, Therese is truly committed to the cause she's monetising, putting herself into the space as a Health and Wellness ambassador for the Mind Foundation and the Health and Wellness Ambassador for Australian Certified Organic.

As an entrepreneur, Therese believes her strength revolves around her ability to connect with people, and a fearless, unselfconscious willingness to do anything to get a job done.

"I have an innate love for people. I love people. I love to make a difference.

I also believe I don't think there's anything I can't do. If I was asked to build the Sydney Harbour Bridge, and I didn't know how, I'd find somebody to help me or I'd get them to show me how to do it. There is nothing I won't tackle in life. You can throw anything at me and I'd get it done, that's because I don't live in fear or am not worried about looking good or worried about looking bad."

Mistakes and growth

Therese makes the point that along her journey, she has made mistakes and this is something she tries to learn and grow from.

"Honestly, we have made mistakes in business and in challenging decisions. One in particular nearly made us bankrupt because we invested poorly and they stole all of our money. We, my husband and I, took full responsibility for that."

Therese has also learned not to take things too personally, and sees the fame that has been given to her family as an opportunity for leverage, and to make a difference in the world.

"We are a very public family and the media says what they want to say about us. I used to worry before but we don't worry now, as long as we know the truth, we are using our public family profile to make a difference. We also know as a family that we are trying to align with other people, transform and educate others. There are 15 million people in America on this course of changing the way chemicals are used across a range of products."

Lessons from Therese:
- Don't live in fear or worry about looking good looking bad.
- Stand in what you believe and don't let anyone talk you out of it.
- If you don't know how to do something, find someone to teach you.

Her vision for the future, for upcoming entrepreneurs, is one of abundance.

"What I would love nothing more is for young people to step into their infinite possibility because we are all born with infinite possibility. Unfortunately, something happens that causes us to reassess that or to change our way of being, that leads us to thinking "oh I can't do that now"".

And what's it really all about for Therese?

"It's about standing in your truth, standing in integrity, standing in what you believe and not allowing someone to talk you out of that and ultimately being and that's where I have come from all my life," she says.

YOU CAN THROW ANYTHING AT ME AND I'D GET IT DONE, THAT'S BECAUSE I DON'T LIVE IN FEAR OF LOOKING GOOD OR LOOKING BAD

EVERY DAY AS MINISTER FOR SMALL BUSINESS I AM INSPIRED BY THE WOMEN I MEET - TRUE TRAILBLAZERS IN THE ENTREPRENEURIAL SPACE. THERE IS NO SUBSTITUTE FOR LEARNING FROM COMPARISON AND EXPERIENCE. THIS BOOK IS A GUIDEBOOK FOR OTHER WOMEN SEEKING TO BE MOTIVATED AND LEARN FROM THE BRILLIANT AND BEST ENTERPRISING WOMEN 'PATHFINDERS' SHAPING AND REMAKING OUR MODERN ECONOMY.

_____

The Hon Bruce Billson
Federal Minister for Small Business

NICOLE KERSH

Founder of 4Cabling

4CABLING

Founded
2006

Awards
OVER 13 INCLUDING NSW ERNST
& YOUNG ENTREPRENEUR
OF THE YEAR 2013

Inspiration
CREATING SOLUTIONS WITH
AUTHENTICITY AND INTELLECT
AND FINDING THE BALANCE IN
DRIVING PROFIT WITH A NOT-
FOR-PROFIT MENTALITY

Digital strategist and ecommerce consultant Nicole Kersh has been recognised as a leading lady in the online business space and an inspiration for young entrepreneurs across Australia.

In mid 2014, Nicole sold 4Cabling to private equity firm Gernis Holdings for an undisclosed sum and honestly attributes the exit to reaching her own experience cap within the company. 4Cabling, Australia's leading direct-to-consumer manufacturer, wholesaler and retailer of cabling and IT management accessories, was turning over $10 million and Nicole felt her personal development could not keep up with the growth rate of the business. Not only did Nicole free up the business to scale appropriately, but she also freed herself up for her next venture and ultimately the beginning of her journey as a serial entrepreneur.

Future dreams

It was a dream that began in her parent's garage. From a young age, Nicole watched with fascination and excitement as her parents worked from home.

"It inspired me to look at the way my parents interacted in their business and Internet," she explains.

Nicole's enthusiasm for business stayed with her. At 21 she taught herself HTML and began laying the foundations of 4Cabling, the only direct-to-consumer manufacturer and retailer of cabling and IT management accessories currently in Australia.

It was a combination of fierce independence and strong self-belief in her abilities, which saw Nicole turn her garage start-up into a multi-million dollar business.

"I've always had a strong sense of intuition," she says. "I just thought, 'I know this can work.' I had a feeling it would be something worthwhile pursuing…"

The result of Nicole's belief in her dream speaks for itself. After 4Cabling sold in 2014, there were also talks of plans to expand across Perth, which Nicole says was the most exciting part. "Leaping from where it was going, it was huge. It was a great business. A really, really great business," she says.

Turning an idea into a reality

For Nicole, learning the "how" of making 4Cabling a real business was an interesting challenge. She notes that she made "…a lot of mistakes, but you have to read and talk to people and not be afraid to ask people what you want and need." Which, she says, was her biggest obstacle when she was young. "At that age you can't do anything but share your vision passionately. You don't have experience or skills as such; you just have a vision and a passion."

It is what Nicole calls, 'finding your secret sauce.'

"It's finding a way to share that with people and recognising traits in people that show they can do it better than you can do it yourself. At 18, 19, 20, that's all you can do, recognise in people what you can recognise in yourself."

And, it was finding the right people that played a key role in the success of 4Cabling as a business. Nicole explains that 'strategic hiring' was a big part of it. "Instinct in hiring takes a big part, especially at that age."

After hiring her mother, an admin assistant and salesperson soon followed. A warehouse manager was also found, "because now…we were bringing in sales I couldn't pack myself."

Within the hiring process, Nicole says there were specific things they looked for. "It's not just that people need to get along perfectly, but you want enough sameness and enough difference – you want people to push and you want people to follow.

So, it would just be things like really looking at a resume and a lot of one-on-one stuff… you want people to be hired who have the same life goal and then aim to facilitate that."

Nicole, who was responsible for the hiring and firing, is thankful there weren't too many mistakes in that area, though she acknowledges that even her good instinct can fail her. "We once hired what we thought was the best bookkeeper because she was so feisty and I thought that would be great for chasing bad debt, but it worked against us in the end. Everyone's made mistakes and hired the wrong people…but you learn quickly."

Learning and growth

Learning and growing as an entrepreneur has been intrinsic to Nicole's journey. She has had her fair share of ups and downs in the online business space but counts it as good experience. "If you make a mistake, who cares? I don't judge, I support being brave enough to take the chance. I'll wear it. I fail and keep failing."

Ego also played a part when it came to failure and success, Nicole says, but she viewed failure as part of your ability to succeed. "More than at the success, the ego comes in at the failure, because you put in so much of yourself and you believe it with such conviction, that when you do have moments of failure you question: 'What didn't I see?'"

Or, 'why didn't that work?' It's a double-edged sword, because while I would question myself it's also a testament to how much I believe in myself too. Because it's equal parts success and failure."

Nicole took a big chance in selling 4Cabling and it proved a success. Not only was it a risk, the choice to let it go was difficult.

"The decision to sell the business was not an easy one," she says. "It's a massive part of

IN BUSINESS, IT'S IMPORTANT TO FIRST SOLVE THE PROBLEM, BUT UNDERSTAND WHAT IS THE PROBLEM? WHY DO WE HAVE THIS PROBLEM? IS IT CULTURAL? WHAT'S THE FLOW-ON EFFECT?

---

who you are and a defining portion of your life. It's hard to walk away from. There's also a fine line between health and unhealthy in that world. My passion was never in manufacturing; it just grew to a point where I wasn't comfortable with the future of it."

But the experiences she gained from 4Cabling have been invaluable. Her passion and enthusiasm has seen her take new directions in the online business world as a problem-solver for others. Now 'unplugged' from 4Cabling Kersh has set herself up as an e-commerce consultant and digital marketing strategist.

"People look at problems, solve them and move on. But I think they're an opportunity to change something for the better and to innovate so I would try the project one more time, I love solving problems."

For Nicole, change keeps her brain keen, and she also sees it as part of the role of being a businessperson. "I think as an entrepreneur you're naturally inclined to juggle

many things and your ability to adapt and change is what sets you apart from people who aren't entrepreneurs. Strategically problem-solving and watching your dreams and plans eventuate; it's a passion.

Kersh's passion has been clear from the very beginning. "It was my dream – from when I was little, standing in my Dad's garage... looking at it, going, 'Wow, this is so exciting,' and 'Wow, one day I can have this!' It was my dream to have built something and it needed to be ok for me to live that. "

Her enthusiasm for chasing goals is infectious and she exudes a fearless attitude to potential obstacles. It's not just about making and breaking on a business level though, Nicole keeps herself fuelled by engaging in the community, helping others helps her to keep going. "Giving. Giving keeps me going. I teach Scrabble at an old people's home in Woollahra and a lot of them are survivors of the holocaust. That's what fuels me: perspective.

Seeing that and seeing the joy of will, it's astounding...that's a choice they've made to keep going and that's what pushes me."

It is this, paired with what she calls "an intense thirst for knowledge," that prompts her to keep moving and she encourages others to do the same. "Just keep learning. Keep being inspired and keep sharing information too."

{ *We are Inspiring Rare Birds* }

Inspiration

Personal inspiration comes from Ronni Kahn – "a great part of me is drawn to social entrepreneurs, I believe I live my life like one personally on a small level" – as well as self-starters who began their entrepreneurial journey with very little or nothing at all.

"People building something from nothing; that blows my mind, like the Apple story – just fascinating! And more so, just the push behind it, how as people we trust it. We're on board and it's collective," she says.

But Nicole's own story of building something from nothing is inspirational in its own right. Under 30 Australian Anthill Winner (2011/2012) to Ernst & Young Entrepreneur of the Year (2013), her achievements in such a short amount of time are astounding.

Lessons from Nicole:
- Learn quickly.
- Today is the day; there is no such thing as tomorrow.
- Read and talk to people, and don't be afraid to ask people what you want and need.

To young women wanting to enter the entrepreneurial space, Nicole had this to say: "Be cautious of what your motivations are, then try and solve it by creating a community. Help them achieve their goals and give them someone that can keep them as humble about it as possible."

And the best way for people to achieve those goals?

"The absence of fear would be the biggest gift in that environment. Just to block out the white noise and keep going. Picking the right people, not rushing decisions, from there it's careful consideration to what comes next because you've got to see the end and that's big picture stuff...find a niche; you have to look at your life, how you interact in the world. Find a niche and find a way to monetise it."

Nicole adds that while having strategy and being innovative is important, so is finding passion and motivation to keep moving forward. "We know when we're coasting and when there's more to give and more to get...that's where the hunger and passion comes from. You never know what's around the corner...you just have to wake up and think, 'today is the day'; there is no such thing as tomorrow. You have to live now."

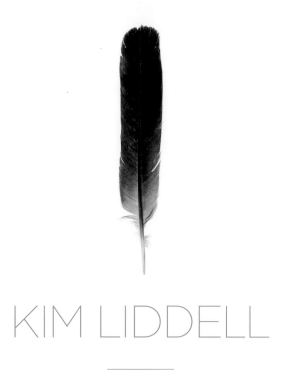

KIM LIDDELL

Founder of Non Destructive Excavations Australia Pty Ltd

NON DESTRUCTIVE EXCAVATIONS AUSTRALIA

Founded
2005

Employees
12

Inspiration
TO CREATE A BUSINESS THAT WILL PROVIDE INCOME FLOW TO HER FAMILY

Of honest and humble origins, Kim Liddell has always been intent on spending her time outdoors and amongst nature.

Kim is the founder and managing director of Non Destructive Excavations Australia Pty Ltd. Her company provides specialised non destructive (vacuum) excavations and service locating in order to maintain a safe working environment for the building & construction industry. Using state of the art custom technologies, Kim and her team efficiently and effectively deliver the desired results every time. Kim has five trucks and employs more than half a dozen staff. Non Destructive Excavations manages small and large contracts across NSW. Major projects such as Sydney's Barangaroo and the North West Rail Link project have benefitted from NDEA's services.

Expanding horizons

In 1991, Kim fell in love with tall ship sailing whilst on the Young Endeavour negotiating Bass Strait. A year later, she was selected to sail with the Young Endeavour from Greece to America where she took part in several regattas and tall ship races including the Columbus Regatta celebrating 500 years since Columbus discovered the New World.

Driven by the pursuit of proving there was a better way for the excavation industry, which was not only a profitable business but also one that made a difference, Kim Founded NDEA to do just that. Today, her company Non Destructive Excavations Australia has been leading the non destructive hydro vacuum excavation industry for the best part of a decade.

Back to her beginnings, Kim spent more time traversing the country and exploring Australia.

"I then lived overseas for a couple of years, followed by a few years in the Whitsundays, where I married my childhood sweetheart, then the Torres Strait, followed by Central Western Queensland, the Sunshine Coast, back to Adelaide, then Melbourne and finally to settle in Sydney. My eldest son was born in Nambour, Queensland. My middle son was born in Geelong, Victoria and my daughter was born in Sydney, NSW."

SUCCESS IS A STAIRCASE, NOT A DOORWAY

Success is a staircase, not a doorway

While Kim is a fierce lover of what she does, it hasn't been all smooth sailing. Diagnosed with Melanoma in her first year of business, when her daughter was only eight weeks old, Kim was met with serious struggles. One which now helps her appreciate the, "Independence, freedom and creativity" running NDEA has given her.

"Supporting my husband though a turbulent few years of depression and bi-polar diagnoses and losing a major client that had attributed to 50 percent of my revenue," have also been significant challenges for Kim.

"I've had low times where I've lost money, lost contracts and even lost friends but at no time have I ever felt that I'm a failure. I believe that failure is a powerful word that has the potential to damage one's emotional state and should be wiped from the books, particularly in light of the rising depression statistics. We are all human, hopefully striving to be the

best that we can be, we all make mistakes and yes, I hope that we learn from them, but are we failures for doing so? Absolutely not."

From these lessons she learnt to spread her eggs more liberally and found the ability to continually strive for a better way. She also attributes a great deal of her development as an entrepreneur to belonging to the Sydney Chapter of the Entrepreneurs Organisation, "they are a great bunch of inspirational people and also a brilliant support network. I also have a wonderful business coach," she says.

What makes Kim tick

Always optimistic, for Kim, "Success is a staircase, not a doorway," and she feels it's important to lead a happy, fulfilled, caring life along the way. "I hope that my friends, family and colleagues would say this of me," she says.

Inquisitive about finding the right recipe that works for her, she enjoys asking other entrepreneurs what makes them happy.

And, iterates that the life of an entrepreneur isn't easy, if it were, everyone would do it.

For others looking to follow in her footsteps, she encourages them to be persistent.

"Don't count the days, make the days count. Life isn't about waiting for the storm to pass, it's about learning to dance in the rain. Be true to who you are, be passionate about what you do. We can't be good at everything so surround yourself with experts in the areas where you need a boost."

She prefers purpose over clarity, citing that 'purpose' seems to be a current buzz word that can have the ability to put the pressure on.

"I prefer Clarity, it's calmer and gives us space to breathe and live in the moment. For me it is always changing, evolving, maturing."

Kim loves to inspire and motivate wherever possible. Ending world hunger and poverty is important to Kim, including the removal

of patriarchy, the right to education and equality for all women and children.

"I feel very strongly about global equality for women and that perhaps a small bit of ego in this area would be beneficial. "I think some ego around this issue helps us hold ground and strive for a better life for the undervalued, mistreated and abused in today's world," she says.

For her personally, Kim values seeing her children grow and achieve. On the brink of a new startup that will completely disrupt and monopolise a segment of the excavations industry, Kim says the future is busy and bright.

Quiet and humble, she leaves us lingering with this one line, "Watch this space" and we certainly will.

CHRISTINE MANFIELD

———

Restauranter

Christine Manfield is a prominent Australian chef, author and food and travel writer whose culinary work is inspired by the tastes and flavours of cultures around the world. Her achievements have been driven by a passion and energy that overcomes obstacles in her path. But before her great success, came a humble beginning.

Christine's expansive work portfolio as an Australian culinary ambassador reveals a range of diverse culinary projects focusing on the sustaining nature of good food, wine, people and pleasure. This is where the restaurants Christine owns come in: Paramount and Universal in Sydney and also East@ West in London. Her love of spices and her understanding of the home cook's need for authentically flavoured, simple yet sustaining food choices provided her with the foundation to create and establish the Christine Manfield Spice Collection: a range of spice pastes and condiments available nationwide.

RESTAURANTER

———

Founded
1990

———

Inspiration
PASSION FOR CULINARY
EXCELLENCE

An unorthodox route to the top

"I have always been an amateur cook," Christine explains. Returning from overseas, after ending a teaching career she began cooking. "It was just baby steps, I had no idea. There was no game plan. Within a few months I knew I wanted to do it seriously."

Christine says she has always had the desire for doing something and doing it perfectly: "I think it came about by really wanting to achieve. I didn't want to do anything half hearted, even when I worked."

But it wasn't just a keen sense of perfection. It was passion. "You have to be totally smitten with what you're doing," Christine says. "As a chef I had it, and you either do or you don't. You just know straight away. I have never trained, I just started cooking. I bypassed the institutional learning because I didn't need it. I was being nourished in much better ways by being around people who were teaching me the same thing."

From South Adelaide to Sydney, Christine set a benchmark for herself to learn from the very best in the business. "Philip Searle, who I knew from my Adelaide days, had just opened his restaurant, Oasis at the top of Oxford Street. I thought if I am going to do this, I want to be the best I can. That was the benchmark."

For Christine, passion was also the key element during the hiring process. "I always employed on passion and practicality," she explains, "rather than you had a piece of paper or you were training to get a piece of paper. You can teach skill but you can't retrain attitude."

She also says that team spirit is everything "keeping that in balance and in check, that's probably the hardest thing to learn and the hardest one to manage. You're in a small room, tight environment, basically shoulder to shoulder; you have to get along."

Proving to herself that she was "incredibly resilient across all levels," Christine opened her first business with her partner. From there, the only way was up.

By the mid 90s, Christine was starring as a guest chef at international hotels, and turning her role into an ambassadorial one to promote high quality, modern Australian food. Promoting "the best of what's happening in Australia," as she puts it.

Christine's working life as a restaurateur spans more than two decades, with Paragon and Phoenix in Sydney (1990-1993), Paramount in Sydney (1993 – 2000), East @ West in London's Covent Garden (2003 -2005) and Universal in Sydney (2007-2013). Her role as a chef, food ambassador, author and travel writer has seen her build an impressive reputation in the hospitality industry.

Labels and other boxes

Christine does not identify herself as an entrepreneur. "I think I have always been too hands on to consider myself in that role. Even though with Universal I wasn't working in a section or working on the stoves I had to be in a role that was supervisory, directing, but I always had someone with me directing because people want to see you; it's your business."

Christine closed her restaurant Universal, in 2013 and has remained busy ever since. "The business was booming (when it closed) and it's the very best way to finish a business. You get all the really great things from it without sliding into it."

Knowing your business inside and out was a key learning point for Christine during her years as a restaurateur. "You have to be totally on your business. Not just working in your business but working on your business and understanding how it all operates; the dynamic, what a spreadsheet is, what your daily food taking is like, what your costs are."

Christine says the driving force behind her hard work and learning the business side of hospitality was belief. "What kept me going was believing in it. I thought if this could work it's my retirement fund and self-finance. I still oversee things from a distance and I know exactly what's going on with the system and the ordering. I do a lot of work promoting it."

Lessons from Christine:
- Be totally on your business - not just working in your business, but working on your business and understanding how it all operates.
- Be passionate. You can teach skill but you can't retrain attitude.
- Be resilient across all levels
- Believe in what you're doing.

While overseeing operations from a distance, Christine has also immersed herself in other projects. "The last four years I have been doing more philanthropic work. I find it

really nourishing. I did a food documentary in Zimbabwe, that was eye opening, I have been involved in Room to Read and I am an ambassador, particularly for girls literacy." In Australia she supports the Cathy Freeman Foundation and is an ambassador for Oz Harvest and Artisans of Fashion. Christine contributes and lends her support to Room to Read, a brilliant educational program for girls in third world countries. Christine believes that world change starts with education.

Christine travels regularly as a culinary ambassador for Australia's diverse gastronomy and continues to work on various global projects. She has been a

mentor and judge for Electrolux Appetite for Excellence Young Restaurateur of the Year since 2008 and also mentors young female apprentices through the NSW Tasting Success program. Christine has appeared as a guest chef and judge on Masterchef Australia, Series 2 (2010), Series 3 (2011), Series 4 (2012) and Junior Masterchef (2010).

Christine also hosts regular luxury bespoke gastronomic travel adventures to exotic locations including India, Morocco, Africa, Sri Lanka, Myanmar, France and South East Asia, working with Jennifer Wilkinson of Epicurious Travel.

She also believes it's not necessary to start big to start a successful business. "Learn as much on the job then make a decision and do something you know is going to be manageable," Christine advises. "You don't have to spend $3 million dollars to open something. Set yourself a budget so if it goes down the toilet you're not owing silly money."

DANIELLA MENACHEMSON

—

Director of B Seated Global

Passion and focus. Two key traits for success, which 'B Seated Global' Director Daniella Menachemson possesses by the truckload. She takes a moment to reflect on how both contributed to her achievements with the family-owned furniture business.

B Seated Global is an all encompassing, designer, supplier and manufacturer that produces high-quality bespoke commercial furniture for the hospitality industry. With either being locally produced or imported, B Seated Global is convinced that "you don't need to spend $1000 on a seat to get a high quality fashionable chair".

B SEATED GLOBAL

Founded
2005

—

Inspiration
HER CHILDREN. THAT THERE IS A SOLUTION FOR EVERYTHING AND EVERY CLOSED DOOR LEADS TO ANOTHER ONE OPENING.

—

Achievements
SUPPLIER TO MAJOR FRANCHISE GROUPS

A passion for business

Daniella's passion for the business world was evident throughout her childhood in South Africa. From charging her mother's friends for doing their nails to relieving her father's receptionist during her lunch break, Daniella loved the idea of being professional and in charge of her responsibilities. Growing up in Cape Town, the eclectic mix of styles, people and colourful personalities influenced her own sense of style and eye for furniture and products.

Daniella's father, Jack Klein had been in the furniture business for more than 35 years before his venture was transformed into the B Seated Global online business it is today. He initially focused on selling furniture to the event-hiring market. But Daniella had other ideas for her father's business.

For Daniella, starting a business with her father happened "by accident" in 2005. At the time, she was working in marketing and went on maternity leave with her first child.

"My father had started a new venture on his own, so I helped him build the website content etc," says Daniella. Eventually she joined him, working from a bedroom in his apartment, and immediately began to see opportunities for expansion. "I saw an opportunity to expand the business to focus on the dining and hospitality venue segments."

Branching out into dining and hospitality saw a marked rise with interest. Soon, Daniella and her father were speaking to the architect and design community and designers fitting out pubs and clubs were suddenly looking for B Seated furniture.

"This is the focus of what we do now," Daniella says. "We supply commercial, fashionable furniture to the drink and dining scenes of Australia. We import from overseas and manufacture furniture in Australia for commercial hospitality venues. We offer our clients flexibility and products that meet their budgets. Eight years ago I wouldn't have dreamed of going into a new restaurant and consulting on the entire fit out, now we have the experience, knowledge and resources to do so."

B Seated Global now has around 18 staff with a range of over 3000 products. The company supplies seating and offers full interior design services for cafes, restaurants and hotels nationwide. "Whatever vision you have for your interior, we are confident we can find the perfect furniture for you," the website promises. The team at B Seated Global has worked on pieces for a range of venues and outlets such as renowned Sydney restaurant The Grounds of Alexandria, Criniti's in Woolloomooloo and Manly as well as work at the international airport.

Evolution

Daniella has worked hard with her father to make B Seated Global the high-profile retailer it is today. The company has evolved from an event-hire furniture supplier into a designer and manufacturer of bespoke commercial furniture for the hospitality industry. Daniella's career path has also evolved, into something she is unexpectedly passionate about.

"My career is very different," she says. " I wanted to work in marketing and landed up in furniture. Ultimately, it has set me on a path that I'm passionate about as we are very design-focused and I have discovered it ticks all the boxes."

FINDING THE RIGHT PEOPLE THAT HAVE THE SKILLS YOU NEED IS CRITICAL FOR GROWTH

Daniella loves finding new furniture brands for the business from around the globe. "We go to India, we go to the Philippines, Italy and we also manufacture products in China."

Daniella believes being humble is important and that she is grateful for the success she has achieved so far. As Director, Daniella oversees the financial side of the business as well as product sourcing, marketing and the website. She also handles clientele, management and suppliers and export documents.

The structure of the business is also key to reaching marketing and financial goals. For Daniella and her father, the flat-team makeup of B Seated Global is vital. "There's no hierarchy, we work collectively on projects," says Daniella. "Finding the right people that have the skills you need is critical for growth and the internal wellbeing of the business."

The skills they have brought into B Seated Global include interior design, graphic design and web design. "We want to give the customers a complete visual experience," Daniella says.

Daniella says she is always willing to give a concept or business idea a try instead of discarding it straight away.

"I believe and have an intuition that it can be done. Even if I am unsuccessful I will always give something a chance and pour all my energy into it as you don't get anywhere without trying."

Balancing life

For her the inspiration to try ideas comes with the wholehearted support from her own family.

"I have three young children so they challenge me constantly and put running my business into perspective," says Daniella. "They have taught me not to sweat the small stuff and that has helped me in how I operate in the business. Having a supportive husband who has a complete understanding of the industry is brilliant; I can always bounce ideas off him and reach the conclusion I need."

Daniella's advice for anyone wanting to achieve personal goals is, "always follow your passions. If you don't do something you enjoy you won't go after it with vigour." She adds

that failure is important to reaching our goals. "How can we learn if we don't fail? I think that's critical to being successful in our ventures."

Lessons from Daniella:
- You don't get anywhere without trying.
- Don't sweat the small stuff.
- Do things to help your business and personal lives be in harmony with each other; as much as they can be.

When asked about balancing work and family commitments, Daniella believes there is no true balance. "I have searched for it and I now can confirm it's a myth. But we can do things to help our business and personal lives act in harmony with each other; as much as they can really be."

"As a business owner and a mother I'm pulled from pillar to post. I believe there is a solution for everything; seek and you shall find. I am always on the path of discovery and learning and as long as that continues I'll be happy with that." Daniella is proof that even the unexpected can be an opportunity for successful change-making, if you have the right attitude, and a passion for making things work.

IVANKA MENKEN

Founder of The Art of Service

Mother and keen horse lover, Ivanka learnt to depend on herself from a very young age. She remembers always playing shop or playing teacher, it is no wonder she's grown up with the mentality of 'everyday can be a school day if you choose it to be'.

Ivanka is the founder and CEO of The Art of Service, a fast-growing IT Service Management education company which is one of the most trusted sources globally for the career-driven IT professional. Her time is distributed between two other businesses which she is involved in: Horses-store.com, where Ivanka imports fashion for horse and rider, exclusively being a distributor for Equi.Linn Sports Lingerie and Complete Publishing where Ivanka's aim is in helping authors self publish, print and distribute their book globally to book retailers and libraries.

THE ART OF SERVICE

Founded
2006

Author
PUBLISHED OVER 100 BOOKS

Awards
NOMINATED FOR ITSMF HIGHEST ITIL SERVICE MANAGEMENT EXAM SCORE IN 1998

Inspiration
TO PURSUE HER PASSION IN TECHNOLOGY

SUCCESSFUL ENTREPRENEURS, AND BUSINESS PEOPLE IN GENERAL, ARE DISCIPLINED AND FOCUSED. THEY HAVE A CLEAR VISION AND GOAL

The story that's a bestseller

Today, Ivanka is the CEO of the world's premier IT service framework company, The Art of Service.The company is one of the most trusted sources globally for the career-driven IT professional. The Art of Service provides online training for career driven IT Professionals. Ivanka and her team help IT professionals to improve their career by offering them short courses and certification programs on demand and browser delivered. Ivanka has spearheaded the company's Cloud Computing Certification Scheme that is becoming the industry benchmark. A wonderful humour and people person, she is a sought-after speaker at global IT events and has addressed the renowned IT Service Management Forum numerous times on IT service and cloud computing.

The Art of Service has served more than 800 corporate clients and 500,000 individual clients and students in 87 percent of the world's countries. Ivanka is based in Queensland, Australia. Naturally with a knack for publishing, Ivanka is also the owner of Emereo Publishing, which she founded in 2005. Insatiably hard

working Ivanka mentions that no matter what type of work you do, you are always on display. Perception is everything she says.

"Every day your work is scrutinised, and the way you come across is important. (after all – perception is reality). First impressions count and you will need to work very hard to change people's minds about the first impression they have about you."

For Ivanka, one of her key skills is presentation, hence first impressions becoming so important to her. "I am great at explaining things, you have to be when you're a teacher and you're teacher enmasse. Presenting is key to people's learning, it's a two way street," she says.

Ivanka started her career as a vocational education teacher. After years of teaching, she decided to pursue her passion for technology and launched a career in the expanding IT industry. She has worked in both public and private companies throughout

Europe, Asia, North America and Australia. Recognised for changing the way people

think about IT Management, Service Management and Cloud Computing, Ivanka is the driving force behind the company's educational programs, she is an engaging and motivating public speaker and author of a number of technical management publications. Her irrepressible speaking style and no-holds-barred blog have helped her create a large following around the world. In October 2010, the itSMF USA Awarded Ivanka with the highest Professional Recognition for IT Service Management.

Ivanka indicates that keeping on track has helped her maintain a steady path. "Successful entrepreneurs, and business people in general, are disciplined and focused. They have a clear vision and goal. They know exactly why they have their business and why they want to be involved in it. Write everything up that you need to do this week. Not just the urgent items, but the important ones as well. Each item goes on a yellow post-it note and stick it somewhere.

This will give you a clear and visible overview of all the things I must do this week. All these little tasks will add up to at least being proactive in achieving your goals for this week, month, quarter and year."

Ivanka's latest book, is an industry bestseller, appearing on the Amazon bestseller lists. It's about the most powerful form of IT

Delivery-Service Management, and how IT activities and processes have to be aligned to create IT Services and products that matter.

Fast tracking growth

As a lover of horses and life-long rider Ivanka is also the owner of Horses-store.com, an exclusive importer and distributor of Equi. Linn Sports Lingerie for Australia. Helping female athletes be stylish and supported in all the right places at the same time.

"Horses-store.com was developed because of our need and desire for quality horse products and we continually aim to offer you the best possible products available at an affordable price. This means that we continually travel the world to find the best possible products

available, whether that is in Europe, the US or Asia. Our connections with the international equestrian community means we have access to the latest research and industry trends."

In order to fast track growth Ivanka says sometimes you have to make the tough decisions. "You have to make decisions faster, and if you have to cut, cut deep to get your outcome, don't play around that."

What Ivanka has truly become successful at is being an expert in her field. She is world renowned for her field of expertise and offers the advice that is aspiring entrepreneurs can become so knowledgeable within their own field, then it will accelerate not only their business, but their personal profile. She offers three golden rules for owning your niche.

Learn it properly the first time

When you have the correct technique you don't have to un-learn yourself later down the track and you'll benefit in the long run. When you are new to an exercise you benefit from having

an instructor to show you the correct way, but you also benefit from having monitoring tools so you can self-manage your progress.

Have consistency and frequency

When you need to learn a new discipline, you need to get used to a new routine. The best way to achieve this is to increase the frequency of performing the new technique or discipline. It takes at least 3 weeks (21 days) for new habits to form so you need to stick with the program for a lot longer than you initially anticipated.

Finally, increase the intensity and level of difficulty. Add more weight to increase the level of difficulty; expand beyond the initial pilot phase and do a full scale deployment.

LISA MOORE

Founder of Rodeo Show

Rodeo Show's headquarters is brimming with feminine floral dresses and an air of quirkiness. A little bit like Lisa Moore herself, with her ever-present smile and relaxed Bohemian temperament. Under her, Rodeo Show has become one of Australia's leading high-end, high-street brands for women, one that aims to provide premium designs and quality to the mass womenswear market.

Lisa has a vision to create beautiful quality garments that are 'fashion fun, easy and accessible for everyone'. The distinct aesthetic of Rodeo Show garments comes from a bohemian influence setting itself apart from other boutiques and designers. Now, after 11 years in business, Rodeo Show has withstood the ever-changing retail climate and online eruption.

RODEO SHOW

Founded
2003

Stores
8

Inspiration
CHOSE TO PURSUE HER PASSION FOR FASHION OVER ACCOUNTANCY

The harder you work the luckier you are.

With the motto, "there is always a solution", Lisa is the type of person you feel instantly at home with. Genuine and generous with her time, she believes her entrepreneurial ability rests in identifying a need or gap in the market, then the skills to take the required steps to fill it, while also understanding the necessary risks along the way to reach her goals.

"Resilience and attitude also makes me a true entrepreneur. It's the ability to bounce back from setbacks and believe that anything is possible. Leading and inspiring my team and the surrounding community makes me an entrepreneur and not just a business owner," says Lisa.

Lisa describes that it's not just the thrill of achieving and winning along the way that has driven her Rodeo Show journey, with a deep understanding of hardship, she's been able to work harder than her competition. Lisa came to Australia with her parents as boat refugees. They arrived when she was only two and the only assets they had were $US14 and few pieces of gold jewellery.

"My parents spoke no English. They were 24 yrs old at the time and had to work multiple jobs to get us set up in a new country. We had little money when I was growing up but we were so happy. I have grown up appreciative of little things and understand the meaning of hard work. Our fortunes changed when I was ten years old when my parents bought a business. I started working in the business after school and weekends. That's where my favourite saying of "the harder you work the luckier you are" was instilled in me. I would not have wished for a different childhood as it has made me who I am today."

Rodeo Show made its debut in a shopfront on Oxford Street in Paddington, Sydney. When Lisa first set out, her goal was to own and run a fashion boutique. However, she remembers that as the brand grew, she had to shift both her mentality and also create new goals for the business.

Originally, the boutique offered a selection of feminine pieces featuring creative prints and textures, but with consumer demand that store evolved into a more accessible brand offering prestige for the masses.

"As the business grew the goal posts shifted, and I never thought Rodeo Show would become a retail chain. I have always wanted to create a fashion brand that is wearable and not pretentious and that has remained the same today. We don't take fashion too seriously. Our brand resonates with our loyal following as it's for girls who know their mind and are confident in themselves. We are a strong minded community and appreciate the beautiful things in life."

Ambitions, challenges and lessons

A cap on growth for Rodeo Show was waiting too long to change her business model back in 2009 when the GFC hit. "We were primarily a wholesale business with two retail stores and when our wholesale customers were dropping off we didn't react fast enough and ended up with two years of financial struggles," she says.

In hindsight, Lisa says she should have grown the Rodeo Show stores faster and not wasted time.

"I believed in my gut that the retail model was the way to go. I wanted to offer our own brand direct to the end customer and have control of the brand in the marketplace. With our own stores we are able to clearly communicate our brand direct to the customer across all the touchpoints. This has since turned the business around and has helped our cashflow and profitability immensely."

Lisa admits she'd like to see her business grow stronger still and says she wants to be a brand that represents strength, beauty and individuality.

"Our brand essence is "Strong, Beautiful, Me" and I want to take that global one day. Our clothes are for those who are self confident, and love who they are. We capture moments and want to be a part of our girl's journey growing up whether its her birthday, graduation, engagement, hens, wedding, anniversary... My goal is to have someone wearing Rodeo Show at every single special event in someone's life." But, success for Lisa is not all about making a profit.

"I won't lie that it helps but personally it's about creating a work/life balance. With three kids under the age of two, including a set of twins, the ability to spend valuable time with my young growing family and work the flexible hours is what it's about. But right now, as we grow, the business needs me. Success is when I can have the business working without me".

With Donna Guest, from Blue Illusion as a role model and mentor for her, Lisa envisages global potential for Rodeo Show. Like Donna, she hopes to build an extraordinary business whilst having an amazing family life as well.

Lessons from Lisa:
- React fast, and adapt to changing markets.
- The harder you work, the luckier you are.
- There is always a solution.

It has only been recently that Lisa, has really worked out why she does what she does.

"I've kind of never thought about it as its just what I do naturally. I love solving problems and giving to others. I love to nurture people and be mother hen. I have always put other people before me and helping people out. It applies to my family, team, customers, community, charities and all the people I come across in my life. I want to create an engine, being the business whereby I can help make a difference to each person's life whether it's helping grow and develop my team or making girls feel beautiful or supporting a charitable cause."

PAULINE NGUYEN

Co-owner of Red Lantern

RED LANTERN

Founded
2002

Awards
MANY INCLUDING AUSTRALIA'S
FAVOURITE RESTAURANT

Inspiration
PASSION FOR HER FAMILY, FOOD
AND VIETNAMESE CULTURE

Pauline Nguyen is no stranger to success. Co-owner of the award-winning Vietnamese Red Lantern restaurants in inner Sydney, she also authored the acclaimed cookbook and memoir, Secrets of the Red Lantern, which tells the honest, difficult story of the Nguyen family, following the journey of her parents from their homeland in Vietnam on their escape to Thailand as refugees, and then on to their eventual resettlement in Australia.

Pauline is proof that success can come from the right mix of leadership, communication and values, with a baseline of passionate drive and hard work. From refugee to industry leader and female business icon, Pauline's journey is a shining example of an Australian-grown entrepreneur building an empire from the ground up.

Work ethic, roots and roles

Having come from humble beginnings, Pauline's prominence in the food industry is the fruit of years of hard work. She arrived in Australia by boat at age four as a refugee from Vietnam, and her family settled in Sydney's most vibrant and notorious Vietnamese enclave. Her parents instilled a strong work ethic in their children at an early age. "I started working when I was seven," she says, "in my parents' restaurant".

Red Lantern began thirteen years ago as collaboration between Pauline and her younger brother, Luke Nguyen. Pauline's background in film and television production and management matched well with Luke's passion for food, and the siblings found early success. From the beginning, Pauline has handled the commercial side of their business.

Pauline believes that there are three roles that are essential to a successful business partnership: the artist, the manager and the entrepreneur. The artist, she says, "...whether they love cooking or designing clothes, inventing or creating," is the one whose creative passion is often the instigating drive for a business. Maintaining a sustainable enterprise, however, requires all three, and involves complementing one's own weaknesses with others' areas of expertise.

"With our business, it took a little while. My husband Mark is definitely the artist; he is the chef of the restaurants, always creating. My brother is also an artist with what he

WHEN YOU GIVE UP, YOU MISS OUT ON LEARNING RESILIENCE AND PERSISTENCE

does, but at heart he's a manager. The three of us work very well together. Over the years we have discovered it's good to say, 'That's not my forte, please can you look at [it].' Over the years I've found my groove and I'm the entrepreneur." Communication is essential to keep those roles working smoothly together to enhance one another.

As a business owner, Pauline believes that leadership by example, clear communication and unwavering values are crucial to creating a good professional environment. Growth is central to both her personal and business philosophies: "Growth in relationships, growth in development, growth in friendships with our customers as well as each other." As a leader, she believes that in order to instil such values, actions speak louder than words. "You can talk all you want but unless you live it and embody it, it doesn't become the truth."

Pauline is also quick to highlight the importance of delegation. In the first year of Red Lantern, she recalls, "We were working 70, 80, creeping on 90 hours per week." Relinquishing

control, she says, can be difficult for business owners. In hindsight, Pauline believes that if they knew sooner to "employ people who were smarter than us, who enjoyed doing things we didn't enjoy doing, people who were faster than us," that their early years may not have been quite as challenging.

However, Pauline is not one to shy away from hard work. "I haven't been rostered in the business for a good nine years but I work every day because I choose to." She eschews the term "work life balance" because of the inherently negative assumptions attributed to the term "work", which she believes is an important part of a fulfilling life. "You find your creativity and inspiration in the space of work," she says. "It's an ongoing journey and there are so many highlights."

Resourcefulness and adaptation

Pauline's determination and flexibility has only been strengthened by the tests of challenging experiences. During the Global Financial Crisis that began in 2008, the team

made the decision to overhaul Red Lantern's supply model to improve sustainability, which was not undertaken without financial strain. "My husband is a big supporter of [the] advocacy and ethics of what we eat and where our food comes from," Pauline says. "We changed to waterless woks, compost recycling and our seafood, fish, meat are all [from] sustainable producers now."

In tough economic times, Pauline emphasizes the importance of resourcefulness and the need to better oneself rather than waiting for the going to get better. "I have seen so many of my industry competitors shut up shop. It's times like these that make me innovate more, connect more, think outside of the square more, inspire my team more, think of different ways of doing things." As a businesswoman, she notes that resilience is vital; "When you give up, you miss out on learning resilience and persistence and you miss out on the opportunity of mastering your craft."

In 2012, Red Lantern was voted Australia's Favourite Restaurant (I Love Food Awards)

and in the same year it won the NSW Telstra Australian Business Award. Since its conception, Red Lantern has evolved into a renowned Sydney establishment that is a perennial favourite of the industry and public alike.

Womanhood and mentorship

For now, Pauline has her sights set not only on the growth and continuing reinvention of Red Lantern, but also on inspiring other businesswomen. "Ultimately, [I want] to serve women entrepreneurs and to help those who don't love what they do yet. Not only in the workspace but in life's journey."

She is a professional mentor to several people and is a strong proponent of the virtues of mentorship. Speaking about starting Red Lantern, Pauline wishes she and Luke had known "to get mentors and coaches in at a very early stage." She still has her own mentors, individuals who challenge and push her. "I get so inspired by people who are better than me in [different] areas."

For young entrepreneurs, Pauline believes that getting guidance is paramount. "I don't believe that young entrepreneurs are disillusioned by how much work they have to put in or how many times they are going to fail until they get there; if they're smart enough they will get mentors who will keep them in line."

Lessons from Pauline:

- Lead by example. Have unwavering values, and be clear about those values throughout.
- Communicate clearly, and identify your role within a business.
- Get mentors and coaches in at a very early stage.
- When you give up, you miss out on learning resilience and persistence and the opportunity of mastering your craft.

One of the biggest obstacles holding women back, she believes, is that they "think they are not good enough." The other, she adds, is the "fear of what other people will think of them." As a mother, Pauline understands the pressure of maternal obligation that affects

working mums. "I have two kids and went back to work straight away," she says. Essentially, she wants to "inspire and help women to live an enriched life", which involves not being held back by guilt and fear. "There is support," she counsels, "from this book, for example."

Primarily, Pauline emphasizes the need to discover your purpose and passion. "I think the biggest advice I give to women starting up would be to really grab onto your 'why'. If you have a compelling 'why', you are going to make it work and get out of bed every day." Finding it, Pauline advises, requires a combination of inquisitiveness and perseverance. "Be curious to find out. No one's going to deliver it to you on a platter. You have to work to discover it." To do this, she adds, requires courage and "stepping out of your comfort zone and dancing in it. Not being afraid."

For Pauline, her 'why' is her family. "I have kicked some big goals and the most rewarding thing I have done is obviously my kids. They are full of love; they are talented, confident, funny."

Above all, what does she believe the entrepreneurial journey is about?

It's about grit. It's about resilience. It's about not giving up.

DEB NOLLER

—

CEO of Switch Automation

With five successful businesses under her belt, Deb Noller is well acquainted with the entrepreneurial journey. Big data and innovation are where she makes a home.

Deb co-founded Switch Automation with John Darlington (CFO), in 2005. Switch handles energy management for commercial and residential properties, with a focus on environmental sustainability. Switch Automation has firmly established itself as a key player in the growing automation industry. Since its inception, the company has since grown to become a serious player in disruptive technologies. With projects in the US and Australia, Switch Automation delivers enterprise operations and portfolio management via its "software-as-a-service" (SaaS) platform through a flexible and scalable cloud-based global framework, powered by the Microsoft Azure infrastructure.

SWITCH AUTOMATION

Founded
2005

———

Awards
SEVERAL INCLUDING DELL FOUNDERS 50 (AUSTIN)

———

Inspiration
DEB LOVES LIFE, NATURE, TECHNOLOGY AND BUSINESS. SHE FERVENTLY BELIEVES THAT BUILDINGS CAN BE CHANGED BY TECHNOLOGY TO BE LESS WASTEFUL, BETTER ENVIRONMENTS AND MORE POSITIVE EXPERIENCES FOR THEIR INHABITANTS.

The drive to succeed

Deb is a powerhouse of drive and energy. She is an avid cyclist, "I ride my bike when I can, it is wonderful," she says, "to get out and about and think about stuff to clear my head. Other than that I work seven days a week." It probably makes sense that even her choice of relaxation is a vigorous one.

Work is something that Deb clearly values and enjoys. It forms a crucial part of the Switch Automation company culture and ethic. "John and I are extremely driven and we expect everyone else to be too," she says, "we reward people who work hard." Amongst other things, she believes work is the key to success.

She recounts, "I grew up with parents that got pregnant straight out of school so we had no money, we were really really poor. We went to public schools. The only way I knew I was going to make it in life was to work hard; I got that from my parents. The value of working hard and being smart, taking advantage of education and taking an element of risk in what you do."

Deb does admit, however, that she's sometimes too quick to judge people by her own high standards. "I write people off quickly if they are not prepared to work hard," she says. Striking a balance, while tricky, seems to have been achieved by Deb in her partnership with John. "John's more likely to persist with people; if he thinks they have knowledge and skills, he's more likely to turn people around." Much of their business success is attributable to the strength of their collaboration. Deb is quick to point out the necessity of having a great co-founder. "You have to totally understand each other, have different skills, let the other person do their job," she says. "You really have to find someone that's

I ALWAYS FOUND IT REALLY HARD TO SIT THERE WATCHING A BAD DECISION BEING MADE WITHOUT SAYING SOMETHING

totally compatible with your managing skills. This is our fifth business together and we have a similar goal to build something really big."

Speaking frankly, Deb admits that the path to entrepreneurship wasn't initially a deliberate one. Part of the drive to begin her first company stemmed from the frustration she felt, while working for other people, in witnessing and being unable to prevent bad business decisions. "I always found it really hard to sit there watching a bad decision being made without saying something," she says. "My first business came about because I was working for someone I didn't enjoy working for in Cairns. I left to have my second baby and the guy I was working with, who also didn't enjoy working for that company – he knocked on my door and said, 'Why don't we go into business together?' " Deb was happy to take a chance and the deal was sealed: "Because I was off having a baby it didn't really bother me whether it was successful or not, so I was happy to take a risk." Expansion occurred rapidly thereafter. "We went into business and started a company that grew from two people to 36," she says. "We were offering logistical software solutions for mining companies in Indonesia."

With modesty, Deb maintains that it was partly serendipity that led her to the position she is now in. "Everything has been accidental really," she says, "because you kind of see an opportunity that you didn't go looking for originally." While her journey may not have begun by design, it has undoubtedly progressed as a result of her following her passions. The history of her tertiary education is a fitting example. "I went into a business degree and discovered computer science. It was just one of the courses we had to do in our business degree and I loved it," she recalls. "It's interesting the way life works."

So what is her company aiming to achieve? In her decisive, well-spoken manner, Deb outlines without hesitation the goals of Switch Automation. "Our vision is to build the standard by which people will manage their buildings in the future, globally," she says. "We are growing something we think will change the way people fundamentally look at buildings worldwide."

"We started the idea of automation in high-end homes in 2002. We found there was nothing available for apartments in multi-residential buildings. When we started out, there was no

solution for all stakeholders, (including property managers and everyone who lives in the building). We thought there was an opportunity around automation for green buildings."

"It took around two years to develop the infrastructure. We changed the whole business model in 2006 to become a cloud-based platform rather than a hardware-based system."

Environmental sustainability is also high on the agenda while corporate social responsibility has become a must. "If we can fundamentally change the way people manage their buildings, and get more buildings around 30 percent energy efficient, that's saving the world's resources. If you just look at the way the world has changed from when I was a kid to now, we're not leaving much of a planet for the next generation if we don't start addressing that."

The future for the company seems bright. "The next ten years look fun," Deb says. "We've already started to kick some pretty good goals into the US. We have a small office here in Australia, we are going to bring on some large partnerships and will also grow the platform from Asia into Europe."

Uphill work

With plans for global expansion of Deb's fifth business well underway, this active and motivated businesswoman appears unstoppable but, fortunate as she might have been, Deb has worked tirelessly to build her businesses from the ground up. One of the major challenges she encountered, and which she believes is also the case for all start-ups, was to do with funding. Being realistic, she

says, is of utmost importance. "You should go into business with the mindset you won't get funding because that's the likely outcome. If you're going to be successful you need to work out how to get money into your business as quick as possible." The best way to do this, she advises, is through sales. "If you can get the sales then you have proven you have something that's viable. That should lead to funding." If money doesn't come from external sources, Deb believes that it is also possible to grow a big global business through self-funding, "if you build the right technology and are reliant on it." She also advises, "Sometimes you need to also downsize and let people go. If you haven't got the money and you can't find it, people need to go. It keeps you focused on sales and where the revenue's coming from." The focus, she says, should be on "growing business, getting sales and managing cash flow."

Deb believes that the term "entrepreneur" has evolved in Australia over the past several years. She thinks that if the term were thrown around even five years ago, tall poppy syndrome would have been the result. "Entrepreneur" is now a label that she is comfortable bearing. "It means someone who is prepared to take risks and put everything on the line to create something amazing that doesn't exist in the world yet."

She feels inspired by the growing community of entrepreneurs we have in this country. "There are some amazing people doing amazing things. They are all entrepreneurs but just don't do business as usual. It's about reinventing. We have got to be more excited about what innovation can do and how much innovation can be good for Australia." With regards to women in business, Deb believes

that their approach is quite different to their male colleagues. "They are much more team orientated than most men," she says. "They tend to be quite collaborative and supportive."

Lessons from Deb:
- Dream big.
- Find a good collaborator who enhances your strengths and moderates your weaknesses.
- Being realistic is of utmost importance.
- Work incredibly hard on something that makes you want to work incredibly hard.

Deb is optimistic about the future of business, "The whole younger generation is amazing. People that whinge about generation Y are crazy!" She does believe, though, that young entrepreneurs still have a lot to learn and emphasises the need for them to "dream big".

With some big changes for Switch Automation planned for the future, only time will tell what is next in store for Deb Noller. Regardless of whatever venture comes next, one can be sure that she'll remain firmly at the helm.

JAN OWEN (AM)

CEO of Foundation for Young Australians

Jan Owen is fueled by shared purpose. Passionate about engaging young people in difficult situations, Jan has met challenges with a head on enthusiasm.

Articulating a clear vision through her work as CEO of The Foundation of Young Australians, Jan inspires those around her to share her passion, and work on creative solutions to perennial problems. As the only national independent non-profit organisation dedicated to all young people in Australia, FYA's role is to provide the tools and connections that equip them to change their world.

FOUNDATION FOR YOUNG AUSTRALIANS

Awards
INCLUDES THE DEGREE OF DOCTOR OF LETTERS (HONORARY CAUSA) FROM THE UNIVERSITY OF SYDNEY (2014) AND WAS NAMED INAUGURAL AFR AND WESTPAC GROUP 'WOMAN OF INFLUENCE' (2012)

Inspiration
ORIGINALLY TASKED WITH INCREASING OPPORTUNITIES AND ACCESS FOR YOUNG PEOPLE WITH DISADVANTAGED BACKGROUNDS

The beginning

Jan Owen is inspiring; a character steeped in positivity and change. Jan began exhibiting these characteristics from a young age in her hometown of Brisbane. "I was one of those entrepreneurial kids who tried to sell lemonade at the end of my driveway; only problem being my driveway was on a road that about two cars went by each day," says Jan. Repeated yet undaunted by failure is the characteristic of truly successful people, and at the age of 11 Jan found a niche market, catching toads for the University of Queensland Veterinary Department with her three younger brothers. "Toads Inc. was a bonanza for a while there, fifty cents a toad at fifty toads per night. We oversupplied the Uni."

Jan has come a long way from selling lemonade by the side of the road. Today, as the CEO of the Foundation for Young Australians, she has contributed to the establishment of social change organisations and has served on a wide range of boards, advising the forward momentum and shape of the business community. Jan insists that getting involved in community organisations or artistic pursuits at an early age can significantly grow leadership skills and allow young people to find their talents and capabilities in safe and supportive environments. In 2000, Jan was awarded membership of the Order of Australia for services to children and young people, and was the inaugural winner of the Australian Financial Review & Westpac Group 'Woman of Influence' in 2012. In 2014 she was awarded an honorary doctorate from the University of Sydney.

As an adopted child with a debilitating stutter, Jan's non conformist, strong will and driven aspirational spirit emerged early. She decided to tackle her vocal disability head on by enrolling in terrifying and potentially humiliating activities such as debating, acting in one woman plays and singing.

A sense of purpose

Jan's sense of purpose was deeply influenced by her family life. "I was brought up…helping others. [It] was part of your religious and societal contribution," says Jan. "My folks helped set up Lifeline and were some of the organisation's first phone counsellors. It was generous. It was without judgment. I gained a strong sense of social justice from a young age…I saw people turn around, pick up their lives, and move on to better times."

Attracted to social justice issues and supporting others, Jan started out trying to make a difference in drug and alcohol education across Queensland with children and young people. She says a 'fairly creative' approach was used to establish youth support services in a style she now terms 'guerrilla entrepreneurship'. "We 'borrowed' unused assets like service stations and turned them into drop-in centres for kids and young people in the inner city."

Jan worked as a national youth advocate and Chair of the Youth Affairs Council of Australia, before working in child protection where she saw young people who were not treated as equals and who were not given a voice in the dispensation of their own lives. This led her to set up the CREATE Foundation, an organisation aimed at meeting the needs of the 20,000+ children and young people in foster care. One of the key initiatives of CREATE was a social enterprise, which employed young people themselves as consultants to the government bodies and NFP's who provided their care. "It was pretty radical," Jan said. "We transformed the state care system from the inside out by bringing these young people, the 'customers' to the table."

After nine years under her leadership, CREATE had grown into a national organisation with offices and staff in every state and territory. Jan moved on.

The next step was Social Ventures Australia with Michael Traill. "We were yin and yang – one from the business and one from the social sector," Jan says. "SVA pioneered new social investment and HNW philanthropy models. We sought to find and back the best social entrepreneurs in the country and invest in them to grow and scale their impact."

MY LIFE'S WORK AND PASSION HAS ALWAYS BEEN WITH YOUNG PEOPLE. THEY INSPIRE AND SURPRISE ME EVERY DAY

After eight and a half years there, Jan left to run the Foundation for Young Australians where she has been CEO for the past four years, and feels she has found her place. Jan explains. "My life's work and passion has always been backing young people. I am relentlessly optimistic about their capacity to create change in their world. They inspire and motivate me every day."

Entrepreneurship and identity

But what has her long career as a businesswoman taught her about the word 'entrepreneur'? Jan says she didn't relate to the word entrepreneur until 15 years ago when someone introduced her as a 'social entrepreneur' at a conference.

"I had never even heard the term," she admits. "Until then I had variously been called an advocate, a founder, an innovator, a leader, a maverick and a disruptor."

When she met Michael Traill; he called her a 'serial social entrepreneur,' and the term seemed to bring all her roles and descriptions together in a way she felt suited her. Most importantly, she finally felt that she belonged to a known and very real tribe after a lifetime of feeling like an outsider.

Jan adds that she now sees that her ideas and approaches to issues and opportunities have always been entrepreneurial, though she says "I don't consider myself a typical 'lone' entrepreneur."

Throughout her career, Jan says she hasn't stopped learning new things about business and effectively achieving new goals. "I feel I actually have too much stuff in my head! There is such a propensity for us all to keep trying to seek more and more, new knowledge without understanding the deeper meaning in what we already know. Most of my learning has been from doing. I encourage my team to experiment and we learn, live, every day."

Womanhood and the entrepreneurial challenges

Jan admits it wasn't until a few years ago, at a gathering in Mexico City of young entrepreneurs from around the world, that she really appreciated how "uniquely difficult" it was to be a female entrepreneur. A females-only session was arranged during the event, which Jan thought would focus on female leadership. "Instead, we ended up having a slumber party where we spent hours discussing how to be a female entrepreneur and have children, a partner and balance being passionate about your work and feeling you could fulfil your purpose and mission in life."

She also says the insight into the pressures on young women from many countries to conform to societal norms were "powerful and oppressive" and for those for whom conforming was not such an issue, the day-to-day realities of being a wife, mother and entrepreneur were "significant hurdles."

Jan attributes her continued success in her field to a combination of natural ability and effort. "I have always been good at spotting an opportunity and articulating a clear vision when it presents itself." After that, the work comes in "motivating, inspiring and galvanising people around that vision or goal and finding like-minded people to help design and implement the strategy to achieve the vision."

Failure and learning

Jan believes that failure is necessary to success as a businessperson. Development comes in the process of experimentation and iteration, but the experience of repeated failure is instructive and useful in itself. She points out, "Failing is not just about learning how to do things faster and smarter; it usually entails acquiring a certain humility, deeper self awareness and understanding."

Jan admits she has been unsuccessful in many things throughout her career. Most of her experiments and failures have taught her lessons in doing her due diligence on partners, both individual and organisational, and ventures where she didn't allow for enough fast, lean prototyping with the end user. The language of business entrepreneurship has given her tools to make those lessons useful.

Jan says that previous failures and personal battles are good reminders of her own strengths and capabilities.

"Whenever I am overcome by self doubt or I am feeling nervous because I am about to take on something significant or attempt something I haven't previously, I always remind myself that I if could survive those life events then nothing worse could possibly happen or be more stressful and painful. It is the way I unlock courage in myself."

And courage is just one value she draws on in her everyday business life. "Courage to innovate...to be bold, to be wrong, to listen, speak out, stand up, show up, to be present, to take risks and back yourself," she says.

Imagination and willpower were also key. "Keep thinking outside the square. Stay open to the endless...possibilities. Keep learning,

I RARELY REFER TO MYSELF AS A FEMALE ANYTHING, ALTHOUGH I AM ACUTELY AWARE OF BEING A FEMALE LEADER AND ROLE MODEL. I CONSCIOUSLY ENCOURAGE AND PRACTICALLY SUPPORT WOMEN TO STEP UP AND BACK THEMSELVES

capture and be captured by others' ideas and be passionate. The determination to work hard and get things done (is incredibly important). Believe in what you are doing."

Inspirations and lessons

"I have been gifted with many mentors and coaches, including some incredibly strong feminists and some extremely influential men in my life. I have also learnt an enormous amount from the people I work with and now they are often way younger than me, which I love. It is a privilege to spend time learning with and from young people."

Lessons from Jan:
- Learn from those around you, whether they're older or younger. Everyone has a lesson to teach you if you can figure it out.
- Most learning is from doing: experiment and learn, live, every day.
- Have courage to innovate...be bold, be wrong, to listen, speak out, stand up, show up, be present, take risks and back yourself.

She believes Australia has the potential to be 'a lighthouse nation' in the world. "I have a clear vision about the future I want to be part of creating... I believe it will take a new form of open and collective leadership to realise our future potential as a country. It will also take a generation of young entrepreneurs in all endeavours science, business, civil society, government, the arts and more to discover what we are yet capable of. I believe FYA is contributing to that vision in a very real way engaging and inspiring young people Australia to be enterprising, outward focused, global citizens."

DAWN PIEBENGA

Founder of Injury Management and Rehabilitation

IMR

Founded
1995

Team
12

Inspiration
TO BE HER OWN BOSS

Dawn Piebenga is founder and managing director of Injury Management and Rehabilitation and Interface Medico-Legal Services. The company was founded in 1996, with no more than a post office box, a computer and a mobile phone in her rental property.

Dawn's professional experience lies within a range of clinical settings including physical, drug and alcohol and psychiatric rehabilitation settings in England. Since her arrival in Australia in 1994 she has worked within the NSW WorkCover, ComCare, Income Protection and CTP schemes.

As managing director, she works at a strategic level to address the needs of IMR and Interface's customers. She and her team are passionate about the application of "evidence-based best practice."

Small steps to big progress

Managing director and senior occupational therapist Dawn Piebenga has built a company that's now become one of Sydney's leading Rehabilitation Providers, IMR. Dawn's entrepreneurial ventures began in 1996, first with IMR and then Interface Med Legal. Both companies have been running for 18 years and within the first year Dawn's team had grown from zero to 50 staff.

One could say Dawn was genetically predisposed, born into an entrepreneurial family from the New Zealand countryside of New Zealand. Her father, a self-employed farmer and her mother a self-employed artist. As a child Dawn was exposed to an environment of self-sufficient, hard-working tradespeople forming role models that would inevitably equip her with invaluable life skills and learnings.

"A job I had when I was a child was picking blueberries, my parents worked out that it cost them more to go and get the blueberries than to pay me to go and pick them. Unfortunately, for me I was a blueberry lover so that co-evened. I also did work in the shearing shed, for the road works holding the snow sign

and made a lot of money by catching calves through the local stock station," Dawn reflects.

For Dawn, immigrating to Australia was a natural progression after becoming a qualified Occupational Therapist in New Zealand in 1989.

"When I arrived in Australia in 1994, I was 25, I started working for a small private practice. I was their first employee and in a year I grew their business to 9 staff members. I actually went and asked for a promotion and a pay rise but I didn't get it. They offered me a small pay rise but no promotion. I was disappointed because I was the leader in the business."

Australia provided the rich soil for Dawn to complete her masters majoring in Ergonomics at the University of New South Wales, this coincided with the organic growth of her first business IMR and first self-employed role. Understandably, as first time entrepreneurs we will encounter many problems for the first time. This often requires time spent on re-strategising or re-structuring the company. For Dawn, her first obstacle came when her team called for too much micro-management. With 50 staff members in her team, Dawn found herself having to closely observe

and control their work. Downsizing and empowering staff seemed her only option.

Prioritising

"I just made the decision that I just didn't want to be managing managers. Then I realised I was going to have a baby and yet at the same time micro-managing managers, I went this is ridiculous. You've been employed in a management role, you've been told what to do, just go and do it please."

Having a supportive team during the time of Dawn's pregnancy was fundamental to the health of her and her baby. When the time did come for Dawn to have children she realised that "children have this very confronting way of making you prioritise or re-prioritise everything pretty quickly".

Post downsizing the team of 50 down to a figure of 12, Dawn felt she didn't have to step in to make decisions and could let the business operate under the watch of those who she had strategically hired. The second time around she felt comfortable to grow and spend important time with her family.

"For me having children, I changed. Things that were really high and important and that I would have prioritised are less important and you face some realities around what you love."

Having been through child birth Dawn was able to empathise more with her team and those women who have gone through the same experience while trying to manage their working careers alongside.

"I have always employed a lot of mums so flexibility has been really crucial for them. I have always prioritised that for my team and it's something I really respect a lot more now and understand when mum's feel conflicted about having a baby," Dawn openly says.

The relationship between staff and company culture plays an important role within Dawn's business. Women need the support network to feel they can have the freedom to begin a family and also know that their job is still available when they return from leave. Dawn noticed that her companies culture grew stronger in her absence.

"I went off to have my son, I just only had the team around me that knew how to do their job and I didn't have to step back in. It really gave me the freedom to take time off, even more so three years later when I had my daughter. I had the same number of people who had been in the business for years and they had a lot of respect for me to take time out."

Dawn is an example of a resilient woman entrepreneur who juggles multiple acts.

"I have a much smaller business now, I still juggle especially with the competing demands of my family, I have to do some work around not feeling guilty and constantly compromised". From IMR to Interface Med Legal to her husband and children also factoring in important "me time". Her skills vary from rehabilitation to investigative interviewing and business coaching.

"For me business is really around flexibility and really allowing you to have the freedom to make the choices that you need to make for your life outside your work life. I love work, work is part of who I am but I also want to have the flexibility to be able to take my children to do their activities."

Lessons from Dawn:
- Don't micromanage. Hire people you trust, and empower them to be entrepreneurs in their own right.
- You're more likely to succeed as an entrepreneur if you have entrepreneur role models in your life.
- An entrepreneur doesn't blame anyone when things go wrong. They figure out the solution.

In addition Dawn is also an active member of the Entrepreneurs' Organisation which is a non-for-profit that sees a congregation of entrepreneurs from around the world. A relevant conversation point when analysing the background of a business person is are entrepreneurs predisposed with the special "entrepreneurial streak?".

Dawn acknowledges from her own experience that having key figures around during childhood allows an added strength over others. "You're more likely to succeed as an entrepreneur if you've had entrepreneur role models in your life. The key thing around that sense of personal responsibility is an entrepreneur doesn't blame anyone when things go wrong, if they do it wouldn't be very successful for them, but my sense is that it's a combination".

RARELY DO YOU SEE A BOOK WITH THE CALIBRE AND VOLUME OF WOMEN ENTREPRENEURS IN ONE TITLE. RARE BIRDS FILLS A MAJOR GAP AMONG ENTREPRENEUR AND BUSINESS BOOKS; AND IT ISN'T JUST FOR WOMEN. A THOROUGHLY ENGAGING READ.

Mark Moses
CEO Coaching International, business coach (and billion dollar business builder)

CATRIONA POLLARD

Founder of CP Communications

Sydney PR mogul and personal brand builder, Catriona Pollard has created a platform where she can help entrepreneurs, consultants, coaches, and anyone who is looking to become more recognised in their field, do exactly that.

Founder of CP Communications, Catriona runs one of Australia's most respected and innovative PR and social media agencies.

She is recognised as an industry influencer, an international speaker and trainer, author and popular media commentator. She has over 20 years experience in developing public relations and social media strategies that engage both consumers and businesses. CP Communications is one of Australia's most respected and innovative PR and social media agencies. She works with world-leading brands as well as up-and-coming organisations, and is regularly featured across the media landscape.

CP COMMUNICATIONS

Founded
2001

Awards
AUTHOR OF POPULAR BOOK, FROM UNKNOWN TO EXPERT, NAMED ONE OF THE TOP 100 PR PEOPLE TO FOLLOW ON TWITTER,

---

Inspiration
TO USE PUBLIC RELATIONS AND SOCIAL MEDIA TOOLS TO INSPIRE BUSINESSES AND PEOPLE TO ACHIEVE THEIR DREAMS AND DRIVE BUSINESS GROWTH

IF WOMEN CAN SEE THAT IT IS ACHIEVABLE THEN THEY CAN ACTUALLY GO AHEAD AND BECOME ENTREPRENEURS

Shaping up

Catriona Pollard grew up in a family that instilled self-belief. "We were told that we could do anything and achieve anything we wanted to achieve. I knew that I was going to go to university from the day I can remember even hearing about it."

Catriona remembers growing up with the appreciation that girls can be tough if they choose to. "My parents took my sister and I out of school for six months when I was 13. We literally backpacked around South East Asia for six months. I think because I was 13, it really influenced how I perceived the world. I saw poverty, which allowed me to understand and appreciate that this is how life is and that what we do in our lives is depended on how we perceive it and what we do about it."

After working in the PR industry, Catriona started her own business when she was 30, "I woke up one morning and said "I can't do this anymore I am going to choose a different path." And so my path was being an entrepreneur."

Catriona is passionate about social media, public relations, business and bringing them all together to create real financial success for entrepreneurs and organisations. She founded CP Communications in 2001 and has built it into one of Australia's leading PR and social media agencies. She believes that CEOs can be celebrities, that as figureheads they are increasingly able to develop recognisable personal brands and reputations.. "I actually find that a lot of women who are working in corporates don't spend enough time thinking about their personal brand or using PR and social media to develop a robust reputation because they think that other people are going to help them along with their career. I think a lot of work still needs to be done with women in terms of them understanding the power of personal branding, PR and social media for their careers."

Identifying the importance of having visible women entrepreneurs in the community, Catriona acknowledges how critical it is for women to see other women entrepreneurs with strong profiles and solid reputations. "I think women need to understand that entrepreneurship is whatever you want it to be. I think that there should be a number of different perceptions of entrepreneurship. If women can see that it is achievable then they can actually go ahead and become entrepreneurs," she remarks.

Cultivating courage and conviction

Women entrepreneurs often feel that modesty and a humble approach is important, but that humility can lead to them undercutting their own profile. It was a long time into her business before Catriona would feel she could call herself an entrepreneur. A strong fear of failure in her first year lead Catriona to say she was consulting rather than admitting she was a business owner. "I had to come to the realisation that we all have a different definition of entrepreneurship and we all have a different definition of success. Success to some people might mean having that CEO position or getting paid a million dollars but other people define success as sitting in their sunroom and just doing as many hours as they want before going to their yoga class."

While successful entrepreneurship has begun to develop a rockstar glamour that is entirely at odds with the grit and effort of real business, challenges are faced for emerging entrepreneurs to own their risks and successes. "There is a lot of attachment to the word entrepreneurship and I think that was one of the things I had to go through, thinking, "Oh but I am not Bill Gates, therefore I'm not and entrepreneur." But I am an entrepreneur because I'm a risk taker, I think up new ideas, I follow through with them I try them they even if they don't work, then I move onto the next thing."

As an international speaker, having spoken live at TEDx Macquarie University in 2014 in front of 500 people and streaming to an online audience of more than 200,000 people, Catriona feels other women need to be braver when it comes to putting themselves in the spotlight.

"What I am trying to say to women is that it's not about you. When I got up on stage for the first time and I looked down at the audience I had this massive realisation that I had been holding myself back because I didn't want to be standing in the spotlight. I didn't know whether I deserved to be there or not but at that particular moment in time I realised it's not about me at all, it's about the audience and the women who are thinking about becoming entrepreneurs but don't know where to start. It's about women who are in their careers but don't know where their next step is or the women that say "I have this bit of knowledge and I want to share it but don't know how."

"You have to work really hard, you have to take action, you will have these moments in time when you feel you can't do this but keep on pushing through and by the end of it you will be a recognised expert."

Lessons from Catriona:

- Build a personal brand.
- Ask the big questions. "Who are the people that I need to influence? Who are my target audiences?"
- Be brave when it comes to putting yourself in the spotlight. You're never ready for a thing until you've done it.

Over the years, Catriona has worked with women in banking and finance, women on boards as well as the Macquarie University Leadership Program. Her advice is to ask the big questions. "Who are the people that I need to influence? Who are my target audiences? And actually applying that strategic thinking to careers the same as business. Whatever stage of the career that you are at, the more that you see it as where you have to start building your personal brand the better it will be."

Her personal mission:

"I wanted to have a voice that reached the hearts and minds of the audience because I wanted to influence their lives and I wanted to influence their business. So it was about the action as opposed to "Oh I'm too humble or I'm not an entrepreneur." that's just all labels and holding women back from their responsibility to actually share their experiences, their journey, their vulnerabilities, their failures and their successes."

MEGAN QUINN

Co-founder of NET-A-PORTER

NET-A-PORTER

Founded

1999

Awards

SEVERAL INCLUDING NAMED
ONE OF AUSTRALIA'S MOST
POWERFUL WOMEN IN RETAIL BY
INSIDE RETAIL

Inspiration

PASSION FOR HIGH FASHION AND
RELEVANT INNOVATION

**Megan Quinn has applied a cutting-edge mind
to re-engineering online retail with her forward
thinking and impeccable execution.**

Named one of the most powerful women in Australian
retail in 2013, Megan Quinn co-founded Net-a-Porter.
com in 1999. Based out of London, in its first month of
sales, Net-a-Porter.com saw a turnover of £18,000 and
doubled turnover each year until it was sold in 2010 for
£350 million. It's currently valued at £600 million and the
website is host to over 50,000 viewers a day and 2.5 million
a month. The success of the company arises from Megan's
understanding of the customers changing needs and wants
within the market of high fashion. Megan made an exit
from Net-a-Porter in 2004, now wears the shoes of a non-
executive director, consultant and international speaker.

Taking a market

Luxury fashion is sought after by some of the world's most discerning customers, a target market that is highly demanding and difficult to please. To produce an e-commerce platform in the luxury space is a task in itself. That the model Megan pioneered is still running successfully more than 13 years later is indicative of the strength of her ideas and execution.

Megan is fastidious when it comes to details and customer experience. Net-a-Porter's end-to-end customer experience is attributable to her hands, right down to the detailing and care in the wrapping and packing of the garments. Megan's personal taste lead her to the experiential element of simple, clean old customer service values. This would set Net-a-Porter apart from their competitors, from the landing page to the delivery aesthetics - black boxes with a black ribbon. In turn, with the attention-to-detail that goes into one delivery, the clientele of Net-a-Porter can experience a smooth but satisfying end-to-end purchase.

Megan is careful to be realistic about her strengths and weaknesses. "I know how to run a business, I know how to make staff happy and lead them, I know how to make customers happy, I have a very healthy respect for the bottom line, but as a creator that side of me costs money. I am commercial to that extent but don't put me in charge of finance."

Given there was no face-to-face communication with the customer, communication through the Net-a-Porter website needed to be clear and intuitive. Megan's focus on the user experience, and a strong business plan meant that functionality could be a primary focus for the website, making it easy to navigate.

For Megan, balance has been key in the formation of what was her multi-million dollar company, "I talk about the importance of the Ying and the Yang, the IQ and the EQ." She points out that creativity and technology can make good partners if you are conscious of balancing apparently incongruent elements in your business, and enhance their ability to work together. For example, while Megan has the creative gene, her partner had a technologically wired brain which saw the evolution of Net-a-Porter. "I was the creative director, I designed the packaging, I loved the process. It was exciting. I was immersed in what I did: building, leading people, designing, creating stuff. I hired everyone until I left so I knew we could work together, my creative team sat right next door to the technology team."

Step on the runway

Net-a-Porter.com has become a brand in itself, a golden gateway that offers access to the shopper to over 350 designers. Customers can choose among pioneers in the high fashion market, including Alexander Wang, Balmain, Burberry, Gucci, Karl Lagerfeld, Oscar De La Renta, Roland Mouret, Saint Laurent, Stella McCartney, and Australian talent Zimmermann and Dion Lee. Megan points out that Australia has the capacity to rise to the level of the rest of the world, but that it needs to share knowledge and encourage growth in order to develop its full potential as a business nation. "We are so stagnated as a country. We have lost so many opportunities and I fear for Australia. We are losing our grandeur, our sovereign wealth should be so much more than it is."

"Look at the amount of offshoring we do. There's next to no manufacturing going on here. It's annihilated entire communities and the foundation of them breaks because you get a movement offshore. Then how are they going to get apprenticeships for young people? It creates social issues, it's a ripple effect. I was in Bendigo and there was a nice manufacturing community, I want to give them exposure and liberate what they are doing." Megan says.

On the other hand, Megan is hopeful about the potential of our future, and the strengths of upcoming business people, particularly young women. "There is so much knowledge with these girls starting a business out of university. It's great for the country".

In addition, Megan's passionate thread strings from the urge to help Australian manufacturing and also onto her role as a non-executive director at UNICEF Australia. "We can create the change that needs to empower ourselves and other people. As an entrepreneur we don't sit around waiting for policy to change you just do it. We move faster than governments."

**Values and womanhood:
Speaking from the heart**

Megan is clear about the balanced values of confidence and realism, "I speak from the heart and not the head. I don't need an island or a plane. I don't see myself as superior to anyone, but I also don't see myself as inferior to anyone either".

Megan explains that leadership of a team is as much about empathy as it is about command; "walking with them, leading from the centre, leading by example, actually caring and empathising," rather than an approach that lacks connectedness which can impede a business. In addition to guest speaking at universities, large corporations, events and seminars Megan is a graduate of the Australian Institute of Company Directors.

"I often get asked to speak about diversity and I have to be apologetic because I've had really great experiences," Megan says. Though she acknowledges that she comes from a privileged background and attributes much of her success to a good upbringing, good values and a solid skill base. "I worked hard, was polite, got to work on time and in interviews I could speak. Back then manners and elocution were prized in my background." She worries that these 'soft' skills are undervalued by newer workers. "the work ethic of kids these days, they turn up and want to work their own hours. They have obsession with their appearance, lack of manners, of empathy. Conversation skills are dying."

Lessons from Megan:
- Don't sit around waiting for the world to change. Make the change yourself.
- Work hard, be polite, get to work on time.
- Balance confidence with realism. Know you can make anything happen, if you have your head around what you can do, and what you need help with.

When asked to define success, Megan put forward a quote from a commencement speech by a writer from the New York Times, "success is an open mountain that you keep climbing and as you get closer to the summit it grows again and so often we can spend our whole lives on whatever this perception of success is and when large matters go largely unanswered and life matters". She pointed out that this successful writer had regrets about his lack of empathy and compassion, "The underlying message is that he could have spoken about all of his successes but instead he chose to talk about kindness as it was his one regret. He said he wish he had been kinder along the way. I think this is important."

Observing Megan's achievement with Net-a-Porter, there are many who can appreciate what she's already accomplished and eagerly await what's next in her journey.

SARAH RIEGELHUTH

Founder of Wealth Enhancers

WEALTH
ENHANCERS

Founded
2009

Employees
19

Awards
MANY INCLUDING INDUSTRY
THOUGHT LEADER

Inspiration
THE TWO SAW AN
OPPORTUNITY TO CREATE A
SPECIALIST MODEL FOR GEN
Y CLIENTS, WITH A FOCUS ON
AN INDIVIDUALS LIFE GOALS,
INSTEAD OF JUST THE NUMBERS

Authentic to her core, Sarah Riegelhuth is the type of woman that has entrepreneurship dripping from her fingertips. The co-founder of Wealth Enhancers,

The League of Extraordinary Women and now We Love Numbers, Sarah is a strong advocate for women in business but also passionate about addressing gender disparity as a broader social issue. With her charismatic and upbeat business partner and husband, Finn Kelly, Sarah is changing the Australian entrepreneurial landscape as we know it. Sarah is co-founder of award-winning financial advisory firm, Wealth Enhancers. Her partner, Finn Kelly, began offering a flat-fee model for financial and lifestyle coaching, focused on helping members reach their financial goals. The duo nearly tripled Wealth Enhancers' revenue in just three years and continues to grow today.

Early growth

Sarah realised in her early 20s that life can be whatever you want it to be. "It was a very liberating time for me," she says. Making her life her own, and teaching others to take control of their destinies became a driver for her, as she started to make her way in the world. "I am obsessed with business and personal finance, I think mainly because these two things for me represent living a life of your choosing, and being in control of your destiny. To me entrepreneurship is all about finding a sustainable way to solve a problem that you care way more about than most people do...helping people make the most of their money and get it under control is a big driver for me for similar reasons, without having your money working for you it's pretty hard to live the life of your dreams."

Wealth Enhancers started in 2012. The company began as a private wealth management firm, with a specific focus on Gen Y clients.

"We realised that Gen Y just wasn't being catered to by financial advisers, however we are an amazing purpose-driven generation who actually want to manage our money and our lives well in order to create the lifestyle we want for ourselves," says Sarah.

I THINK BIG AND DREAM
BIG, BUT THEN I BREAK
IT DOWN INTO A PLAN
AND GET IT DONE. I DON'T
PROCRASTINATE ON DETAILS

Forward momentum

Since then, the goal hasn't really changed; to be Australia's first choice for Gen Y when it comes to financial advice and lifestyle coaching. Sarah sees this as both a business and a social goal, changing people's lives in a very real and practical way. The only thing that has really shifted is that the business plans to expand to global clients. After recent research trips taken to New York, San Francisco and Singapore, it became clear that the niche of this huge market was wide open. Part of this small player's confidence in the future of their business lies in the strength of their employees and a strong team. "We have an incredibly aligned team and I think we're at the start of a big journey for WE," says Sarah.

Not content with one game changing business, Sarah is also founder of the League of Extraordinary Women. Beginning as a single event in Melbourne for 20-30 women, instead they sold 160 tickets in three weeks and the buzz on social media quickly alerted them to the fact that they had tapped into a powerful need. Women entrepreneurs were craving a community and network. And again, Sarah's ambitions are not limited to Australia. "We now have a goal to put Australia on the map as a leader in raising the profile of female entrepreneurs, we are also expanding into other countries who need the platform just like we did."

Challenges

While successful and a much admired entrepreneur, particularly to younger women, Sarah has overcome some major difficulties along the way to her current inspiring position.

"By far the hardest thing I've had to deal with was my dad's passing in May 2013. Dad was my friend, my mentor and the person I went to with every business challenge I ever had." This personal grief outweighed other challenges for Sarah, though she acknowledges that every business has hurdles. "Of course there are always challenges with staff, with managing growth and cashflow she says. "Everything you can think of goes wrong at one time or another, but losing my dad put all of those things into perspective."

Sarah is also an author, publishing her first book, Get Rich Slow as a way to articulate her commitment to help Gen Y members realise their potential, both financially and in all aspects of their lives.

Sarah is values-driven, which helps her make decisions and keep her on track toward reaching her goals and creating the life she wants. Some values close to her core:

Self-leadership. Taking full responsibility of where one is now, and where one is going.

Constant improvement. Constant reflection and work on innovation and development of self / business.

Having goals. Where does one want to be? Where is one now? Make a plan and execute.

Raising the bar. Being involved with community and making lasting positive changes.

One life. To be driven by passion, to live in the moment, and everyday work toward one's vision.

Sustainability. The ability to determine what to say yes to, and what to say no to. To focus and never give up.

Advocacy for Women as Entrepreneurs

Named as one of Melbourne's Top 100 most influential, inspiring and creative citizens by The Age in 2011, Sarah is recognised as one of Australia's leading female entrepreneurs. She is also an accomplished keynote speaker, a popular blogger, writer and columnist for several leading publications including Women's Agenda and Money Management. She regularly appears on Sky Business Your money Your Call.

TO ME ENTREPRENEURSHIP IS ALL ABOUT LIVING ONE LIFE AND NOT SEEING WORK AS SEPARATE FROM LIVING

Sarah was a finalist for the Money Management Financial Planner of the Year Award in 2012, and for the AFA Rising Star Award in both 2008 and 2009. She has received nominations for the Telstra Businesswoman of the Year Award, and the AFA Adviser of the Year Award.

On how to get things done, Sarah says, "I think big and dream big, but then I break it down into a plan and get it done. I don't procrastinate on details, I just get started and figure the rest out as I go along. I've always been like this, and for the most part it serves me well. I've learnt that taking action on an idea is far more important than the idea itself. I also think I am very good at building and maintaining relationships because I genuinely like 'people', and I love to collaborate on projects. I have employed so many friends and people I know over the years because my preference is to just be around people I love! It doesn't always work out, but when it does it's amazing."

Lessons from Sarah:
- Find a problem that you really care about solving and then start working on it. Think about it every which way you can and come up with a sustainable solution to fix it.
- Dream big and never give up.
- Innovate, create, be the master of your own destiny.

In 2010, Sarah became the youngest Board Member in the history of the Association of Financial Advisers (AFA) and championed the launch of the inaugural Female Excellence in Advice Award. The award has been more successful than any other award established by the AFA.

Speaking passionately and frequently on the topic of women as entrepreneurs, Sarah sees an abundance of numbers in this respect believing the problem lies in the conversation.

"I think there are actually plenty of female entrepreneurs in Australia, what I think there is a need for is recognition of these women. I also think we need more encouragement for the females who do start businesses every year, a number that is pretty much equal to the number of males who start businesses each year, to involve themselves in the entrepreneurial community. We need more platforms, like Rare Birds and The League of Extraordinary Women, to tell the stories of these women, until it gets to a point in society where it is normalised and we don't see a difference between a male entrepreneur and a female entrepreneur."

MARGOT SPALDING

———

Founder of Jimmy Possum

JIMMY POSSUM

———

Founded
1995

———

Awards
MANY ACCOLADES INCLUDING
NATIONAL WESTPAC BUSINESS
OWNER AWARD

Inspiration
TO TURN NOTHING INTO A MULTI
MILLION DOLLAR FURNITURE
& INTERIORS BUSINESS

With ten stores across the country, Margot Spalding's business, Jimmy Possum, has made Australian manufactured furniture popular again.

The Bendigo-based businesswoman first founded Jimmy Possum in 1995 with her husband Allan as a way to support their seven kids. Margot's tale of success is also a story of resilience and effort paying off. Initially struggling to get clients when she first started, 11 years later, Margot was awarded the National Winner of the Westpac Business Owner Award and named Telstra Australian Woman of the Year in 2006.

The beginning

Before launching Jimmy Possum, Margot originally began in children's clothing manufacturing and gourmet food products, while Allan was in furniture making. When the two decided to go into business together, they chose furniture as the best route for a shared business venture. Jimmy Possum Furniture was born.

Their previous experience in the industry was for Margot and Allan a starting point from which they were able to figure out what to do with Jimmy Possum. In the first five years, they established what and who their market was and how they were going to tailor their product to that market through research.

"We didn't know if it was going to work, but in a previous furniture business we had made custom things and we did the designs. We were purists in what we would make," Margot said.

"We realised what we wanted to do was to really focus, not custom make things, or huge ranges of furniture. I had been working in a mainstream furniture store, so I knew what customers wanted and so we thought we got it right. When we established these collections of furniture we wanted to make, nobody was producing it. We were pretty much an instant hit because the product was so different."

After selling to wholesalers and retailers for years, Margot and Allan eventually opened their own store in Fitzroy, Melbourne. Another store in Sydney and then in Melbourne followed the success of the Fitzroy store, and soon enough, there were ten Jimmy Possum stores across the country.

Hardship, and the importance of family in a family business

"There were lots of things we had gotten wrong previously that we were getting right now," Margot explained.

It hasn't always been smooth sailing for Margot, however. The first 18 months of Jimmy Possum involved a lot of cold calling while trying to find clients, which she describes as a "hideous" experience. Eventually they made the cut to participate in a trade show, which turned things around for Jimmy Possum.

"At the trade show we took on 22 stores, which was amazing for supply...I had sold enough in four days to keep the boys in work for nine months. We had to make swift moves then. We worked all day everyday for 18 months. The kids were around it. We would work nights loading trucks and we just worked and worked and worked."

"It was a really positive affirmation that we were on the right track. That was fantastic," Margot said.

With Jimmy Possum growing at such a fast rate, Margot and Allan's children, Georgia, Eliza, Emily, Jessica and Todd, all joined the business. For Margot, having her family involved is a great benefit, having lost her parents and sister at a young age. "Losing my parents and then my sister made me value people because you don't know when people can be taken away from you in a heartbeat. Living at a furious pace, you need to take advantage of every day and that's what I've done, 36 hours into every 24 hours."

With an ever-growing family, Margot's daughter-in-law Olivia and sons-in-law Dave and Borris, have now become part of the business. "There were areas suitable for all of the kids that wanted to come into the business to utilize their skills and interests. We say that everyone should be able to either make it or sell it," Margot said.

"You get to spend so much time with them, and families tend to have a level of commitment that most other people don't have, which is good. We all enjoy each other's company, which is a bonus. That's not to say its all perfect where we all agree on things, but it is good working with family and we enjoy it. We can turn things around in a couple of weeks. We can call a family meeting and adapt very quickly."

Transparency

Despite the good working relationship the Spalding family has, the business would not be what it is if not for the level of transparency between the family members. Margot says that it is also important that people outside of the family, too, are given positions of leadership within Jimmy Possum.

Though hiring people in Australia is costly, Jimmy Possum Furniture employs more than 150 people across the country. Margot feels that being able to offer a product to consumers that they cannot get from overseas is more important than keeping costs low.

"Initially when Australian retailers deserted Australian manufacturers and were in favour of cheap China products, the pressure was really on there," Margot said.

"There has been big pressure all of those years, but there is so much product now that it is inexpensive. So if you're going to have a product and offer the level of service and quality that we do, they are going to have to pay for it."

At the same time, Margot stresses the importance of becoming more efficient in order to be competitive. For her, time management and lean manufacturing is an extremely big part of it.

"You have to run your business very lean," Margot said. "We have a just-in-time system where once it's produced, it's out the door. It's all produced for customers or necessary floor stock."

Running their business in this way means that they are able react quickly to demand and change methods swiftly if needed. This is, in large part, helped by Margot's emphasis on being aware of what is current and getting ahead of it.

"Consumer buying changes all the time. You have to constantly be reviewing what sells and what doesn't," she said.

"Having been in the industry for a long time, we have seen some extraordinary

changes. You have to be relying on really good statistics constantly."

Margot cautions against over-research though, saying you run the risk of "Googling your life away" if you're not careful.

Eventually, the company's success led Jimmy Possum into the online world, with an online store which grew at a rate of 700 percent within a week.

"Initially we thought people wouldn't be into purchasing furniture online but that's not the case," Margot said. Margot attributes the success of their online store to trust in the brand, and says that a good online store is made by those who love and understand shopping.

"If you're a shopper, you know what you love about shopping and that's what you try to provide for your customers." She also emphasises being in tune with what works for your business and what doesn't when it comes to online advertising and brand awareness. "You have to trial what works for you. Instagram works well for us, Facebook does and Twitter doesn't," Margot explained.

"It would be really easy to be left behind with social media. It's an enormous part of the business now. If you don't change, there is no question. You'll be left behind." This was not the only lesson Margot learnt when she started Jimmy Possum. She found that it was important to be realistic but passionate, work hard and to value people.

"I think it would be very hard to have a business on your own," she added.

"Having a partner is much better to bounce off opinions. The right partner, anyway."

Lessons from Margot
- Learn from those around you, whether they're older or younger. Everyone has a lesson to teach you if you can figure it out.
- Most learning is from doing: experiment and learn, live, every day."
- Have courage to innovate...be bold, be wrong, to listen, speak out, stand up, show up, be present, take risks and back yourself.

Now that the business has become such a success, Margot hopes to become more hands on in the development of products and that Jimmy Possum will soon be extending their range to smaller products and upholstery. In the next two years, Margot expects that they will open a further four to five shops across the country, and thinks that franchising in certain parts of Australia and overseas might even be on the horizon.

PENNY SPENCER

Owner of Spencer Travel

With her passion for travel and excitement, Penny Spencer has charted the highs and lows of the travel industry for the last 27 years, from unpaid intern to creator of Spencer Travel, with substantial success.

Now a leader in the field she's chosen, she is an inspiring example of how to build a high growth, sustainable business from the bottom.

SPENCER TRAVEL

Founded
1998

Latest Turnover
$50 MILLION

Awards
MANY INCLUDING BEST CORPORATE AGENCY

Inspiration
WANTING TO "DO IT" HER WAY

Working for nothing: working for something

"I can work for nothing." This was the offer Penny Spencer made while seeking industry experience with travel agencies. It seems almost ironic, given her current high position as owner and managing director of Spencer Travel, an award-winning agency, and founder and chair of TIME [Travel Industry Mentor Experience]. However, it was this persevering work ethic, as well as her commitment to maintaining her key values, which saw Penny rise from a 6-month unpaid position to running her own business.

While most people in her shoes may have been disheartened by their situation, Penny began stamping brochures at Adventure World in Brisbane, she took this opportunity to observe and respond to the processes of her work surroundings and was eventually promoted to a paid general helper, what Penny calls 'Girl Friday' and describes as "the girl who does everything." Then she worked her way up.

Working in a predominantly male environment during the 1980s, Penny refused to conform to the status quo positions for women in reception and administration, and became determined to open her own agency once she saw it could be achieved.

"When I was working for men, it was a completely different field. When I saw a woman in business and how she did it, I thought I want to do that."

By age 31, Penny initiated her plans for Spencer Travel, a career move she describes as, "a roller coaster you can't get off." Her genuine love for her work, however, and admirable business values (honesty, communication and fair treatment) saw Spencer Travel evolve into one of Australia's greatest travel agencies which goes "above and beyond" for clients.

"I wanted to do it my way ... Not necessarily do it completely differently but learn from the things I had seen that hadn't worked and things that had."

Adaptation

However, no business is without its challenges and Penny realised a necessary change in her business model was needed in September 2011, when the plane hijackings and subsequent civilian attacks that came to be known as "9/11" devastated people and politics, reverberating through travel businesses all over the world.

"The only time the phone rang was when the people wanted a refund on tickets. I had to re-look at the business to keep it going and that was only domestically. No one was travelling overseas, no one was coming in and there was no outbound/inbound."

Down but not defeated, Penny approached "the corporates" and, after extensive consideration, offered them a better than standard rate for domestic travel. As new businesses were starting to appear online, she continuously competed with lower rates and "created a different model to survive" which could have resulted in mass firings of staff. Penny thought she could do better.

"I put staff on nine day fortnights which they were happy to do ... this wasn't going to be forever and I didn't want to get rid of my really good staff because when it [higher income] came back, I wanted them there."

On the advent of the GFC, Penny also had to combat this dip in business with a daily contingency plan. This consisted of projecting what figures needed to be made to keep the business afloat, as well as planning the next steps to take if things took a turn for the worst. This also involved Penny investing $200k in Spencer Travel.

"... people weren't travelling and they weren't spending money. Instead of five people going business class to London to go to a meeting, they would send one in economy. That was a huge drop in our income."

To sustain morale in that depressed economic climate, Penny constantly exercised the values on which she had built her business.

"I would meet with them [staff] everyday and say, okay this is where we are at today, things aren't great for this week, this is what we are doing about it. If anyone wants to take unpaid leave, this is the time to do it."

While Penny continued to face heavy competition online, she also noticed a key problem many people were having which, proved to be instrumental in keeping Spencer Travel afloat.

"People are getting more time poor ... For example, five years ago, I had one domestic consultant and now I have six because the corporate PA doesn't want to spend his/her time booking Sydney to Melbourne flights for their boss when they could be doing other work-related things ... It's evolved from, Yes! I'll do it myself to Oh! It's too hard, and I think it's only going to get harder. Which is better for us"

Penny also emphasises the professionalism, personal touch and honesty of Spencer Travel as being the factor in making her business a more desirable option for travellers.

"People can go online to find out if the hotel is nice, but we have actually stayed at the hotel. We can tell you the room has a view of the harbor. People want to know firsthand, but the reality is it's better to talk to a person than read something from America."

Above all, however, it is clearly Penny's enthusiasm and passion for her work which has brought Spencer Travel financial security.

"I wanted each traveller to have the best experience she can have … When I was consulting, that's what made me good at it because I wasn't just an order taker. I kept that passion up because I travelled and learned new things and could take that back to my role."

Family and womanhood

When Penny became a mother, she was forced to prioritise her work schedule so that it wouldn't compromise quality time with her new family. Speaking about this quite openly, Penny reveals the "pull" between "the business baby and this baby" and the separation anxiety that all working mothers experience.

Penny also felt her attitude and position shift when she returned from maternity leave and decided to hire a business coach to get back into "the right frame of mind". Her positive experience then inspired her to create the now four-year-old mentorship program TIME which focuses on "that middle level scenario as opposed to entrance." With up to 60 mentees, Penny has felt the rewards of encouraging and advising people who "have been stuck in their career".

When we asked Penny what she believes to be the most important assets of an entrepreneur, she emphasises energy, positivity and innovation.

"You can tell the difference between an entrepreneur and someone who is happy to work hard but not necessarily be a strategist. An entrepreneur has a helicopter view and they are good at that bigger picture."

Lessons from Penny:
- An entrepreneur has a helicopter view. You have to work hard, but also strategically.
- Adapt.
- Be across your industry, and look for things that 'everyone' is doing, which you could do differently.

Penny also reinforces the benefits of having a resilient support and communication network. She is a strong advocate for the CommBank Women in Focus, a community which shares a variety of resources, networks and business intelligence for women to get involved with such as the Australian Businesswomen's Network, Business Chicks and Westpac Ruby.

"I also like EO because it's men and women and you can learn from both, it doesn't just have to be about women. We lead differently to men and that's why we get together, we are more like minded."

When discussing the differences between female and male leaders in business, Penny highlights the noticeable, internal disparities between the two genders, such as a larger guilt complex and lack of self-confidence notable among most women.

"Self confidence [in women] isn't there - especially if we have left the workforce for a while and come back, we have so much pressure on us."

When asked whether she considered these differences as causes for preventing women from pursuing business careers, she is strongly affirmative.

"You have to have an amazing support network around you and you have to have a lot of energy and confidence and a lot of women lack that. My husband is a big support for me … A lot of women don't have that. It's very hard to run a household with two high-powered career people."

From "the girl who does everything", Penny Spencer has achieved great heights from which anyone can aspire to while doggedly combating the overwhelming realities of running her own business and starting a family. To entrepreneurs in any field today, Penny is an inspiration for working hard for your goals, adapting to any situation and upholding the values important to you.

SASHA TITCHKOSKY

Founder of Koskela

KOSKELA

Founded
2000

Employees
19

Inspiration
TO KEEP QUALITY
MANUFACTURING
ALIVE IN AUSTRALIA

"Follow your heart. Trust your judgement. Do it for joy". These simple yet evocative words embody the heartfelt passion and stubborn work ethic shared by the creators of Koskela; Sasha Titchkosky and Russel Koskela. Since the idea of Koskela was born, Sasha Titchkosky has adopted the above sentence as her company motto.

Both Sasha and Russel were from corporate backgrounds when they first met and their shared passion for interior design and local manufacture rapidly inspired them to start their own business and practice what values they believed to be most important. One of the primary values that brought them together was the importance of being environmentally responsible in the creation of products.

FOLLOW YOUR HEART. TRUST YOUR JUDGEMENT. DO IT FOR JOY

Challenges and risks

Their decision to fund their own startup business was a particularly risky move, one which Sasha aptly defends.

"It was important to me that it [Koskela] grew organically and that it needed to be able to fund its own growth."

While this decision kept development slow, Sasha points out that this slow growth strategy significantly increased the stability of her business. Furthermore, owing nothing to funders allowed it to remain a steady a source of revenue.

Very little furniture was being manufactured in Australia and there were certain restrictions on creativity regarding what could be made, due to a scarcity of skilled craftspeople.

"We were recently exhibiting in Milan at the fair over there and you just realise how spoilt you are by the choice in Europe because there's someone to do everything. Whereas for us, we always have to design and suit what can get made here."

But the importance of ethical local sourcing overrode these difficulties:

"We wanted to know and thought it was important that the end customer could feel confident with one of our pieces to know they were made by people who were treated right, who got paid correctly rather than going offshore because there were cheaper wage rates."

This ethical approach has characterised the business, both from a commercial standpoint and as an expression of cultural values.

FOR ME, MY ROLE AS I SEE IT IS TO BE IN A WAY THE CUSTODIAN OF THE CULTURE AND THE VALUES... TO INSPIRE PEOPLE TOWARDS THE LONGER TERM GOALS

In all her years of managing Koskela with her husband, Sasha does not shy away from revealing the 'growing and plateauing' years she experienced.

"I think in the last couple of years the screws have really tightened in terms of costs and there's a lot of people in our industry and the commercial side that are going in just to win projects which I think sets a really bad benchmark...We just had different people that came to us and said: 'I've got this idea, you should do this with me,' and I never felt completely comfortable. They were never the right people, they didn't understand what we were about. The ones that are right, they are really hard to point to."

Success and social change

In the last 14 years, Sasha and Koskela have increased their staff from eight to 19 and expanded their business to collaborate with indigenous communities. With this last development, Titchkosky regards the ongoing design projects with weavers from Elcho Island in Arnhem Land as a move 'to collaborate and effect social change' as well as incorporate traditional weaving techniques to create contemporary design products.

One other ethical priority of Koskela for Sasha was to push for products which the environment could benefit from. According to the Australian Businesswomen's Network, more than 80 percent of Koskela's products are independently certified by GECA as being environmentally innovative and have featured heavily in many of Australia's 5 star green star rated buildings. All Koskela furniture is finished with low Volatile Organic Compound water-based finishes and the company is committed to working with manufacturers and suppliers with sustainable materials and practices. Titchkosky also emphasises the company's take-back policy at the end of a piece's cycle (each piece of furniture is designed to be easily disassembled), so they may strip a returned piece to its components and refurbish it for reuse.

Both Sasha's drive for outside collaboration and focus on the environment defines her as a social entrepreneur; one who uses her business to take the initiative to improve our lifestyle for a better future. In her latest project, she tackled the education circuit by featuring Koskela in a widespread re-design of classrooms to encourage creativity and enable students to be 'more independent and in control of the learning outcomes'. This also an example of Koskela's expanding diversity as a business as well as its ongoing productivity.

In terms of selling to a particular clientele, Sasha confirms that personal choice plays a large role in design but she believes that the gradual expansion of Koskela has zeroed in on a culture (mostly comprised of designers, foodies, artists and homemakers) which is more responsive to their products. For instance, their second gallery in Rosebery (the other is in Surry Hills) also features the modern, vibrant artwork of stylist Megan Morton and her studio as well as the seasonal produce-focused *Kitchen by Mike* cafe which draws on the weekend '5 to 600 people a day.'

"We had the Zimmermann fashion week launch here and we had a big event for Mini. We have thought about a couple of different ideas we could do with the space, like a hub, but somewhere where people can come that has really good facilities".

While the diversity of Koskela seems to be the business's winning card, Sasha claims there are both 'good and bad' aspects to this element, "Sometimes I think it's quite difficult, you feel you're not doing everything perfect. But I think that the speed of what's happening right now is so fast that you won't think you've done something that quickly. For Russell and I, we are always looking at the next idea. It works for us".

Lessons from Sasha
- Collaborate and effect social change.
- Follow your heart, trust your judgement, do it for joy.
- Slow growth can mean a more stable business, more in your control.

In addition to her numerous collaborations, it seems to be the consistently high product quality and sincere message behind Koskela which continues to attract clients. While most other competitors in her market are reselling an imported brand, Sasha reinforced Koskela's image as a mid-priced Australian designed furniture and homewares company that proudly supports local manufacturers.

"For me, my role as I see it is to be in a way the custodian of the culture and the values. To inspire people towards the longer term goals."

For her passion and ethical business priorities alone, Sasha Titchkosky is an inspiring role model for female entrepreneurs interested in pursuing design and social change.

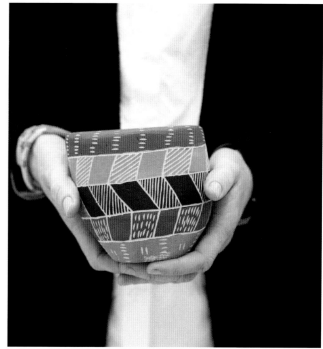

ANNEKE VAN DEN BROEK

Founder of Rufus & Coco

RUFUS & COCO

Founded
2008

Awards
THE ANITA PRABHU
WOMEN LEADERS AWARD -
THE AUSTRALIAN SCHOOL
OF BUSINESS

Inspiration
PASSION FOR ANIMALS

Business coach, mentor and owner of a successful pet care company, Anneke Van den Broek has an impressive history as a senior manager in some of Australia's leading businesses.

Anneke set out to fill a gap in the pet care industry and today, Rufus & Coco is a household name in the pet industry offering original, trusted and inspired products that offers solutions to pet owners and their pets. "Our mantra is to provide 'Best Of Breed Petcare. " Anneke says. While competitors were well entrenched with pet food products, Rufus & Coco innovates in other categories. Rufus & Coco has secured it's range to be sold with supermarket giants Coles and Woolworths. The range is also available in selected IGA stores, pet stores, veterinary clinics and pharmacies and in several worldwide markets.

Starting with love

Anneke Van den Broek had a taste for entrepreneurship from a very young age. "I used to breed mice at about the age of 6," she says. "I would select them according to who had the most beautiful spots and colouring. People used to love them and I'd sell them to the pet shop for 50 cents." It wasn't just mice Anneke loved. "I've had everything from chickens, to rabbits. I've had three dogs...about twenty cats. All my pets were part of the living."

Anneke's history of business management is proof of her ability to learn quickly and to evolve even faster. At the age of 16, Van den Broek began work as fashion show Assistant at David Jones. At 23, she landed the head role as managing producer. Van den Broek moved into other areas of David Jones including event management, PR and advertising before ending in Research and Strategy. It was then that she started her Master of Business Administration (MBA). "It (the degree) gave me the business acumen I needed. I knew, that running my own business one day, I'd need it."

Anneke then moved to natural health brand, Blackmores as marketing manager. After 6 months in FMCG, she was promoted as marketing director. Anneke went and worked as divisional manager for Pacific Brands, where she says she learned, "mostly not what to do in business. I learnt how brands can represent themselves externally and how that cannot match internally...how that ultimately unwinds a brand." She acknowledges that not all forward movement is a good thing, after a brief stint as general manager of Sportscraft.

Anneke left Sportscraft with a number of ideas for starting her own business and called on her community of friends. "I'm fortunate enough to have a group of female friends that are entrepreneurs of just amazing female business people that I've collected over my career. So I got them around a table to come up with brand names. We ended up with the name Rufus and Coco."

Business growth

Since launching, the business has developed an extensive range of products that are sold internationally, and it's continuing to grow. "We have eight, soon to be ten, staff in Australia; we have two, soon to be four in the Philippines," Anneke says. A major turning point came when the business went into Woolworths in 2010. "I met Jennifer Rogers – fourth buyer at Woolworths – in April that year and by October we were secured for national distribution. Every year we grow massively." Two years later in 2012, Rufus & Coco also secured national distribution with Woolworths' rival supermarket giant, Coles.

Anneke believes the success starts with your learning ability. "As an entrepreneur, you have to be able to learn quickly. I think you have to be real about it. Ask yourself, 'Is it not working because of me?' You have to find the source of the problem. Trust your gut instinct. Learning how to trust your gut feel has been a great lesson."

Her early love for animals (those beautiful mice!) became the driving force behind the Australian-owned household pet care brand, Rufus & Coco. Savvy in marketing, Anneke looked for what pet owners were missing out on, avoiding the oversaturated food market to focus on a range of natural toys and pet products.

"The dream at the time was to have a global pet brand that actually stood for having amazing pet stuff," Anneke says. The company originally launched in 2008, with the specific aim of filling in a gap in the pet industry. " I wanted products that were more natural." Van den Broek explains. "Our competitors are well entrenched with food, where we innovate is in other categories. I wanted it

to be fashionable and affordable and that's the gap that we fill in the marketplace."

"I wanted a name that was emotive, that said, 'cat and dog,' not 'children's clothing.' She says it was also important to be, "a brand that is set across all channels and spoke to all people," and knowing that people treat animals like humans and want to engage with their products.

Marketing and strategy

The marketing strategy of Rufus & Coco's products has definitely been key.

"We design the packaging, so it doesn't have a photo of the species," she says. "If you don't own that species the product won't talk to you in the same way." Van den Broek adds that social media has been a particularly strong point of focus for marketing Rufus & Coco. "We pack a punch on social media. Part of what's made us successful is that we're innovators and nimble in a category that's more complicated. We just launched a new website, which enables people to upload photos of themselves with their pets and our products. We also have pet of the month and we find that very successful."

When it comes to being the leader of Rufus & Coco, Anneke believes that being realistic with your team is essential. "Being real is important and with every leader you need to maintain a level of positivity. Things aren't always great, but you have to keep yourself up and it can't just be appearances. People sense when you're not up."

The cohesiveness of her team has seen her personally involved with every hire for Rufus & Coco. "We don't use headhunters," she explains. "I think it's the most important thing you can do; these are the people that represent you. It's going that extra mile in leadership. "

Lessons from Anneke:
- Learn quickly. Be real about the problem – is it you? Don't look for excuses, look for the probem!
- You have to keep yourself up and it can't just be appearances. People sense when you're not up.
- Don't give up. Be persistent, be resilient.

Entrepreneurship and womanhood

"My definition of an entrepreneur? Someone who creates something. It may not be business, but we use it in that context. Entrepreneurs share passion, creativity, determination and resilience. I honestly think that risk-taking is also a huge characteristic."

On women and women in business, Van den Broek says, "The last time I looked, there were more females starting out businesses than men. They're obviously starting…why are they stopping? Why doesn't it succeed for them? What is it that we can do to help them keep going? You may have the confidence but the people around you may be dragging you down. It's not just the person's environment, it's their own critical voice that's stopping them."

Her inspiration to believe in her own ability comes from her father. "He would say, 'Anneke, today you will swim to the end of the pool and back – but before you go, you tell yourself three times, 'You can do anything you want if you try.' That lesson stuck with me." She says when it comes to establishing the business it has been one of her greatest learnings. "But also to not give up; to be persistent, be resilient, they're the greatest skills you can have."

ANGELA VITHOULKAS

CEO of VIVO Cafe

If anyone knows how to turn a business from ruin to reward, it's Angela Vithoulkas. A big business mentality in a small business environment, she's well acquainted with running lean, highly efficient businesses that see obstacles as speed bumps, not a stop sign.

Known to some for challenging Sydney Lord Mayor, Clover Moore's throne in 2012, Angela is determined to not stand by and watch Sydney city deteriorate beneath a mountain of red tape and small business crushing policies. Now owner of Vivo Cafe, Eagle Waves Radio and a Sydney City Councillor, Angela is a figurehead for the development of small business.

VIVO CAFE

Founded
2007

Awards
SEVERAL INCLUDING CITY OF SYDNEY BUSINESS OF THE YEAR

Inspiration
TURNING HER SKILL OF BEING A NATURAL COMMUNICATOR INTO A BUSINESS

AS AN ISOLATED SMALL BUSINESS OWNER AT A VERY YOUNG AGE, THERE WEREN'T NETWORKS AND MENTORS, IT WAS ALL TRIAL AND ERROR ON YOUR OWN

A migrant to serial business owner

Angela has always been and always will be the daughter of migrant parents, something that has influenced her business choices, lifestyle choices, family and friends. Of Greek heritage, whenever Angela feels she is hitting a wall, she recalls her mother, a young girl who came to an unfamiliar country at the age of 15 with no family and no friends, no language skills, and within five years had her own business. A girl that managed to get herself one of the first Commonwealth bank loans without a male co-signer.

"I feel I had all the advantages of the war my mother fought without any of those hardships, but I found the restrictions of my culture very influential in the rest of my life, I still do, it influences my ethics in business and the way we develop our staff - it's a part of our culture."

She is the daughter of great parents, a girl that at nine years old had to learn to understand and read a lease in the solicitors office because someone had to interpret for her parents.

"I somehow had to have the capacity to understand what the solicitor was saying

in one language and then translate that to two other people who didn't have any business or language skills. Still, they didn't let any of that stop them."

Angela caught her first shop lifter when she was three. That's the way it's always been, thinking bigger and beyond herself, she recalls.

"If there was anyone else predestined to do something, it's me. It was never going to be anything else. The hunger is always there to try and change things on a bigger scale. If I see something I want to do I'll do it."

Big business brain in a small business environment

A big business brain in a small business, Angela's forté is buying businesses that are facing ruin and re-building them, or starting businesses from scratch. Re-evaluating, re-structuring and re-organising are some of her key skills. This means she's constantly in startup mode, which she says is hard but incredibly rewarding. To date she has owned and sold almost 30 businesses and now focuses solely on Vivo Cafe and Eagle Waves Radio.

Her tight rein on her bustling cafe on Sydney CBD's busy George Street, allows her to flex her entrepreneurial strengths in the construct of a smaller enterprise. A tracking platform that analyses and forecasts their customers desired appetites, allows Angela to predict the business will sell ten times more vegemite toast than any other toast and that 70 percent of Vivo's coffee sales come from flat whites, along with other consumer patterns. Her confidence as a business owner was confirmed when she won her first award, the 2005 City Of Sydney Café of the Year Award.

YOU SINK OR SWIM FROM YOUR DISASTERS AND THEN YOU EITHER KEEP REPEATING THEM OR LEARN FROM IT

This love for data and ability to track buying power may be quite everyday for big business, but when adopted by a small business it's something quite revolutionary. "We don't let our size stand in our way but we do invest a lot in it, which is what would hold back a lot of other small businesses," says the small business queen.

Angela's out of the box thinking led her to question why other small businesses weren't implementing new methods in order to get to a higher level of operation .

"Why aren't businesses much more proactive about issues that are going on around them? The bigger the environment you are in the less you know about what your neighbors are doing. The less you know about what the business across the road is...we are not a community and I'd like to change that."

Eagle Waves Radio was born from this, a place where Angela has once again taken a small business mentality into an area where small business have not yet ventured down. She affirms she's tackling big business media and has been self funding the digital station for the last three years.

"I have no technical background in radio, no experience in audio but I love the way it sounds, I love the way it connects with people on a very intimate level. I can't own a TV station and I can't own a commercial radio station but I can build my own digital radio station and the playing field is very level in this world. It doesn't matter which brand is behind it, it's an opportunity where I have the advantage by not being a big business. Not being a commercial radio station, I have an advantage because we can run lean. Small business knows how to run lean. We also know about punching above our weight and the kind of power you can produce."

The station attracts 6,000 live listeners a month with a couple of thousand downloads on their podcasts. Angela would like to see the station grow and become so successful that it spins off into other media platforms. But, ultimately she would like to see it handed back to the community, which she believes is part of her purpose.

Believe in your own experience

Making decisions for Angela comes through relying on her belief in her own experience. "At the end of the day we all stand the same chance of being wrong. It's the experience of your life that has the best odds in making the most appropriate decisions, that can equal success but mitigating a disaster is sometimes all you can hope for."

While she has always viewed the self employed lifestyle as the fastest way to make money, Angela says small business is a lot more difficult for the emerging generations.

An education system, mentors and clearer guidance are things Angela believes would

have taught her to think differently. "As an isolated small business owner at a very young age, there weren't networks and mentors, it was all trial and error on your own. You sank or swam from your disasters and then you either kept repeating them or learnt from it."

A result of what she's learnt along the way, Angela wants to create real change for small business in the city of Sydney, a space she sees as having huge uncapped potential with realistic outcome.

"The online world and people that can develop a business that doesn't require fixed space, has changed the playing field where everyone can be a small business owner. We have gone from being insignificant, to significant, to running the mill."

From migrant to serial small business owner, big believer and big thinker, Angela knows small businesses work, for both the community and economy, but it's something to be embraced by individuals first.

"I draw attention to the fact that I am self employed and I will finish my business life being self employed. If you have a small business that employs you, you are successful. You have achieved what you had hoped even if you didn't verbalise it."

CATRIONA WALLACE

Founder of Flamingo & Fifth Quadrant

FLAMINGO & FIFTH QUADRANT

Founded
2014
2005

Awards
MANY INCLUDING 2014
AUSTRALIAN BUSINESS
WOMEN'S HALL OF FAME

Inspiration
TO AFFECT SOCIAL CHANGE
THROUGH COMMERCIAL

To look at Catriona Wallace, with all her glamorous eccentricity and caustic wit, you never would have known that all she ever wanted to be was a farmer.

Operating in Australia and the U.S, IT software startup Flamingo focuses on enabling businesses to personalise experiences for individual customers. Flamingo helps enterprise win and retain customers through providing digital customer experience tools, co-creation labs and analytics. The company is one of the first significant vendor relationship management (VRM) platforms globally.

No limitations

A child of four with a father who was an entrepreneur, Catriona did not grow up with boundaries around gender roles. "There was no difference in the expectation of what the boys would do as to the girls. We were both brought up with the same level of education and if we wanted to do a business on our own, we could very much do that," she remembers.

While she might have been a self-confessed rebel, a fiery red head constantly trying to disable typical conventions as a young girl, Catriona also recalls growing up with an instilled sense of gratitude.

"I was very much brought up with the view that we are very lucky to be middle class, that it is a position of great privilege and that position holds great responsibility. That responsibility is to build resources and effectively give them away. All of my siblings were also brought up with that mindset - so it wasn't to be an entrepreneur and enormously wealthy or commercial success, it's for a stronger purpose."

Take a 'sista' wherever you go

Though the word entrepreneur may have turned highly mainstream, according to Catriona, it is the year of the female entrepreneur in Australia. A strong advocate for this space, she believes we're beginning to see a breakdown in the traditional masculine hierarchy leading to the rise of the feminine archetype in business. From a commercial point of view, the things women are naturally good at are more highly valued.

Because of this, Catriona sees it as the perfect time for females to start businesses. Away from the conventional social discussions around equal opportunity and women on boards, she sees structural global shifts occurring and feels that if we, as women, can all invest in this shift then it will happen far quicker than we think.

"The tide is already turning, don't compete with each other, take a sister wherever you go and the more of us that succeed, the bigger the swell is going to be. Now is the time. For us leaders, it's important to make sure it's a smooth not rocky path for these upcoming women."

Catriona believes the insurgence of automation and artificial intelligence will actually reinvigorate the need for these skills.

"The logic is that machines and computer learning can take away a lot of the traditional things that were masculine orientated around tasks, results focus, planning, rostering, executing...a lot of that can be automated now. What can't be automated and what was typically a feminine archetype: social networks, collaboration, reduction of hierarchies, rise of empathy, customer, development of distributed leadership. All of these things come naturally to women so we are seeing organisations having to build these into their company."

On her own journey as a female entrepreneur, originally, Catriona was not interested in business, but it has been her diverse career choices that seem to have set her up with this unique entrepreneurial acumen that makes her who she is today. "25 years ago it wasn't common for men let alone women to become entrepreneurs and I knew I didn't want to go into a corporate environment. I did what I thought was interesting and became a cop and worked as a detective in Kings Cross and went on to become a prosecutor training people in that branch."

It was a great lesson for her, which she believes is responsible for her now unshakeable confidence.

"I had to survive because the system would eat you up and destroy you if you didn't. I was dealing with murderers, drug addicts, prostitutes, felons of all types, dealing with a corrupt system, the public doesn't like you, criminals don't like you and most of the cops are crooked. I did that for four years and at the end of that I was like that's enough, I don't need to rebel against what I'm destined for anymore."

I AM VERY CONFIDENT TO TALK ABOUT MY SUCCESSES. I CAN CONFIDENTLY SAY WHO I AM, THIS IS WHAT I HAVE DONE, THIS IS WHY I AM THE BEST IN THE WORLD AT WHAT I DO, AND I ABSOLUTELY BELIEVE IT AND I CAN MAKE OTHER PEOPLE BELIEVE IT

Finishing a degree in Economics and English literature spiralled into graduate recruitment at a management consultancy. But she became dissatisfied realising they were charging her out at $1000 while she was on a salary of $25,000.

"I set up my own business when I was in my early 20s. I was the only person I knew who had done that. My father, who is probably the only mentor I have ever had, was watching over me so I was able too. It was just okay to try and okay to fail."

Catriona started a management consulting practice, walked into Prudential Insurance, sold herself at $800 a day and was astounded at the ease of it all. "I made a fortune and that's when I started to do philanthropic stuff, I really gave it all away and essentially continued on that path of building my own practice."

At 27 Catriona unexpectedly fell pregnant and was a single mum for five years.

"I have deep empathy for women who are trying to run a business and have little kids, it was a really hard time because most of my mates were out partying and traveling and I was trying to look after this baby on my own."

Out of adversity often comes triumph, Catriona indicates just how important her support group is when faced with obstacles.

"Of all the women entrepreneurs I know, it's not really the business stuff that's difficult, it's the 'my partner,' 'my family,' 'my kids,' this is the really hard stuff. There's a spotlight on us and we don't want to look like we are failing. We don't want to look like we

haven't balanced it out and there needs to be a lot more conversation around that."

Lessons from Catriona:
- Take advantage of market place trends.
- Don't be afraid of what you don't know, it's an opportunity.
- Be proud of and own your successes.

Entering new markets takes guts

A keynote speaker, Catriona frequently shares her thoughts on resilience.

"Being an entrepreneur is about being knocked down and getting back up, and sometimes by people closest to you. I thought nothing was harder than surviving as a single mum in your twenties, so bring me any business problem because I will deal with it."

Perhaps the most exciting thing to date is Catriona's transition into the startup world with Flamingo. A new generation platform under vendor relationship management, it focuses on empowering customers to have tools to better manage their vendors rather than the other way around.

"It's like a co-creation laboratory; on one side customers come into the lab and on the other side is employees from another organisation. It allows customers to express what it is they want, what product, the channels they use, who they are as a person, the way they communicate, the price they want to pay, but that is all within the parameters of what a business can deliver to an employing customer to co-create a whole experience that a customer wants. The system then puts that back into contact centre and delivery so next time that customer makes contact with an organisation their experience will be changed and delivered to them."

Catriona closed a $2.1 million funding round from a number of angel investors in late 2014, which will see Flamingo launch the startup into the United States in 2015, to be followed by a proposed Series A funding round open to US investors in the mid-year.

Truly solving a problem, Flamingo is the first of its kind in the world and as a result, the company has attracted a huge amount of interest from both the media and industry.

"From 150 startups, Flamingo was voted number 2 interesting startup to watch. It was chosen into the Springboard of women entrepreneurs, and we have attracted a partnership with Oracle, alongside some really high profile investors as well."

Most telling of Catriona's strengths as an entrepreneur has been her ability to navigate the startup up world, in particular Silicon Valley. She is not too proud to acknowledge that this is all new to her, but rests in the confidence that she can always learn from others.

"I am very confident to talk about my successes. I can confidently say who I am, this is what I have done, this is why I am the best in the world at what I do, and I absolutely believe it and I can make other people believe it. I have grown up having to deal with senior executives who want to give me a run for my money so I have had to master it and know confidentially how to present myself."

Catriona is nothing short of accomplished, she has a PhD from the graduate school of management, has written a book, owned a night club, taught on the MBA program and paid her way through university. She is now married to Mark whom she had to children with, Indigo and Saxon to add to a family of five kids, Hunter her first and Mark's children, Jake and Dan.

LEONA WATSON

———

Founder of Cheeky Food Group

CHEEKY FOOD GROUP

———

Founded
2002

———

Inspiration
PASSION TO CREATE A FUN
AND INTERACTIVE 'SPACE'
FOR TEAM BUILDING AND
CLIENT ENTERTAINING
THROUGH COOKING.

Making people smile is Leona's currency. She has a brilliant way of using food to cultivate an environment of togetherness. Schooled in Mount Isa, Queensland, a town which appeared of limited opportunities to Leona Watson, she needed tenacity and ambition to become the successful woman she is today.

Leona Watson is the managing director of Cheeky Food Group, founded in 2001, following her passion for cooking, marketing and business. Cheeky provides team building, conference and client entertaining activities across Australia and New Zealand. Throwing several hundred cooking parties every year, involving groups of 7 to 700 colleagues all cooking at the same time.

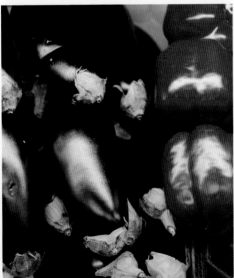

The Cheeky journey

Leona worked at Optus for 18 months, but came up against an internal restructuring, which threatened to change her employee status, and not for the better. Leona says, "I said: well I saved you millions and made you millions in other areas so I said I'm going to think about it for a few days. I went and had the weekend and came back and resigned. I said, 'I am going to do my Le Cordon Bleu training', I thought, I have worked my ass off, earned good money and I did really good work and I thought I am going to do something that's for me."

The 10 months of grueling training prepared Leona for the practical challenge of creating Cheeky, her first real business venture. In the fledgling stages of the new business, Leona also worked doing part-time marketing consultancy for two to three years, for both large and small corporations, including Microsoft in the UK, Optus, CBA, QANTAS, Virgin Mobile and MBF, until the Cheeky Food Group could stand on its own. Leona thought that her passion was for food, but during the Le Cordon Bleu training, she realised it wasn't about the food but the togetherness of people that food brought. "So with the food thing what I realised really quickly, back when I was in my 30s doing the Le

IT'S ABOUT CREATING THE SPACE FOR PEOPLE TO FEEL TOGETHER... I THINK THAT IS WHY I DO WHAT I DO

Cordon Bleu training I had a few people pick me up in a restaurant and when I realised it wasn't the food and the preparation that gave me the joy, it was that they'd have big long boozy lunches and all end up in the kitchen with me. Half the food would come out very different to how I planned it in my head but it didn't matter because I could see them all having fun with it. That's what I was doing years before I started Cheeky and to me it's all about how food brings people together." Now Cheeky is an interactive event company which does cooking parties for numbers up to and exceeding 700 people, bringing people together in very real ways.

"I stand on stage sometimes and I might have 350 CEO-level men who are the most interesting characters on the planet. I'll get the best of the best of everything then there they are, all laughing their heads off, and all I've done is create a space for them to be the best of the best people they are outside of business. All of a sudden they are looking at each other differently. They might get a little medal they win for being the winning team, and they are getting around like five year olds; they wear them out afterwards. They wear them in bars, these 50 year old men who are running million dollar companies," Leona says.

Leona also took on the demanding role of event managing for the company. "We do 600-700 people or eight to ten people. Senior Executives, some of them are a bit wild, out of control, then some are quieter more controlled. At the heart of it, food is my passion and it's interesting how the product has developed if I look at my old business partner. He came at it from a totally different view-point. The focus was very much on the food and not the chef. That's not what I wanted. It's not a cooking class. They can go to a cooking class and pay a lot less money. I am going to give them something they will remember - not just the food but an experience of being together and who they did it with. I am going to give them that space. That's my thing."

Leona's motivation, challenges and the woman question

At one early point, Leona was having mixed thoughts about her new venture and its daunting logistical challenges. She had dinner with a friend and mentor and reminded herself of her first food memory. She remembers how that conversation affirmed her in why she's doing Cheeky.

"... I was in a restaurant and I just cried. It was when we were kids, we'd all get together on a Sunday morning, pitch in five to ten cents and go grab a bag of flour, lemon and sugar and we would just hang around making pancakes. It wasn't just pancakes it was creating the togetherness that everyone belonged. It doesn't matter whether it's a pancake or a ten course Thai banquet. It's about creating the space for people to feel together... I think that is why I do what I do," Leona recounts.

Leona said that she's never thought of herself as a female doing a job, or felt that her femaleness has held her back in business.

"I'll be honest about one thing: I don't rate myself as male or female. I was raised in a male dominated area, Mount Isa where the ratio was three to one and you had to be able to hold your own against men. I have one brother and my father died when I was quite young so I didn't have that influence. When I went into advertising agencies they were very male heavy back then, very male heavy. I just never, I've never seen myself as a woman doing a job, I've just seen myself being a person

doing the job. Do I hide from being a woman? No. Even when I worked for Microsoft it was another very male dominated company, I just never thought there was any difference. That was my view, even two years ago I went to a conference they had a group that was just for women only it was all about going through the glass ceiling and there were women there who were 10 years older than me and some younger, the older women were dominating and I put my hand up and said do any of you even know what the glass ceiling is?".

Failures and turning points

Leona said that during the Global Financial Crisis, the phones stopped ringing. This meant no business and a low point where Leona felt a dizzying fear and lack of confidence.

"We're something you'd hire when you're staff are a bit iffy and you want to get them revved up. You are not what you hire when you are laying off staff. You can't be seen to be spending money like that and literally the phones just stopped. I went into a state of "I'm a failure." I was just a mess. I had never considered myself as a failure at anything until then. I looked in the bank and there was nothing there. I thought, oh my God, am I going to have to lay people off?" Leona recaps.

Fortuitously, a friend from her support network offered for her to travel interstate for a business seminar, assuring Leona she might get something out of it. Little did Leona know that that was exactly what she need to pick herself back up. For Leona the

"further you withdraw, that's your natural instinct but at some point you need to get out there and look. You're not going to all of a sudden get a big order out of the blue, you need to make that happen," Leona says.

"One of the things they were talking about when they looked at top entrepreneurs around the world was that these people like Murdoch, Branson, Bill Gates...they all have the same stuff happen. If they make a bad decision for the business, they are publicly humiliated. They have all that same life stuff that happens to you and I and they hurt just as hard but they have the ability to get up so much quicker. That was the turning point for me, something just twigged: I'm just one of a billion companies around the world who are going through this same thing," Leona recounts.

Evidently the ones that survive events such as the Global Financial Crisis are the ones that get back up and rethink a new way to approach it. Leona had thoughtfully protected everyone in her office from the outside climate as she didn't want to lose her hard-working, valued staff. Her strategy was to be open and honest.

"I came back and sat down with them and said we are in deep trouble, I'm scared about losing all of you guys, I'm scared about losing the company. I said not a lot of leave is going to come in but what can we do to make this company survive? They would even turn off the freezer to ensure we weren't using too much power. Like awesome, awesome stuff, figuring out how we could offer cheaper products. We had to react to the world," says Leona.

Mentoring and change

"Having done a lot of mentoring, I've seen a lot of people make bad business decisions because they were worried about cash flow. If you're not worried about that, you can make a lot stronger decisions, because you're not caught up in the stress. You don't enjoy the process of growing your business either if you're constantly stressing. If you're not enjoying your business growth in the first two years you're going to be seriously struggling in years three, four and five."

Leona points out that for successful entrepreneurship, you need a balance of risk and routine. Many entrepreneurial types have a million ideas and want to execute them at once, which is why the going consensus is that if you've owned a company for 15 years you either get a partner, sell, merge or evolve. Through this, greater successes come about. Leona discusses change as a key element of why she has achieved success.

"Change doesn't faze me. 90 percent of the population needs a baseline. They need no change, roof over their head, knowing what their income is... some people can take away that security factor. It's about recognising what you need for yourself. That's me. I'd say most entrepreneurs are like that. It's working out your own risk level. You either need to be a leader in your own organisation or you can be a leader in another organisation. If there is something inside of you in another organization that goes, 'no you can't do it', that's when you start to

think about running your own show and doing part time work to support you developing that."

Although in many ways, success can be defined by some by income and profitability, for Leona it's defined by "the number of smiles created. If I am smiling, if my clients are smiling, my friends, my staff, a lot of good can come from that. If other people are smiling with you that will make you feel better."

Lessons from Leona:
- Work out exactly what you want: Owning a business isn't for everyone and people shouldn't feel any less about themselves if they're not an entrepreneur. It's important to hone in on skills that you already possess and channel them into something that will be of benefit to the world. The trick is figuring out how you are going to do that.

- The experience of running a company can be very stressful but incredibly joyful. It's worth fighting for. If you have a message, if it's going to create good in the world, you've got to get it out there. There's plenty of people out there ready to spend money. Your idea might be great,and sometimes people just need a little nudge to give it a go.

- Your first year will be the best and worst: The first year, that's when you have no staff, no rules, no departments - that should be the fun time. My recommendation is if you can manage it, see if you can find something that brings you in part time work. Don't expect to get holidays

within the first two years of starting a company; you have to say goodbye to a car and all those kinds of things.

- Cash flow is important, know funding sources: When you rely on someone else to support you then that support disappears, you're in a vulnerable position. Keep a part time income coming in.

- Just see it through for a little bit. That's what I do in times of stress and hardship. I say to myself 'this too shall pass', hang onto feeling. The natural progression of things is that you can't stay down there, you can't, you have to come up.

Leona also says that "you're able to make better decisions on things. If everyone's smiling you have a general feeling that the world's okay. Now whether for some people and if they can only smile because they are in a fabulous expensive boat or if they are smiling because they're out camping, it doesn't matter and I can't judge people, but if they're feeling that and seeing that around them,that's success."

INSPIRING RARE BIRDS SHOWCASES THE OUTSTANDING ENTREPRENEURIAL WOMEN WE HAVE IN AUSTRALIA. IT PROVIDES ROLE MODELS AND INSPIRATIONAL STORIES FOR YOUNG GIRLS TO ASPIRE TO. PUTTING THIS BOOK IN THE HANDS OF YOUNG WOMEN AND GIRLS WILL PROVIDE BOTH INSPIRATION AND THE PATHS TO FOLLOW. LEADING THEM TO SAY - IF SHE CAN, I CAN.

Sally-Ann Williams
Engineering Community & Outreach Manager, Google Australia

GLOSSARY

—

ACN (Australian Company Number) – Under the Australian Corporations Act, each registered company is issued with a nine-digit identification number. This number is used to identify the company on formal documents. It is sometimes replaced by the similar ABN - Australian Business Number - which is used when dealing with the Australian Taxation Office.

assets – Business assets are property owned by a business and are typically used to run the business. For example: assets might include cash at the bank, vehicles, land, or plant equipment such as workspaces or factories. Successful entrepreneurs look after their business assets as though they were their own.

brand – A brand is the way businesses identify their products, services, or the organisation itself. The better brands are distinct, easily identifiable, and provide a strong personality and bond of trust between the business and the consumer.

bricks & mortar – Bricks and mortar businesses have a physical presence, offering a face-to-face experience for their customers. These physical experiences are in contrast with internet, or e-commerce transactions and businesses.

Many entrepreneurs now operate both internet and bricks and mortar businesses. (Refer also to e-commerce.)

business – Entrepreneurial activity is driven by people – by business owners who are known as entrepreneurs (if they own the business in question) or entrepreneurial managers (if they are undertaking entrepreneurial activity and employed within a business).

This entrepreneurial activity utilises many vehicles, and many of these are known as businesses. These businesses can be unincorporated and unregistered ventures, or formal organisations (such as companies, partnerships and trusts). They are recognised in many stages of business life (whether startup, early-stage or mature ventures).

Remember – all entrepreneurs run businesses, but not all businesses are entrepreneurial. Similarly, all social entrepreneurs run social enterprises, but not all social enterprises are socially entrepreneurial.

capabilities – see resources

cash cycle – see working capital

cash flow – Cash flow is the movement of money in to and out of a business or project. It is usually measured over a specified period of time such as month or year.

Being profitable does not necessarily mean having cash (refer working capital). Entrepreneurs must focus carefully on their cash flow, as it is cash not paper profits that pay wages and other expenses.

CEO – A Chief Executive Officer (CEO) is typically the most senior manager or administrator of a business. This does not mean they have no boss - they typically report to a Board of Directors of a company, or other group of people if there is a different legal structure.

chain of supply – see supply chain

costs – Money that leaves the business as costs (also known as expenses) is the expenditure incurred to create and sell products. For example, businesses need to pay for staff, ingredients, electricity, or printing. Some of these costs will grow sharply when production increases, others will remain much the same. These can be categorised as variable or fixed costs:

- Fixed costs are those cost that are constant, such as those paid every month regardless of the business activity and revenues. For example, for most businesses this includes the rent, salaries of permanent staff and registration costs.

- Variable costs are those that change with revenues. For example, if during summer an entrepreneur sells more, and as a result she has to employ 2 more people, or pay more for petrol, these extra costs are variable costs.

creativity – All innovation begins with creative ideas. 'Creativity' is the ability to produce work that is both novel (i.e. original or unexpected) and appropriate (i.e. useful, valuable or meeting the task constraints) with no clear or identifiable path to solution. That creativity could appear an artwork, invention, or discovery.

Creativity is rare, and requires the simultaneous presence of a number of traits such as intelligence, perseverance, unconventionality, and the ability to think in differently. The output of that creativity can be protected by patent, copyright, trademark, designs, or plant breeders' rights.

(See also Intellectual Property).

distribution – For an entrepreneur, distribution is the process of making a product or service available for use or purchase. Entrepreneurs may distribute and sell their products directly to their customers, or indirectly through other businesses such as retailers or salespeople.

e-commerce platform – E-Commerce refers to businesses that trade in products or services using the internet rather than physical shops or face-to-face sales.

entrepreneur – There are many definitions of an entrepreneur. For example, one of the earliest was given by the Frenchman Cantillon in the year 1730, who considered entrepreneurs to be people who are the bearers of uncertainty: buying at certain prices in the present and selling at uncertain prices in the future.

The number of definitions of entrepreneur continues to grow.

Essentially, entrepreneurs reach different markets, sell different things, and/or do things differently. They seek to generate value, whether that is economic, social or cultural, by undertaking business and economic activity.

Entrepreneurial businesses are significant as they do not typically 'replicate' other businesses or 'share the pie.' On the contrary, entrepreneurial businesses 'create a bigger pie.' It is this 'difference' that has been shown to create enormous value for the entrepreneur, their business, and the communities surrounding the business.

entrepreneurial activity – Essentially, entrepreneurial activity is that which aims to generate value and change by identifying and exploiting new products, processes or markets. Measures of success for entrepreneurs can include financial, social or cultural outcomes (for example, a social entrepreneur might be running their business in order to generate employment for people with disabilities) but no matter what the motivation and mix of outcomes achieved, all entrepreneurial businesses must be financially sustainable and operate as businesses.

environment – External conditions can have major impacts on a business: For example, if the economic cycle is booming business conditions will be very different to those encountered in a recession or depression. Similarly, if commodity prices are rising – industry performance will be very different from when prices are falling and businesses are competing ruthlessly on price. Many entrepreneurs use the following framework to ensure they thoroughly explore the external environment, asking:

- Political factors - for example, are government officials and political parties supporting small and medium enterprises in the country or province?

- Economic factors - for example, is disposable income increasing? Is the exchange rate assisting or hindering industry growth? Is there stability in salaries and workforces?

- Socio-cultural factors - for example, what are education levels? How accepting are people of changes in technology? Are people happy to spend money on luxuries?

- Technological factors - for example, how pervasive are mobile phones? How is the Internet utilised by businesses? Do people have good access to information?

- Legal factors - for example, how stable or transparent is contract law? Are business activities regulated and controlled?

- Natural factors - for example, what seasonal factors impact an industry? How are changes in the local environment impacting the industry? Does the wet-season impact sales?

- Entrepreneurs think of these aspects on a large scale, that is – these phenomena are impacting on a large scale (i.e. all businesses in an industry), and over the long term (this might be over 5-10 years).

forecasts – Entrepreneurs seek to make accurate forecasts to manage and avoid uncertainty, risk and loss – They forecast revenues and costs to ensure that their business is profitable, but also to ensure there is sufficient cash to pay bills such as salaries and utilities as they fall due.

Making good forecasts helps entrepreneurs understand the profitability of their business, track their performance against benchmarks, and identify potential risks before they are major problems.

Entrepreneurs often create their forecasts in the same format as their daily reporting, allowing them to check performance regularly

GFC (global financial crisis) – The financial crisis, which commenced in 2007, was also known as the Global Financial Crisis (even though it mainly impacted the economies of North America and Europe). It has been considered by many economists to have been the worst crisis since the Great Depression in the 1930s. It negatively impacted many entrepreneurs' businesses, with many customers forever changing their purchasing behaviours.

industry – To define an industry, entrepreneurs often border it by geography, and look from the user's perspective. Common industries include agricultural grains, food services, education, garden supplies etc. Sometimes an industry is unique to a country, or to a province. Quite often buyers are unable to cross physical boundaries such as rivers as much as unable to cross national boundaries.

An entrepreneur's 'choice' of industry can have major implications for their business strategy. For example, if they define it too broadly (e.g. I am in the food industry) they might distract themselves worrying about too many competitors (for example, anyone selling food in supermarkets, restaurants, commodity markets etc. will be their concern). If an entrepreneur defines it too narrowly (e.g. I am in premium restaurant industry) they may ignore some of their industry (e.g. home food delivery, self-serve buffet etc.).

Intellectual Property (IP) – Intellectual property is a legal term that refers to creations of our imagination and minds, and are recognised as property. Typical intellectual property includes discoveries or inventions, artistic works such as music or writing, and designs and symbols. There are laws that protect the rights of the owners of that intellectual property, with many entrepreneurs..

innovation – To innovate is to make changes in something established, or introduce something new (especially by introducing new methods, ideas, or products). One way of considering innovation is bringing creativity to an audience.

To innovate does not automatically mean that an entrepreneur will capture the value associated with that change. Entrepreneurs must take care to control and capture (or share) the value associated with that change.

institutional investors – Business assets are property owned by a business and are typically used to run the business. For example: assets might include cash at the bank, vehicles, land, or plant equipment such as workspaces or factories. Successful entrepreneurs look after their business assets as though they were their own.

investment banking – Investment banks do not accept deposits from customers, but rather assist organisations raise financial capital, merge with or acquire another business, or provide other services such as trading currencies and commodities. The corporate advisory services provided to entrepreneurs are often essential to support the growth and health of businesses.

leadership – The entrepreneur must be a leader. Leadership is focussed on people:

on doing the right things, and creating multiple helping relationships. To lead, the entrepreneur's task is to build the right team around them, draw on the right minds, and create shared purpose. To do this entrepreneurs devote time and resources to allow relationships to be built.

Entrepreneurs ensure that each person in their team is aware of their role and responsibility in the group, as well as the 'softer' and less visible aspects of leadership. They:

- Lead the economics of production (creating a profitable organisation)

- Take responsibility for the legals (and operate within the letter and intention of the law) of the organisation

- Take moral responsibility (to meet the moral and ethical expectations concerning the environment and society), and

- Set the example (stating the 'mindset' of personal ethical behaviours expected of the organisation).

liabilities – Liabilities are the things that a business owes to others. Sometimes it is good for a business to have liabilities, as the business can grow faster, as long as those liabilities are used to grow revenue (for example, buying a bicycle on credit so that home deliveries can be made).

But an entrepreneur must always be sure that they can pay back these debts when they are due.

loss – Entrepreneurs also potentially lose – as we all occasionally suffer loss. Entrepreneurs must minimise these losses to ensure they are not devastating but educating. Before a business 'does' something on a large scale, or to a level that would impact the health of the business – the entrepreneurial leader should tests or pilots the action and learns before any large losses are suffered.

mass customisation – Entrepreneurs are often chasing a holy grail of marketing - mass customisation. This allows customers to design or feel as though they have bought a unique and differentiated product, customised to their wants… and at the same time allow the manufacturer or provider to benefit from low unit costs from mass production.

Through modular design and computer input, some entrepreneurs are able to bring together these unlikely opposites.

mentors – Mentors are experienced people that take a personal interest and role in the career and development of another less experienced or developed person (the apprentice, protégée or mentee). Many long term relationships are formed between more and less experienced entrepreneurs.

opportunity – Opportunities for entrepreneurs are essential, as they can bring new revenues and grow profits. Sometimes an entrepreneur can be alert to opportunities (the customer finds the entrepreneur). Sometimes the entrepreneur must be more active in finding opportunities (the entrepreneur must find the customers). This requires understanding of resources and capabilities, but also of possibilities and opportunities.

Entrepreneurs are often challenged by the question of whether there is a gap in the market, or no market in the gap...

patents – see intellectual property

philanthropy – Philanthropy is different to social entrepreneurship or social enterprise. It is similar to charity, in which philanthropic donations attempt to solve the root causes of a social problem (charity is said to be more focussed on relieving the pain of the social problem).

positioning – (see also about market segments and market targets)

Entrepreneurs produce a product or service that their target market would like to buy. How they position that business or product in the market is critical. For example, entrepreneurs could position themselves as the best quality provider (perhaps they have nicer packaging, better quality products, and

higher prices)? Or they could position themselves as the best value (perhaps there is no fancy packaging, there is little difference in quality offered, and they always offer the best prices).

PR (public relations) – Public relations is the practice of managing the flow of information between an organisation and its public. The aim of public relations is to inform or influence the public audience, managing the communication without paying for advertising or other paid endorsements.

For many small companies, writing press releases, managing websites and social media, and writing public speeches is an essential part of their communication activities.

profits – Profit, for a business, equals revenues minus costs. If an entrepreneur carefully manages the costs of her business (for example ensuring they don't have to raise their product's price) and also grows the revenues of the business (for example due to its good product, cheap price, or good service) the business will be making strong profits.

resources (& capabilities) – Resources are essentially the things entrepreneurs have, such as land, cash, computers and machinery. Capabilities are essentially the things that entrepreneurs and their businesses can do, and include things such as labour, experience, education, and time.

Entrepreneurs consider both their resources and capabilities, but also think about the nature of these resources and capabilities:

- Are they valuable to them and a consumer? For example, an entrepreneurial farmer might ask – Does the land rented or owned have good access to water? Is the business growing a crop in demand?

- Are they different, unusual or rare? For example, if an entrepreneur has a retail shop, are they selling a product that is not sold everywhere in town?

- Are they difficult for others to copy? For example, if the entrepreneur is manufacturing a product, is the quality or workmanship difficult to copy? Is the brand clear and protectable?

- Are they things that the entrepreneur can well utilise and enjoy utilising? Are these resources and capabilities things that the entrepreneur is happy to utilise and build? Using resources and leveraging skills should be something that is enjoyable.

reporting – Tracking performance usually means keeping records – that is, recording in a simple and organized way the key information about the business. This information usually includes the revenue, costs, assets and liabilities of the business. But it can also include other transactions,

for example if an entrepreneur takes some money from the business it is documented as either wages (for the entrepreneur) or withdrawals from the business (if the entrepreneur needed the money for a family emergency).

An entrepreneur's business reporting and tracking typically have three purposes: understanding – to determine how well they are performing; communication – to manage uncertainty, expectations and set milestones; and credibility – to build teamwork, confidence and integration.

The entrepreneurial manager will need to track: i) the flows of money (revenues and costs); ii) the stocks of money (savings and owings); as well as iii) the timings of transactions.

There are many ways to keep records, from a simple book to complex computer software program. For some entrepreneurial business, a simple book may be all they need to use.

Each time a transaction is completed, it should be recorded against one of these categories (revenue or cost) to inform the entrepreneur of their profit, and working capital needs. It is easier to record these payments as they occur, or in summary on a daily basis. If there is an expense that is paid each week or each month (as fixed costs) be sure to forecast these as a daily basis.

revenue – Money that comes in to the business is simply the quantity of products (or services) sold multiplied by the selling price of each item. Growing revenues is the first challenge of a business – build revenues before costs. The enterprise must focus on providing good quality products at an appropriate price (i.e. not too expensive that the customer is unhappy, and not too cheaply that the enterprise goes broke). Revenues will include income:

- From regular sales of the entrepreneur's product or service (for example, daily quantities and revenues of the products)

- From special orders of the entrepreneur's product or service (for example a corporate order)

- Any other income.

risk – Entrepreneurs also face risk, which can be managed with a good team, good supervisors, and her market knowledge. Risk cannot be avoided, and entrepreneurs will need plans to implement to manage that risk if it eventuates. For example, perhaps a major customer will disappear, or a valued employee will leave the business. The chances of these things happening may be moderate, but the implications major. Entrepreneurs must understand these risks and act accordingly.

(see also uncertainty and loss)

segmenting the market – Divide the market (= all potential customers) into clusters. The first obvious cluster will be whether an entrepreneur has business or individual consumers. Cluster again – perhaps the entrepreneur can organise businesses customers that buy a lot, or a little, or those that buy based on certain performance criteria. Similarly, with individual consumers entrepreneurs' could divide (for example):

- By male or female (differentiating between the different sexes)

- By age (perhaps recognising that younger consumers behave differently to the older consumers)

- By geography (perhaps recognising that it matter whether people live in certain districts or regions)

- By income (if people with lower incomes buy different volumes or quality of product?).

How finely entrepreneurs segment these markets will depend on the product or service they are selling. For example, if they sell beauty products, entrepreneurs would likely be interested in differentiating: consumers living in big or small cities, whether they are men and women, and whether they have low or medium-high incomes.

(see also targeting)

series A funding – Series A funding, or Series A Round, is the name typically given to a company's first significant round of capital investment. The shares, or stock, is typically sold to professional investors such as venture capital funds.

shelf company – A shelf company is one that is created by someone but then left alone. It is then sold to someone wanting to avoid all the procedures of creating a new company.

social entrepreneur – As with the definition of 'entrepreneur', there are many definitions of social entrepreneurs. One could be as follows:

Social Entrepreneurs are those people (key stakeholders) who seek to generate change (creating social, cultural or natural value), through the creation or expansion of economic activity, by identifying and exploiting innovations such as new products, processes or markets.

Note the differences between this definition, and that for a commercial entrepreneur.

startup – A startup is a company, a partnership or other organization that is particularly young. These companies are in a phase of development that requires rapid growth to take advantage of a new opportunity.

strategy – Strategy refers to the art and science of leading a business. Business strategy is about being different, and deliberately choosing a set of activities and products that will create value. Successful entrepreneurs know their strategy, as its articulation can help guide their decisions and communicate purpose.

Strategy will help the entrepreneur align: their vision, their internal resources, and the external environment. Entrepreneurs can ask multiple questions to determine whether their strategy is integrated, such as: who, what, where, when, and how.

supply chain – Businesses buy things from someone (the manufacturer or the fabric, for example) and they sell it to their customers. As an example, cotton growers sold their product to cloth factories. These factories then sold the fabric to the people who sews the dresses. The owner of this business then sells her finished dresses to shopkeepers or individual customers. All these together buyers and sellers together are like a line, or chain, of businesses. This is known as the chain of supply. At each step, the cost of the product gets higher, as each business adds their expertise and value.

Entrepreneurs seek to understand what parts of the chain of supply they can, and can't, participate in. For example, if they grow vegetables, do they also want to be also selling them to the public, or cooking them in a restaurant?

targeting markets – (read about segmenting the market first!)

When an entrepreneur has segmented her market, they choose the segments that have the most potential for their business as target customers. (From the example above, an entrepreneur may not be interested in selling cosmetics to old and poor men from small villages in the county.) Not all the customer segments will be targets for an entrepreneur's business... some might not have any interest, or not have the purchasing power for their product. For example:

- If they are selling beauty products – they might target women who earn higher income, who live in the cities, who are younger...

- If they are selling dresses for women – they might target women who would like a good quality dress, who are older (and more traditional) and rarely spend money on themselves...

(see also positioning in markets)

uncertainty – Businesses are faced with the uncertainty of the political climate or the seasonal climates. No matter what the business does, there is nothing the entrepreneur can do to impact these changes. The entrepreneur cannot see into the future (no matter how confident they are), and we are all faced by uncertainty. Entrepreneurs must get used to uncertainty, but be prepared for any eventuation.

(See also risk and loss.)

vision – A vision statement typically states what a business does, and what it could possibly be if it became the best version of itself. For many entrepreneurs, it should clarify, engender confidence, and inspire. There are aspects that hint whether a vision is appropriate – entrepreneurs seek to answer these questions:

- Does your vision utilise your strengths and performance? That is, will it encourage you to do better at the things you already do well (if they are the right things to do)?

- Does your vision look outside your business to external opportunities and needs? That is, you are able to make a difference and impact?

- Does your vision look towards what it is you really believe in? That is, is the vision yours, and is it a personal expression of your dreams?

People's passions are what arguably differentiate one business from another. Entrepreneurs have belief in what their business stands for (rather than just what products it sells), and they can shape and articulate that passion.

working capital – Working capital is the money required to fund the normal daily operations of an entrepreneur's business. For some businesses the operating cash cycle can be long (for example, it may take many days between purchasing supplies, manufacturing a product, finding a customer, supplying the product, and collecting the money from that customer). To cover the timing differences between these costs incurred from suppliers and payments received from customers, working capital is required.

This operating cash cycle can be shortened – for example, by ensuring that an entrepreneur receives payment on delivery from their customer, by limiting the credit provided to their customers, or by asking for advance (part) payments for large orders. Successful entrepreneurs manage carefully their cash, stocks, and invoicing.

RESOURCES

—

Flavia Abbate
Bolster Trading Pty Ltd
bodybolster.com

Narelle Anderson
Envirobank
envirobank.com.au

Natalie Archer
Bendelta
bendelta.com

Jacqueline Arias
República Coffee
republicaorganic.com.au

Shelley Barrett
ModelCo
modelcocosmetics.com

Layne Beachley
Aim for the stars
aimforthestars.com.au

Jo Burston
Job Capital
jobcapital.com.au
Rare Birds
inspiringrarebirds.com

Carden Calder
BlueChip Communications
bluechipcommunication.com.au

Rebekah Campbell
Posse
posse.com

Karen Cariss
Pageup People
pageuppeople.com

Nahji Chu
MissChu
misschu.com.au

Carolyn Creswell
Carman's
carmanskitchen.com.au

Topaz Conway
Biothoughts
biothoughts.com
Springboard
sb.co

Andrea Culligan
Harteffect
harteffect.com

Nicole Eckels
Sapphire Group
sapphiregroup.com.au
Glasshouse Fragrances
glasshousefragrances.com

Audette Exel
Adara Group
adaragroup.org

Simone Eyeles
365cups
365cups.com

Lauren Fried
Pulse Marketing Group
pulsemarketing.com.au
Joule
hellojoule.com

Jodie Fox
Shoes of Prey
shoesofprey.com

Donna Guest
Blue Illusion Aust Pty Ltd.
blueillusion.com

Kylie Green
Apollo Nation
apollonation.com.au

Mandi Gunsberger
Babyology
babyology.com.au

Janet Hamilton
THE Shed Company
theshedcompany.com.au

Avril Henry
Avril Henry & Associates
avrilhenry.com

Jo Horgan
Mecca Cosmetics
mecca.com.au

Emma Isaacs
Business Chicks
businesschicks.com.au

Adina Jacobs
STM (Standard Technical Merchandise)
stmbags.com.au

Pip Jamieson
The Dots
the-dots.co.uk

Kristina Karlsson
kikki-k Pty. Ltd
kikki-k.com

Therese Kerr
Divine by Therese Kerr
divinebytheresekerr.com

Nicole Kersh
4Cabling
4cabling.com.au

Kim-Louise Liddell
Non Destructive Excavations
Australia Pty Ltd
ndea.com.au

Christine Manfield
christinemanfield.com

Daniella Menachemson
B Seated Global
bseatedglobal.com.au

Ivanka Menken
The Art of Service
artofservice.com.au

Lisa Moore
Rodeo Show Clothing
rodeoshow.com.au

Pauline Nguyen
Red Lantern
redlantern.com.au

Deb Noller
Switch Automation
switchautomation.com

Jan Owen
Foundation for Young Australians
fya.org.au

Dawn Piebenga
IMR
imr.com.au

Catriona Pollard
CP Communications
cpcommunications.com.au

Megan Quinn
NET-A-PORTER.COM
Netaporter.com

Sarah Riegelhuth
Wealth Enhancers
wealthenhancers.com.au

Margot Spalding
Jimmy Possum
jimmypossum.com.au

Penelope Spencer
Spencer Travel Pty Ltd
spencertravel.com.au

Sasha Titchkosky
Koskela Pty Ltd
koskela.com.au

Anneke van den Broek
Rufus & Coco
rufusandcoco.com.au

Angela Vithoulkas
Vivo Cafe
vivocafe.com.au

Dr. Catriona Wallace
Fifth Quadrant
fifthquadrant.com.au

Leona Watson
Cheeky Food Group
cheekyfoodgroup.com

JO BURSTON

—

Founder and Managing Director of Job Capital & Rare Birds

—

Recognised as one of Australia's fastest growing companies in 2012, Job Capital catapulted from an idea in 2006 to a $40M business by 2012 having only 12 staff. Job Capital offers outsource payroll, salary packaging and migration (visas) services, while also looking after online tax returns and superannuation refunds for overseas nationals whilst expanding the service offering.

Jo Burston breathes life and purpose into everything she does, making her the successful entrepreneur and natural leader you see today. With over 15 years spent in the outsource payroll, migration and contingent workforce space and has made moves in the technology sector, Jo has a strong belief in the power of dynamic business models matched with a thriving and happy work culture. Her brands, Job Capital, claimyourtax.com, big-data.net.au, cleaningmaideasy.com.au and thecandidatebank.com.au are working examples of her ability to build and grow smart businesses. Aswell as succeeding, Jo embraces failing as her true method of learning along with sharing experience and receiving the value of experience from others.

She is actively passionate about the entrepreneurial space and, true to her nature, is a member of the global Entrepreneurs Organisation which as of 2014 represents 10,000 entrepreneurs in 50 countries and is known as "the world's most influential community of entrepreneurs". She has taken board positions as both Education and currently Strategic Alliance chair from 2012-2016 on a voluntary basis, which involves organising over 30 learning events per annum for 140 entrepreneur members.

Praised as a business role model for women, today, Jo is the founder of Rare Birds, something she attributes to be her "true purpose in life". Inspiring Rare Birds is an Australian based movement that aims to be the largest global database and connector of women entrepreneurs globally. Having launched in 2014 with global expansion plans in 2015 underway, Rare Birds consists of a series of books, a fully comprehensive online community of women entrepreneurs featuring some of the most notable female identities in Australian business. With a heart to increase this population by 1 million by 2020 globally, Jo believes in creating a platform where women can be open and honest about their trials and triumphs while exposing all women to that one empowering thought of, "If she can, I can".

EO History

Joined EO Sydney Basecamp forum in 2009. Board positions of Learning Chair 2012-2014 and Strategic Alliance 2014-2016. Attended Amsterdam University in 2010, New Zealand 2012 and Istanbul in 2011 and Ignite in Sydney 2013. Jo attended The Global Learning Conference in Bahrain 2012 and Athens in 2014 and attended forum retreats with Basecamp in Shanghai, Auckland, Gold Coast (ANZAC Summit), Melbourne and Philippines. Jo has attended over 120 events in her EO tenure and is an active member.

Some of Jo's successes

2011
- BRW Fast100 #13
- SmartCompany Smart50 #8
- Startupsmart - Best Service Company Australia
- Australia's Top Female Entrepreneurs #34
- Nominee Telstra Business and Business Women Awards

2012
- BRW Fast 100 #23 and Faststarters #8
- NSW Pearcey Awards - Tech Entrepreneur of the Year
- Ernst & Young Entrepreneur of the Year Finalist

2013
- SmartCompany Smart 50 #8
- SmartCompany - Top 40 Female Entrepreneurs

2014
- SmartCompany - Top 30 Female Entrepreneur
- Shoestring - Top 50 Females under 40
- Invited delegate for G20 YEA Summit Sydney

REBEKAH SCHOTT

—

Photographer

—

A fashion, commercial and lifestyle photographer, Rebekah Schott is responsible for the majority of imagery you see in this book. A New Yorker at heart, she has been photographing people and the life around her since she was a little girl. She has a bachelors degree in Studio Art and has worked as a freelance photographer since 2005.

Her career began in Redlands, California (Southern Cali), where she was voted the #1 Wedding Photographer in the Inland Empire. While living in California she began traveling to New York City to pursue fashion photography and quickly established herself as a regular test photographer for many modeling agencies including Ford, MSA, Images Management and Fenton Moon Models. She began freelancing for Fashion 360 Magazine covering Mercedes-Benz Fashion Week, and has done so for the past 6 seasons. In 2012 she officially relocated to New York City and in May 2014, moved to Sydney, Australia.

"My photography style is clean, natural and fun.From shooting fashion to business profiles to family portraits my goal is to capture the unique personality and natural beauty of my subject. I love getting to know my clients and helping them tell their story through my photos."

Proudly published by

Inspiring Rare Birds is a profitable smart heart business built by entrepreneurs, for entrepreneurs. We believe that a philanthropic heart can beat in unison with a profitable enterprise to create social and economic change. Our Vision is to see 1,000,000 more women entrepreneurs by 2020 globally and our mission is to give every woman globally the opportunity to become an entrepreneur by choice. Inspiring Rare Birds is built on the foundation of values and the four pillars of Storytelling, Mentoring, Access to investment for women and Community and Education.

www.inspiringrarebirds.com